CORINNE TRUE

Corinne Knight True
Her last portrait, probably in the early 1950s

CORINNE TRUE
Faithful Handmaid of 'Abdu'l-Bahá

by

Nathan Rutstein

with the assistance of
Edna M. True

GEORGE RONALD
OXFORD

GEORGE RONALD, Publisher
46 High Street, Kidlington, Oxford, OX5 2DN

© NATHAN RUTSTEIN 1987
All rights Reserved

British Library Cataloguing in Publication Data

Rutstein, Nathan
   Corinne True : faithful handmaid
of 'Abdu'l-Bahá.
   1. True, Corinne 2. Bahais—Biography
  I. Title II. True, Edna M.
297'.8963'0924   BP395.T7

ISBN 0–85398–263–5
ISBN 0–85398–264–3 Pbk

Phototypeset by Photoprint, Torquay, Devon, U.K.
Printed and bound in England by Billing & Sons Ltd., Worcester

CONTENTS

Preface	ix
1 Corinne Knight's Southern Heritage	1
2 The Birth of a Family	10
3 Tragedy and Faith	17
4 'Found Ye Spiritual Assemblies'	30
5 'Abdu'l-Bahá's Call for the Temple	37
6 Six Days in Akka	48
7 The Struggle for Unity	71
8 A Wonderful Coincidence	80
9 The Master's Protection and Guidance	94
10 'The Money Came . . . Rolling In'	110
11 Two Kinds of War	117
12 Farewell to the Master	133
13 The First Ma<u>sh</u>riqu'l-A<u>dh</u>kár in America	147
14 'In the Center Stands This Youth'	151
15 'Give Them Love'	160
16 The View from Home	167
17 Two More Pilgrimages	172
18 Mother True	180
19 A Tower of Strength	194
20 The Most Venerable Pioneer	202
21 The Hand of the Cause	208
Published Sources	215
Notes and References	217

LIST OF ILLUSTRATIONS

Corinne Knight True, her last portrait   *Frontispiece*

1 Corinne's parents   between pages 20–21
2 Corinne True
3 Corinne and her first four children, *circa* 1888
4 The twins, Kenneth (left) and Katherine, *circa* 1894
5 Nathanael, the youngest son who died in 1899

6 The True family at home,   64–65
   711 West Adams Street, Chicago, *circa* 1896
7 The House of 'Abdu'lláh Páshá, with its arched red-brick entrance
8 The room in which 'Abdu'l-Bahá received His guests
9 The main hall in the House of 'Abdu'lláh Páshá
10 Arna, at about the age of her pilgrimage with Corinne in 1907
11 Corinne at Fruitport in the grounds of their summer home

12 Delegates to the first nationwide Bahá'í   84–85
   Convention, 20–23 March 1909
13 Corinne Knight True (1861–1961)
14 Moses Adams True (1857–1909)
15 The committee of fifteen gathered at the Trues' home, 1 August 1909

16 'Abdu'l-Bahá, the Center of the Covenant of   100–101
   Bahá'u'lláh
17 'Abdu'l-Bahá at the dedication of the Mashriqu'l-Adhkár grounds, Wilmette, 1 May 1912

ILLUSTRATIONS

18 'Abdu'l-Bahá in Lincoln Park, Chicago, 5 May 1912, with children
19 Laurence Knight True (1885–1906)
20 Charles Gilbert Davis True (1886–1912)

21 'Abdu'l-Bahá with pilgrims and other Bahá'ís beside the Tomb of the Báb, 9 November 1919   142–143
22 Dr John E. Esslemont (1874–1925)
23 Edna Miriam True at the time of her 1919 pilgrimage with her mother
24 Five American pilgrims with Shoghi Effendi, November 1919

25 The Bahá'í House of Worship, Wilmette, Illinois   158–159
26 The first gathering of Bahá'ís in Foundation Hall of the House of Worship, 9 July 1922
27 Saichiro Fujita and Wyatt Cooper in Wilmette, 1971

28 418 Forest Avenue, Wilmette, the home of Corinne True   190–191
29 Leo Perron, who was married to Arna True in 1912
30 Davis Perron in the U.S. Army Air Corps

31 Corinne True at the European Teaching Conference in Copenhagen, 1950   206–207
32 Corinne's eighth and last pilgrimage, November 1952
33 Corinne True attending the public dedication of the Mashriqu'l-Adhkár with her daughters, 2 May 1953
34 Corinne with Paul Haney, on the platform of the 1956 Bahá'í National Convention
35 Corinne with Edna, in front of the National Ḥaẓíratu'l-Quds, Wilmette

36 The Hand of the Cause, Corinne True, 210–211
representing the Guardian of the Faith at the
formation of the first National Spiritual
Assembly of the Bahá'ís of the Greater Antilles,
22–24 April 1957
37 Dr Katherine Knight True (1893–1963)
38 Arna Corinne True Perron (1890–1975)
39 Edna Miriam True, member of the Continental
Board of Counsellors for North America and
Trustee of the Continental Fund from 1968
until 1980

Grateful acknowledgement is made to Miss
Edna M. True for twenty-three of these
photographs, and to the Audio-Visual
Department of the Bahá'í World Centre for
their interest and care in reproducing many of
these as well as the seventeen additional
illustrations from their collection.

Preface

Writing the biography of Corinne True was a profound learning experience for me. It was more than becoming acquainted with the essential facts about a devoted servant of the Bahá'í Faith. I was able to probe beneath the surface of the kind of personality I have always had difficulty liking. In essence, I overcame a prejudice and discovered an extraordinary spirit: one that has inspired me and steadied my sight on what is most important in life. Corinne True was a remarkable woman. So is her daughter Edna. It was she who actually launched the writing of this book. About four years ago she telephoned me and asked if I would write the biography of her mother.

Edna has consistently helped me. Not only by patiently answering my many questions. We taped for thirteen hours, and there were the numerous telephone conversations. What she told me has contributed immeasurably to the book, usually without further reference than this acknowledgement. But her assistance was also routed through an extra-phenomenal channel which affected me directly. About midway through the book, I kept getting up in the middle of the night – 2 and 3 a.m. – burning with thoughts and feelings about Corinne True. Dashing to my typewriter provided relief. But this process had some less desirable effects on me. Dozing off in the middle of the afternoon, for example. It dawned on me that I had better call Edna and plead with her to be moderate in her prayers. She laughed when I made the request. I know she made an adjustment, because I started getting up at 4 and 5 a.m., a much closer time to my normal waking hour.

I had never known Corinne True. I had seen her at the 1955 National Bahá'í Convention through the eyes of an eight-month-old believer. What impressed me most was the way she was greeted by the delegates and guests. They obviously knew something about her that I wasn't aware of. I got an inkling of what they felt that day, because the certitude that emanated from her was extraordinary. Usually, little frail-looking ladies in their 90s don't radiate that kind of strength. Little did I know that I would write her biography.

In writing this book I also learned what a struggle the Faith experienced in setting its roots into the North American continent. Corinne True was in the middle of the struggle. I received help in gaining an accurate perspective on the early days of the Faith from Roger Dahl, Archivist of the National Bahá'í Archives in Wilmette, Jackson Armstrong-Ingram, Assistant Archivist, and Robert Stockman, author of *The Bahá'í Faith in America: Origins, 1892–1900*, the first of a projected three-volume series. Their patience and willingness to help were the source of considerable encouragement. And there was Bruce Whitmore, author of *The Dawning Place* and of 'Mother of the Temple', who aided me to gain greater understanding of Corinne True's role in the erection of the Bahá'í House of Worship in Wilmette, Illinois. Finally, I acknowledge gratefully the contributions of Thelma Jackson, Edna's companion of many years, and Marion Hofman, who came to know Mrs True in 1933, to the accuracy of my book and its portrayal of her spirit and character.

There are a few places in the book where I try to surmise what Corinne True's thoughts might have been about certain incidents. I didn't take this liberty without much exploration of sources – and pondering. It was perhaps a daring thing to do, but it had to be done, I feel, for the reader to obtain an awareness of her true spirit. Every day for nearly two years I thought of Corinne True. By reading about her, listening to those who knew her or knew a great deal about her, plus reading letters about her and those she wrote to close friends, I was able to piece together what I believed to be her unique personality.

In order to understand how this great woman grew spiritually, I studied the Tablets 'Abdu'l-Bahá sent her. They were like water and sunlight to a sapling. He knew her reality. And she knew He knew it. His words nurtured her and helped her develop her spiritual capacity to influence, through her steadfast and energetic devotion, the growth of the Faith in America. Certainly Shoghi Effendi, the Guardian of the Bahá'í Faith, understood her spirit and recognized her contributions, for he named her a Hand of the Cause of God when she was 91 years of age.

My sincerest wish is that those who read this book will get as much from it as I received writing it.

Nathan Rutstein

Amherst, Massachusetts
20 March 1987

1

Corinne Knight's Southern Heritage

Considering her heritage and upbringing, Corinne True's life took an unusual turn at the age of 38. When she was growing up, girls in her social class had a good idea of what their role would be as adults. That wasn't necessarily the case with Corinne. Though she didn't know what her life would be like at the turn of the century, she probably sensed that it would be different from her mother's. She was just that kind of person.

Corinne's roots were embedded in Southern aristocracy, perhaps the most conservative social element of America's pre-Civil War period. Plantation owners defended slavery as a legitimate national institution, basing their defense on a clause in their country's Constitution which counted only three-fifths of the black slaves in a State when apportioning Representatives and taxes.[1] Also, respected Christian clergymen could cite Biblical chapter and verse to prove that blacks were inherently inferior to whites. Martha Thomas Duerson, Corinne's mother, was brought up to believe in slavery. It was part of the Southern way of life. She considered the thirty slaves, whom she inherited along with her father's Kentucky plantation, as her property.

Martha's Duerson ancestors were, for the most part, French Huguenots of independent mind who had fled France in the mid-1700s rather than bend to the dictates of a Roman Catholic-dominated government. They joined frontiersman Daniel Boone's Wilderness expedition and were among the first whites to settle in Kentucky in about

1773. Martha's grandfather married the daughter of Captain Trigg, Boone's chief military aide, who was killed by Indians at the Battle of Blue Licks Spring.

The Duersons carved out a farm on a bluff overlooking the Ohio River. Over the years their land grew into a spacious plantation.

Martha never knew her father; he died before she was born. And her mother didn't live to see Martha reach womanhood. As a child and youth, she never experienced deprivation. A personal slave combed her hair and dressed her daily. At 21, she was a highly-respected heiress, intelligent, strong-willed and proud of her Southernness.

No cash crops were grown on the Duerson plantation. The vegetables and fruits produced, as well as the hogs, chickens, sheep and cattle, were used to feed her and her slaves. Most of the horses were used for sport and to pull her handsome carriages. Inside the plantation manor was a large collection of books, including many English classics. The elegant piano that graced the expansive parlor was played regularly by Martha, not to exhibit her musical prowess, but to satisfy her yearning for aesthetic fulfillment. She loved flowers. The hyacinths, jonquils and lilies-of-the-valley that grew in natural patterns around the manor delighted her heart. Because of her love for them, Martha learned the names of every plant on her property, including the trees.

Martha Thomas Duerson was considered quite a catch by all potential suitors in Oldham County where she lived, and among the well-to-do in nearby Louisville. But she was highly selective. The typical young romantic held no fascination for her. Perhaps that's why she married Moses Greene Knight, a Presbyterian minister, who was twenty years older and possessed a stronger will than hers.

Moses' parents were wealthy southern Kentucky farmers. His father arrived in the state from Milledgeville, Georgia, at the age of 10 with his widowed mother. But the Knights' roots go back to Virginia and England. Moses' mother's family was also of English stock.

Moses didn't have a church when he married. A throat ailment kept him from preaching; but that didn't prevent him from practicing Christianity wholeheartedly. He read the Bible daily, using it as his sole code of life. That dependence was passed on to his wife and children.

Moses had a strong and independent mind, and his father respected his son's individualistic nature and firm character. That's why Moses was trusted to carry out complicated, sometimes dangerous family tasks. At 19, he was sent to Missouri by his father to purchase government land that was for sale. He had to make the long journey by horseback. In the 1830s there were no railroads heading toward that part of the country. When Moses reached his destination, he discovered that the acreage wasn't suitable. Instead of turning back empty-handed, he rode northward to Iowa, where the soil was rich and fertile. He bought some choice property in Burlington for $1,800. Though Moses' father was displeased with the purchase, the property proved to be a springboard to a future real estate venture that would make the Knight family independently wealthy. When his father died, he willed the Iowa land, and a slave, to Moses, who promptly freed the slave.

Slavery, Moses felt, was wrong. He disagreed with the Constitution's interpretation of the black man; and no slaveholder's argument, not even his wife's, could dissuade him. Once Moses was convinced, nothing could pry him from his stance. Martha acquiesced to her husband's demand and freed her own slaves before President Lincoln's Emancipation Proclamation in 1863. But most of the blacks didn't want to leave the plantation; they enjoyed working on it. Martha had provided comfortable housing and generously shared with them what was grown and butchered. So Moses hired the black men and paid them a wage. He also had a briarpatch cleared, built a schoolhouse for the black children and hired a teacher to educate them. The building was big enough to accommodate some of the neighbor's children who were white. Probably Moses Greene Knight operated the first racially-integrated school in Kentucky prior to Reconstruction.

Though he was strongly against slavery, Moses was a devoted defender of the Southern cause during the Civil War. In some ways a paradox, because slavery was one of the crucial issues in the bloody conflict between the North and the South. But Moses' loyalty to family tradition and the only way of life he knew superseded any Yankee ideological position even though he was in agreement. He was no traitor to the Confederacy. In fact, he would willingly have given his life for it, as would his wife, who made Confederate uniforms during the war and harbored a rebel commando shortly after it ended. In later years Corinne remembered the incident when Federal troops broke into the manor, searching every room including hers. She was only 3 at the time. Seeing soldiers with rifles plundering the plantation house and barns was an experience that haunted her for years in the form of nightmares. The Union forces never found the commando, who was Corinne's cousin. He had been hiding in the Knights' cornfield. Other relatives weren't so fortunate. A number of them were captured and languished in Northern prisons.

Like most Southerners, Moses Greene Knight didn't trust Yankees. Unhappily, in future this deep-seated attitude would sever a close family bond, an experience that would nearly break his heart.

Corinne was born on 1 November 1861, at the plantation. To Moses, it was a significant event. Not only was she his first child, but she arrived on his birthday. Father and daughter shared other things. Both were independent and strong-willed, and they loved horses. Though it was customary for a Southern man to be closer to his son, Moses favored Corinne over Thomas, who was two years younger and more like his mother. Thomas's fondness for his mother was revealed in a journal he wrote later in life:

CORINNE KNIGHT'S SOUTHERN HERITAGE

Whatever I am, and whatever I have, I owe her. I am proud to have had her for my mother. Whatever talents I may have, whatever ideals, whatever love of literature or nature, flowers or trees, whatever unselfishness, I owe this splendid woman, who possessed them all in far greater abundance.[2]

Growing up on the plantation was fun, even during the war years. Northern Kentucky was far from the major battlefields. The Knights weren't deprived economically, for Moses had invested wisely. In 1857 he and his older brother and a close friend had gone to Chicago by horseback on a land-buying venture. With the $3,000 he received from the sale of his Iowa property, Moses purchased several downtown sites, five acres at Monroe and Clark Streets, as well as twenty acres in suburban Oak Park. Today that property is worth more than 100 million dollars. By 1861 the Knights were earning $10,000 annually from a brick structure on their Chicago lots on Clark Street. That was a great deal of money in those days, and the chances of earning more from their property were great, because Chicago's economy was booming during the 1860s. The city had become a huge supply center for the Union army. With the completion of the Illinois Central and other railroads, Chicago became their hub. Raw materials like iron and coal were shipped to the city via the Great Lakes and channeled to its factories. The railroads transported the finished products to the war fronts. It didn't take long for Chicago to become the nation's greatest railroad center.

Though the Knights had fine carriages, elegant clothes and a spacious house, their tastes were simple. Fun for them, especially the children, was watching the birds – red cardinals, bluebirds and finches – swoop into the orchard in late spring to attack the ripe cherries. There were also the hummingbirds flitting among the morning glories, trumpet vines and Virginia creepers. The children didn't look forward to winter, because it meant wearing shoes.

When the Knight children closeted their shoes, Moses and Martha knew that spring had arrived. There was nothing more liberating for little Corinne than racing barefoot across a field of young spring grass. And there must have been some resistance to going to church, because stockings and shoes had to be worn every Sunday morning.

The Knights were a horse-riding family. As soon as the children learned to walk, they were placed on horses. And they loved it. In fact, one of Thomas's favorite family chores was riding his old mare to the post office twice a week to fetch the mail. It was a ten-mile trip, back and forth.

Corinne enjoyed riding alongside her father, especially when they raced across the meadow. Those were pleasurable moments for Moses as well. There seemed to be a special bond between father and daughter, undoubtedly a bond that emerged from possessing similar natures. They liked being together.

Moses learned early that Corinne was a special child with a keen and strong mind. He discovered that one day when he tried to rebuke her at the dinner table. 'Corinne,' he said sternly, 'you were looking around while I was saying grace.' 'Father,' she responded, 'how do you know I was looking around?'

When Moses talked about the Bible, Corinne cherished every word. Studying it transported her back to the Holy Land, 1900 years before. She surrendered her heart to Christ, and often remarked as a child: 'How wonderful it must have been to have lived in the days when Christ was on earth.'[3] In the future, her knowledge of the Old and New Testaments would help her discover new spiritual dimensions.

Though life on the Knight plantation was comfortable and gracious, there were moments of sorrow. Of the eight children Martha Knight bore, four lived to adulthood; and of the four, two of Corinne's younger sisters died of tuberculosis in their early twenties. You can understand why Corinne and Thomas grew close, although not as close as she would have liked, for Thomas never accepted what she eventually embraced as the most meaningful thing in her life.

Moses and Martha Knight believed in education and gave their children the best schooling. In her early years, Corinne attended the school her father had built on the plantation. Fortunately, she had a mother who made sure Corinne did her lessons. In fact, she tutored her children throughout their elementary and high school years. They marveled at her mathematical ability. There wasn't an algebra, geometry or trigonometry problem she couldn't solve. Her fondness for literature contributed to Corinne's love for reading; and her piano technique inspired Thomas to acquire great musical skill by the age of nine.

When Corinne was 14, the family moved to Louisville so the older children could attend a more advanced school. Moving day was a sad time, because city living wasn't conducive to running barefoot across the countryside and riding a horse whenever you wanted to. They settled in a neighborhood where, in those days, homes were cared for by servants, gardeners, carriage men and butlers. Attending balls was a fairly common occurrence.

When the Knights moved to Louisville, they had no idea they would be living in Chicago a year later. Chicago was Yankee country. But they had to move when the depression of 1873 practically destroyed their income. Those who rented apartments and stores in Moses Knight's building couldn't pay the rent. The situation was even worse than when the fire of 1871 had wiped out downtown Chicago, including the original structure on his property. Then, with a bank loan of $38,000, Moses, his brother John and Major McNeal, a friend, had built a much larger building. But a commercial building, no matter how elaborate and functional, needs economically solvent tenants, especially when the owners have a mortgage to pay off.

The Knights sold their Louisville home, with its carriages and horses, and took over a third-floor apartment in the Chicago building. The family's life style changed drastically. There were no more maids and butler. If they had to go somewhere, they walked. The older children attended a public high school. Though the change was severe for Moses and the children, Martha, who had always been pampered, had to make the greatest adjustment. Scrubbing floors, cooking meals, washing clothes were chores others had always done. But suddenly they were her responsibilities. She did them well – and without complaint. Their mother's attitude toward her new duties deeply impressed Corinne and Thomas. They knew their mother's background, which was theirs as well. If she can do what servants used to do, they thought, then we can do it too. Martha's eighteen months of housekeeping saved her children from pride in their social position.

Two years after the move from Louisville, the Knights' economic situation improved. They purchased a large house in Chicago's West side, and were able to afford a cook and housekeeper. Corinne adapted well to big-city living in the North. Too well, thought her father. She was losing her Kentucky accent and manner. In a way, watching his favorite child turn more Northern than Southern tugged at his roots. To stop the transformation, he sent Corinne to the Miss Mary Baldwin finishing school in Virginia, where students were groomed in the Southern way of life. Corinne took courses in elocution, sewing and piano. She was to become a lady, Dixie style. Evidently it didn't matter that Thomas pursued his education in the North. He was sent to Williams College, in Massachusetts.

The prospect of going South to study for the next few years didn't upset Corinne – though she found life in a city stimulating. Intelligent and curious, she was intrigued by new concepts and people from different places, especially from different countries, and there were many like that in Chicago.

Corinne went South, turning the situation to her advantage. Though she would have preferred taking challenging courses like philosophy and theology, she did well academically. Her fellow students often sought her advice, because she radiated an inner strength, an assurance that seemed so rare in others. Corinne didn't seek leadership; it came to her naturally.

Fortunately, there were relatives in Washington, DC, not too far from her school. The balls they invited her to were fun, not because she sought acceptance in high society, for she never thought of such matters. She loved to have fun. In the nation's capital, which was really a Southern city in those days, the balls were more elegant, the gentlemen more courteous and the orchestras more accomplished. And there was opportunity to meet people with a wider perspective. Talking with them was always appealing. But what attracted her most in others were genuineness and basic honesty. And those were attributes her future husband possessed in abundance.

2

The Birth of a Family

While Corinne was away at school, a family from Maine moved next door to the Knights. They were refined and gentle people. But as Moses and Martha soon discovered, the couple were committed social reformers. Mrs Harriet True, a descendant of President John Adams, crusaded for better jail conditions in Chicago, especially for women. Through her efforts, the police department provided separate cells for female inmates.

The Knights liked the Trues, despite their pure Yankee lineage. New Englanders, the Knights had always felt, were aloof and rather snobbish. But that myth was soon disproved.

The Trues' son, Moses Adams, was especially appealing. He was a generous, friendly young man, with a loving regard for his parents. On Sundays he would escort his mother to church. That impressed the Knights, especially Mr Knight.

Because her parents praised the Trues so highly in their letters, Corinne was eager to meet them. At their first meeting, she wasn't disappointed. The new neighbors fit her parents' description. But there was one thing the Knights hadn't counted on: the immediate attraction between Corinne and Moses Adams. They saw a lot of each other during her vacation.

Corinne left for her last year of school with a heavy heart. She wanted to be near Moses. It took considerable will to keep from quitting school, but the thought of hurting her parents' feelings stopped her from following her impulse. Nevertheless, she remained close to Moses through correspondence. After graduation she rushed back to Chicago.

It was soon apparent to both sets of parents that Corinne and Moses were in love. That frightened Mr Knight, because he knew his daughter well. Changing a course she felt was right would almost take a miracle. He had to act swiftly, because she seemed ready to ask her parents for permission to marry the boy next door. The idea of his firstborn, his favorite child, marrying a Yankee upset him. It didn't matter that he liked the young man, or that he was impressed with his character. His Corinne, he had somehow hoped, would marry into a Southern family, and he was determined that this should happen.

But his daughter was equally determined to follow her heart. After all, Moses Adams was a genuinely good person, someone she could trust. He wasn't obsessed with proving his manhood, an impulse so many men his age were driven to fulfill. It was refreshing not having to probe through a façade to know Moses' true feelings. And he had integrity. If he disagreed with Corinne he would stand his ground, but in a pleasant manner. Nor would he commit himself to a cause he didn't favor. To her, that was far more courageous than leading a military charge in battle. Moses' sense of humor also pleased her.

In one way they were alike. Both were open people. What they felt wasn't hidden. They didn't have to ponder or analyze each other's behavior to know how they really felt.

Mr Knight sent Corinne to his sister Josephine, in Louisville. She was to stay there until her infatuation with Moses waned. And Moses was forbidden to visit Corinne. Though Mrs Knight felt her husband's position was extreme, and she told him so, he refused to budge. Her daughter's sadness pained her; yet there was nothing she could do to change the situation. The clash between her husband and her daughter could easily split the family.

Much to Mr Knight's displeasure, his sister Josephine became Corinne's ally. In fact, she wrote to her brother, pleading with him to change his mind, because she was certain that Corinne and her beau were genuinely in love. Aunt Josephine even offered to give the couple a grand wedding.

Mr Knight wrote to Louisville to make sure his sister didn't do anything rash. As for his daughter, she was grateful for the support she was getting from her aunt and cousins, who incidentally viewed her trials as terribly romantic.

Banishment hadn't changed Corinne's feelings for Moses. They were in touch by mail.

Why, Corinne wondered, would a man who was so God-fearing, so liberal with black folks, be so opposed to someone from a different section of the country? She knew her father liked Moses. She knew he respected her judgment. His position was irrational; she was convinced of that. Nothing was going to stop her from marrying Moses, even though she loved and respected her father. But he was wrong. She felt obligated to protect her future; but more than that – she couldn't allow herself to become an accomplice to an injustice. In her heart she knew that Moses Adams True was right for her and she right for him. She had met many young men, in the South and in the North, men with more education, wealth and social status. But he was special; he embodied those ideals and characteristics she respected most. No one she had met was like him.

In a few months, in November, she would be 21, legally an adult, and free to do what she pleased. Her father would be unable to stop the marriage; but he could cut her out of his will, and stop any flow of trust money to her. But that didn't matter to Corinne. She was certain that Moses and she could manage financially. He was a hard worker and resourceful; and she could work, if need be.

Why wait until November, she wondered, since she was sure her father wouldn't change his mind then, or ever. But it wasn't up to her alone when they should marry. Moses had to be consulted. She sent him a telegram, which was incorrectly transmitted. Instead of reading 'Now or November', it read 'Now or Never'. 'Now' he wired back; and arranged to meet her in a small Indiana town, where a justice of the peace would perform the wedding ceremony.

In her wildest dreams she had never thought that one day she would elope. Like most young women of her age and social status, she envisioned a church wedding, with the traditional white silk gown.

Though Mr Knight wasn't aware of Corinne's telegram to Moses, he knew what he would do in her place. He tried to block her from running away. Among the things he did was direct the Louisville railroad office not to sell Corinne a ticket. But that didn't work. The clerk she approached hesitated at first, but when he learned that she was eloping, he sold her a ticket. He did it, he said, because a week earlier he had done the same thing.

Aunt Josephine and her daughters accompanied Corinne to the train station, and assured her that she was doing the right thing, that the misunderstanding with her father would soon pass. Moses and Corinne were married on 24 June 1882 in a small Indiana town's municipal building, with a stranger as witness.

Mr Knight was deeply hurt and angry. No one in the family, he determined, should have anything to do with Corinne and her husband. He eliminated her from his will, and his life.

The young couple spent little more than a year in Chicago, living with Moses' parents. It was a difficult time. They were certainly welcome there, but the house next door was off limits. That hurt, because Corinne missed her parents. During that year, Mr Knight persuaded his wife and son not to contact Corinne; he even refused to see his first grandchild, Harriet Merrill, born on 20 August 1883.

For Corinne, the tension was unbearable. She knew her father was capable of never speaking to her again. For peace of mind, and to relieve the stress in her parents' home, she decided to leave Chicago. After the birth of Harriet, they moved to Grand Rapids, Michigan, where Moses worked for Encyclopedia Britannica. His large territory kept him away from home for days. But Corinne managed well. Learning to be a mother was a challenge she undertook with enthusiasm, and she made friends with other young mothers.

Corinne really didn't have much time for anything else, because during that eight-year stay in Grand Rapids she gave birth to four more children: Laurence Knight, Charles Gilbert Davis, Edna Miriam and Arna Corinne.

When Moses was home, he always found time for his children. He enjoyed being with them, and the boys and girls knew it. In some respects they viewed him as a playmate. After dinner he would usually organize games, but not mindless games. They were designed to develop the children's imagination, or teach them skills that would be useful when they became adults. Among their favorites was simulating a grocery store or a bank. Though the games often lasted for hours, the children were so involved they never noticed the passage of time. While they played, Corinne would sew, knit or read. Hearing the laughter of the children, and sensing their excitement, drew the ache away from her heart, an ache caused by the alienation from her father.

Corinne couldn't do what Moses did with the children. She wasn't as creative, she felt, or as uninhibited as her husband. It was good to have someone who could amuse them with wholesome activities, and undoubtedly Moses contributed greatly to the happiness of their home. The children's friends knew it, too. Many of them spent more time at the True home than in their own, even during holidays like Christmas.

The children loved their mother, not only because of who she was to them, but because she possessed the kind of strength they could lean on or draw upon when in trouble. Mother, they felt, was a decision maker, a wise woman. She was the strong, sturdy pivot around which the family, including Moses, revolved. Her strength came from a deep belief in God, something her father had helped her form.

Mr Knight's campaign to ostracize Corinne from the family broke down in about a year after the move to Grand Rapids. Not that he contacted his daughter, but Mrs Knight and their son Thomas did. He knew it, but didn't interfere. News that Grandma Knight was coming generated excitement among the children. They loved her not only for her generous spirit, but because they knew she really cared for them and went out of her way to make them happy.

Corinne felt her children would have adored their grandfather too. But she realized he wouldn't budge from his stand, even though it caused him grief: not knowing his grandchildren and being separated from a child he cared for deeply, who had defied him and, of all things, eloped.

For eight or nine years her father didn't see or speak to Corinne. But as he aged, he grew more mellow. He was grateful to his son Thomas, who was practicing law in Chicago, for bringing Corinne back home after so many years. Aware of his parents' desire to make amends, Thomas had gone to Grand Rapids to persuade Corinne to return to Chicago. Uprooting wouldn't be easy for them. They had a home, friends, a school the children liked, and there was Moses' job. But they had to return, because Corinne knew what it took for her father to bend.

But he couldn't bend all the way. Though he gave Corinne his house at 711 West Adams Street, he wouldn't speak to her husband, the man he believed had snatched his daughter away from him. Her father would have Corinne and the children – there were five by then – visit him and his wife at their residence at the Chicago Beach Hotel, but without Moses, a fact that Corinne and the children could not help resenting. Yet Moses remained optimistic, and he encouraged Corinne to visit her parents. He viewed Mr Knight's seeing and speaking to his daughter as the beginning of a healing process, and felt confident that his father-in-law, in time, would accept him. He didn't know what it would take for Mr Knight to change his attitude, but the change would come.

3

Tragedy and Faith

The Knights spent May through October, and sometimes November, in Chicago, but the rest of the year they lived in the South, usually in hotels. Though out of sight half the year, they kept in touch with their son and daughter in Chicago. Mrs Knight was a dedicated letter writer. To her family, especially the grandchildren, she was a year-round Santa Claus, sending gifts regularly. During the months in Chicago she would take them to Marshall Fields' department store and buy them toys and winter coats. She also provided for dancing-school lessons and dental care for the children.

In the summer, they all had a grand time, for the Knights purchased a summer house for the Trues near a spring lake in Fruitport, Michigan, where the children developed friendships and learned to swim, sail and play tennis. For Corinne and Moses, it was an opportunity to reacquaint themselves with old friends from Grand Rapids.

But there was no vacation the first year back in Chicago. What Corinne had always feared, happened. It wasn't something she talked about, nor was it apparent, yet it troubled her heart. Would what had happened to her mother happen to her? Six of Martha Knight's children had died.

The True children found the big house on West Adams Street a lot of fun. It was so much bigger than their house in Michigan; there was so much more to explore. Harriet, the eldest child, was nearly 10, and a delight to her mother; for she loved life, was so curious, so warm and trusting.

Her four brothers and sisters loved and respected her, because she seemed to do everything right in a cheerful way.

It all happened so fast. No warning. Harriet died shortly after falling down the stone basement stairs. Corinne was shaken, while Moses was crushed. For nearly nine years Corinne had nurtured her firstborn, preparing her for adulthood; and she was gone on the first day of June 1892, gone like a fresh flower swept away by a sudden storm.

Why would God take such a tender being away, Corinne wondered. Her child had done nothing to warrant such a fate. But maybe the child's mother had to be punished? Corinne didn't know what to believe. It didn't make sense. And no one could really comfort her. She had to find answers to why such tragedies occur. In time, the answers would come; but they wouldn't fall from the sky. She would have to search for them. There were no answers for her in traditional Christianity. Reading the Bible brought moments of comfort, but only that. Her father's Calvinistic dogmatism didn't help. For a while she and Moses flirted with Unity, a progressive movement within Christianity which tries to give practical application to the teachings of Jesus Christ in daily living. Though the people she met in the movement were nice, she couldn't find what she was looking for. Nor could Moses. They turned to Christian Science, hoping to experience God's protective embrace there. The church's teachings on spiritual healing were appealing: since man is imperfect, whatever healing process he employs is going to be imperfect; only God is perfect, but the challenge was to discover the right channel to His healing power. The Trues thought they had found it in Divine Science, with teachings similar to Christian Science, and they attended Sunday services.

Gradually, the pain of Harriet's loss lessened. Moses still had his good job with Encyclopedia Britannica. The children had recovered well from their sister's death, and those old enough were attending a local private school. About fourteen months after the passing of her eldest child, Corinne gave birth to twins. Katherine was blond and her brother Kenneth had dark hair like his father. Life seemed to be back to normal, with the usual after-dinner antics, except that the children were involved in playing theater. As vaudeville was popular, the children enjoyed going to the matinée performance with their parents, trying later to enact some of what they had seen. With the help of their father, they put up a curtain between the large foyer of their house and the parlor. When the curtain was drawn, the children would perform. Laurence, the eldest child, was the master of ceremonies. He had a reserved and dignified manner, much like the Knights, while Charles Davis, an extrovert, resembled his father. Everyone agreed that Davis, as he was called, was the star of every performance. He loved to play the part of a clown, because he enjoyed making people laugh. Not only was he good at that, but he had a knack for imitating vaudeville actors, be they dancers, singers or comedians. There was always a supporting cast. Edna liked to dance and unpredictable Arna did whatever she felt like doing, which could prove embarrassing to Laurence and Edna who were more conventional. Even Arna's mother would shake her head in wonder sometimes, and say, 'I don't know where Arna came from, she's not like anyone else in our family.' Some thought of her as a rebel, but those close to Arna viewed her as a free spirit. While she would go out of her way to feed a hungry person, she could embarrass some of the family with her table manners. One evening at supper, with guests present, she recited her version of grace in a rapid-fire manner: 'Thank the bread, thank the meat, thank God. Let's eat.'

There were others who participated in the performances: some of the children's friends and an adult neighbor who could juggle and tap dance. At times, theater at the Trues took the form of serious drama. The children made up playlets on the spot, often depicting life as they viewed it. Though Moses would sometimes perform with the children – telling jokes – Corinne was a delighted spectator, usually darning socks or the boys' breeches. But she did get involved, somewhat, when the children were a little older. There were times when the family would sing and Corinne would play the piano, something she did well. As teenagers, they would sing in three-part harmony. Kenneth, particularly, had a natural gift for music. Whenever the family gathered around the piano, little Kenneth (who died at the age of 7) would stand by the keyboard and play some of the notes. One day Corinne remarked in amazement, 'Kenneth never missed a note.' On another occasion, after attending a concert the night before, he described it with remarkable accuracy. Somewhat later the other children studied music, Laurence the mandolin, Katherine singing and violin, and Edna the piano.

Corinne's cooking was nothing like her piano playing. She avoided the stove. Fortunately, the Trues always had a cook. Moses and the children agreed with Corinne's assessment of her culinary ability: 'I'm so bad at cooking, I burn water.'

The True children were basically happy and very close. Their love for their parents was deep, and they weren't afraid to express it. Edna remembers going around the house as a child, leaving little notes to them and writing on almost anything available, 'O, how I love my mother and father.' But being youngsters, they had their rebellious moments and flings, with yearnings that had to be fulfilled regardless of family rules. Davis and Arna had the hardest time following the rules. Not that they were defiant. They were natural nonconformists and prone to fantasize. Once soaring in their make-believe world, it was difficult for them to relate to such mundane things as worldly regulations. One day, Davis and Arna were missing. Their mother was beside herself, for they had been gone for

1. Corinne's parents, Martha Thomas Duerson (1839–1901) and Moses Greene Knight (1819–1903)

2. Corinne True

3. Corinne and her first four children, circa 1888. (Left to right, from the top) Harriet, Laurence, Davis and Edna

4. The twins, Kenneth (left) and Katherine, circa 1894. Kenneth died after diptheria in 1901.

5. Nathanael, the youngest son who died in 1899 at the age of three. Corinne received her first Tablet from 'Abdu'l-Bahá about his death.

several hours. Family friends finally spotted them marching at the head of a Salvation Army parade that had gone way beyond the neighborhood.

Most of the punishment was meted out by their father; but there were times when Corinne would administer it, admittedly more irritating than painful. If a child was unruly while she was darning, and her stare failed to quiet the youngster, she would tap him on the arm or cheek with a thimble-mounted forefinger.

On 17 January 1896, Nathanael was born, the True's seventh living child. He was a joy, with a sparkling personality. Everyone was attracted to him, even the twins who were only twenty-eight months older. A few months after his birth, Laurence and Davis established a ritual with Nathanael. After he had been put into his pajamas and prepared for bed, Corinne would bring him into the parlor so that his elder brothers could lift him over their heads and make him giggle. There were times when the lift turned into a toss. Before going to bed, Nathanael would usually wind down on his father's lap. His sister Edna remembers an incident that best typifies Nathanael's charm: 'While in Father's arms one evening, Nathanael noticed a penny on the floor and exclaimed, "Oh look, there's my penny!" "Are you sure that's *your* penny?" Father asked. "Well, it looks like my penny," the child replied.'

The dreaded diphtheria swept through the Chicago area in late 1898. Several of the True children contracted it. Little Nathanael had the worst case. In those days, there weren't any antibiotics, nor had a vaccine been developed. Physicians tried to treat it, but there weren't any reliable cures. Corinne and Moses had their hands full. Caring for four seriously sick children was an all-consuming effort. Many a night was spent without sleep. They had known of people who had succumbed to diphtheria, a contagious malady that strikes the tonsils, nose and pharynx, creating a false membrane in those areas. The membrane can grow so large that breathing is hampered, causing some victims to suffocate. A bad case can damage the heart. Heavy coughing and a high fever are associated with the disease, as well as a painful sore throat. Because it was highly contagious, there was a chance all of the children would get it. So Moses sent Laurence, his eldest child, to a friend's house and isolated his daughter Edna from the other children.

The Trues' doctor, a good friend and neighbor, worked valiantly with the children. But Nathanael's condition worsened. He had difficulty breathing and lay limply in bed. The doctor gave the baby a new drug which had a good record in overcoming the symptoms. In a few days Nathanael regained some of his vitality, wanting to play again. One night, while Nathanael was sitting on his mother's lap, he seemed to be staring into space, his face luminous. Suddenly he reached up his hands toward the ceiling and pleaded, 'Oh, play with me.' A moment later Nathanael gasped his last breath, dying on 31 May 1899.

Though it hurt deeply to see Nathanael go, being with him when he died was an experience that strengthened Corinne's faith. She believed that during his final moments of life, Nathanael was approached by souls from the next world and that his last wish was granted.

The other children survived diphtheria that year. It had been a siege. Tired and saddened, Corinne didn't have time to grieve. She was concerned about Moses, who was taking the loss of Nathanael hard. He cried for days, and was perplexed, wondering why such an innocent little child would be kept from experiencing the richness of a full life. Corinne wondered about that too, but she was also worried about what Nathanael's death would do to her husband's health. He had a weak heart.

She succeeded in pulling the family together. That didn't mean she wasn't hurt. She was. But she didn't show it. Nor was anyone aware of the wounds left by Harriet's death. She took her questions to God, hoping that He would provide the answers. There was no one else to turn to.

Divine Science had provided some stability during good times. But during a crisis Corinne couldn't find solace in it, nor meaningful answers to the questions that had been raised during Harriet's passing. It seemed that she hadn't made much progress in her quest. She prayed for help, for guidance as to why her children were being taken away from her. They were so young, and desperately dependent on their mother and father. It all seemed so cruel. And yet deep down she knew there was a reason for everything in life. She couldn't explain why she felt that way; and if she tried, she was sure she would fail to be convincing.

Her search for the right answer intensified. This time she wasn't going to allow herself to be sidetracked; only finding the truth would end her quest. But Moses remained firm in Divine Science, believing his wife could find in it the answer she needed.

Despite caring for six children and a husband, Corinne found time to read new and old books about life, human behavior, creation, theology; she also attended lectures by traditional thinkers as well as by leaders of new philosophies and religions. She was optimistic that she would eventually find what she was looking for. In fact, she sensed that it existed in her time. How and when she would encounter it was out of her control. All she could do was try. She was convinced that there is a Great Power operating in the universe that charts the sincere seeker's course in life.

Several months after Nathanael's passing, Corinne met a close friend in the street, who described the illuminating experience she had had the previous night at a free lecture on religion given by three Persians. A sympathetic person, the friend knew that Corinne was suffering over the loss of Harriet and Nathanael. These men from the East, she told Corinne, might provide her with some insight on death and the meaning of life, and she urged Corinne to attend the next lecture.

Corinne went. It was like stepping out of a blizzard into a warm home. What the men from the East said made sense. More than that. Her heart knew that she had been exposed to God's Message. As she basked in a light she had sought, even as a child, she said to herself: 'This is it.'

From the start, Moses never doubted his wife's complete commitment to the Bahá'í Faith. When she returned from the lecture, he could tell that he was looking at a person who had discovered the rarest of treasures.

In the fall of 1899, over half of the 1,400 Bahá'ís in North America lived in Chicago. Since the Faith wasn't really organized in those days, there was no official continental headquarters. Yet Chicago was known as the spiritual center. Thornton Chase, the first American believer, lived and worked in the city. He was a highly respected insurance company executive. Other established businessmen and professionals were a part of the Bahá'í community – people like Arthur Agnew, Dr Chester Thacher, Rufus Butler, Byron Lane and a young printer, Albert Windust. A good percentage of the believers were women, many of them independent souls like Corinne; and they didn't retreat into the background, as most women did in those days. Women like Cecilia Harrison, Elizabeth Greenleaf and Jean Masson sensed that in the Bahá'í social order they would have an opportunity to develop their human potential and speak out, as men did. This, when American women were not allowed to vote in political elections and were restricted from participating in the professions. Though there weren't any clergy in the Bahá'í Faith – and many of the believers had been attracted to the Faith because of that – there were some outstanding teachers such as the charismatic Dr Ibráhím Khayru'lláh, a Syrian physician who had become a Bahá'í in Egypt. He came to Chicago in 1894 and, during the next few years, was able to enroll hundreds of men and women in Chicago and Kenosha, Wisconsin. But shortly after his pilgrimage to Akka in 1898–9, where he had come to realize that his hope for leadership of the American Bahá'í community could not be fulfilled, he defected from the Faith.[1]

Though there were other Eastern Bahá'ís in Chicago, such as Mírzá Asadu'lláh, a personal emissary of 'Abdu'l-Bahá, the Faith took on a sort of Protestant form – maybe because most of the believers were from that kind of religious background. There was little desire to organize. In fact, there was a feeling among a large number of adherents that organization would impede spiritual expression and development. So the weekly meetings were like church services. Excerpts from the *Kitáb-i-Íqán* (*The Book of Certitude*) and the *Hidden Words*, typed on sheets of paper, were read, as well as Tablets from 'Abdu'l-Bahá. So were passages from the Bible. There were no Bahá'í books in English. The most popular literature consisted of 'Abdu'l-Bahá's statements on spiritual matters in reply to questions sent to Him by the believers. His responses were usually copied by the inquirer and circulated throughout the community. At times, someone would speak for ten or fifteen minutes, usually on some millennial theme. The hymns sung afterwards reflected the same themes. They were Protestant hymns like 'Joy to the World, the Lord has Come', and 'Nearer My God to Thee'.

Unlike regular church services, no money collections were made. Quite a few, finding that especially refreshing, became Bahá'ís because of that practice. Many of the believers knew very little of the Faith they joined, but that was understandable since it was so new and translated literature was practically non-existent. But there were those, like Corinne True, who possessed a basic understanding of the Revelation of Bahá'u'lláh which was difficult to articulate. It was a belief that possessed her heart. She never doubted, regardless of the tests she encountered.

The Bahá'í Sunday meetings – usually held in the

afternoon so that people could attend regular church services in the morning – were held in a home with a piano, attracting about fifty to sixty men and women.

Corinne attended regularly. It was there that she became acquainted with members of the Board of Counsel, a group of men who conducted the meetings. Thornton Chase, Arthur Agnew and Dr Chester Thacher were among them. Based on her understanding of the Faith, Corinne felt that women should also be on the Board of Counsel, and it wasn't long before she made her feelings known about the matter.

It was at these meetings that Corinne was able to secure copies of some of the Bahá'í writings read there. She studied them faithfully, almost every day. They were precious, because they helped her to love God more and to grow more knowledgeable about Him. It was the medicine prescribed by the Divine Physician that continually lifted her closer to God. It was a feeling that was difficult to convey, and yet she wanted to, especially to her husband, her brother Tom and to her children. But it was difficult. She didn't want to give the impression of being a fanatic. So she prayed that those close to her would see what she saw and feel what she felt. But she didn't share her new Faith with her parents, because they wouldn't understand. It would only alienate them, especially her father who was deeply committed to Calvinism.

Like most new Bahá'ís at the turn of the century, Corinne was encouraged to write to the Master. She wrote to Him, even though she didn't expect an answer because she knew how busy He was. Though it took several months, she did receive a Tablet from the Holy Land, sent by Lua Getsinger on 12 October 1900. Through His Tablet, 'Abdu'l-Bahá helped Corinne face the reality of Nathanael's passing, providing her with some understanding of what had really happened to her three-year-old son.

O thou who art tested with a great calamity!

Be not grieved nor troubled because of the loss which hath befallen thee – a loss which caused the tears to flow, sighs to be produced, sorrow to exist and hearts to burn in great agony; but know, this hath reference only to the physical body, and if thou considerest this matter with a discerning and intelligent eye, thou wilt find that it hath no power whatsoever, for separation belongeth to the characteristics of the body. But concerning the spirit, know that thy pure son shall be with thee in the Kingdom of God and thou shalt witness his smiling face, illumined brow, handsome spirit and real happiness. Accordingly, thou wilt then be comforted and thank God for His favor upon thee.[2]

A few weeks later, Chicago was battling another outbreak of diphtheria. The seven-year-old twins, Katherine and Kenneth, were badly stricken. Katherine was an excellent student and serious minded, while Kenneth loved the piano.

It was a trying time. The youngsters' high fever and weakness caused great anxiety for their parents. Corinne prayed for their protection, and read 'Abdu'l-Bahá's Tablet again and again. While it strengthened her to accept God's will, she longed for their safe recovery.

The physician who had treated the children during the previous diphtheria outbreak was looking after the twins. He gave them the same drug administered the year before. Though their fever diminished and both seemed more alert, Katherine appeared to be stronger than Kenneth. Moses worried especially about him. One night Kenneth grew weaker, struggling to breathe. It all came on suddenly, for he seemed to be recovering, but he died that same night, 14 January 1901.

Another child gone, the third in eight years – two in less than two years' time. The surviving children and Moses were crushed. Once again Corinne had to hold the family together.

'Abdu'l-Bahá's Tablet concerning the passing of Kenneth,

sent in May 1901, was reassuring:

> O thou who art patient and resigning thyself to the judgment (of God)!
> Be not grieved at the calamity which hath unexpectedly come upon thee and for the misfortune which heavily weigheth upon thee. It behooveth one like thee to endure every trial, to be pleased with the decree and to commit all thy affairs to God so that thou mayest be a calm, approved and pleasing soul before God. Know thou, that thy beloved son hath soared, with the wing of soul, up to the loftiest height which is never-ending in the Kingdom of God. Rejoice at this great prosperity which the chosen ones were longingly asking from the Holy and Exalted Threshold (of God). Truly, I say unto thee, wert thou informed of the position in which is thy son, thy face would be illumined by the lights of happiness and thou wouldst thank thy forgiving Lord therefor and thou wouldst long for ascending to that praiseworthy position.[3]

Katherine recovered from the illness. A few months later, however, the Trues received disturbing news, that Kenneth and Nathanael hadn't died of diphtheria. The drug had had side effects, weakening the boys' hearts. Heart failure was the real cause of their deaths.

Despite the loss of Kenneth, Corinne gradually developed a sense of well-being. Strange, she thought, considering what had happened to her in recent years. She knew that without the Bahá'í Faith and 'Abdu'l-Bahá's Tablets she would have been consumed by grief. Through 'Abdu'l-Bahá she had gained an awareness of reality that books and revered ancient and modern philosphers had been unable to provide her. Corinne's husband was amazed at her strength, and so were the five remaining children. They all drew comfort from her.

Corinne knew that direction from the Master was divine guidance, creating in her a feeling that encompassed and fortified her spirit. The feeling was difficult to describe in words. Yet she communicated it to others by the way she lived her life. She grew calmer, more patient and faithful. Friends, not familiar with the Faith, marveled at the way she endured such grievous hardship. But she recognized that what impressed them was not herself, but the power of the Faith. How could she tell them that? Nevertheless, she had to. 'Abdu'l-Bahá had urged all Bahá'ís to share the healing Message of Bahá'u'lláh with others. It was the Word of God for today, and so many people were looking for something to really believe in. Deep down, they were dissatisfied with what they were accustomed to. Not to share the Message would be like refusing to cast a life preserver to a drowning man. But Corinne was reserved by nature, one who respected people's privacy; and though she was well versed in the Bible and had studied the Faith deeply, she had never tried to teach it. She was a housewife, with five children to rear and educate and a husband to nurture and keep happy.

And so, though plagued with feelings of inadequacy, Corinne began to teach, even while on summer vacation in Michigan. She introduced the Faith to that state, establishing Bahá'í communities in Grand Rapids, Grand Haven, Fruitport and elsewhere. Of course, she also taught in Chicago and traveled to Milwaukee, Racine, Kenosha and other Wisconsin towns throughout the rest of the year.

It wasn't long before Corinne discovered that being a Bahá'í wasn't going to be easy. There was so much to contend with – people's differing backgrounds, characteristics and biases, as well as her own shortcomings. These could create barriers between people, even those who professed the same faith.

4

'Found Ye Spiritual Assemblies'

For most American Bahá'ís in 1901, an administrative order was a foreign concept, especially the kind outlined in Bahá'í writings not then translated and which is presently operating in the Bahá'í world. Most of the believers were of evangelical Protestant background, and accustomed to churches loosely organized by the clergy, where the minister was accountable to the congregation. Though they were familiar with working in church groups, they would have viewed an elected body of nine people, with sole authority in a spiritual community, as strange. Of most interest to them was the theme of the Return of Christ. The fact that He had come in the person of Bahá'u'lláh, and they knew it, catapulted them into a rarefied state of mind. Now, they felt, the Kingdom of God would soon follow; and that would come about through some great cosmic event.

In Chicago, there was a core of Bahá'ís who believed that organization was essential to the survival of their fledgling Faith. A few sensed the correlation of an administrative order and the formation of the Kingdom of God on earth. They had seen a copy of the *Kitáb-i-Aqdas*, which mentions the development of Houses of Justice.[1] So, even though the Master didn't request the believers to organize administratively, some prominent Chicago Bahá'ís felt they should. After all, He hadn't said they couldn't. Besides, they were assured that 'Abdu'l-Bahá was following the development of the Faith in North America, making certain that the believers remained united. Moreover, people like Thornton Chase believed that organizing the Faith would protect it from confusion and schism.

'Abdu'l-Bahá had sent special emissaries to the West to promote unity among the Bahá'ís. Mírzá Asadu'lláh was one of them. Based in Chicago, and adored by the Bahá'ís, he helped to transform the Board of Counsel, which was conducting the Sunday meetings, into a nine-member administrative body. His suggestion that it be called a House of Justice was adopted by the newly-elected unit. But that name was soon dropped when 'Abdu'l-Bahá said that a different title should be used. According to Thornton Chase, the Master felt that the term 'House of Justice' would indicate to the public a political unit, especially in countries where the Bahá'ís were being persecuted. Because 'Abdu'l-Bahá didn't suggest a name, much effort was devoted to devising one. They finally agreed on 'House of Spirituality', which the Master approved.

Corinne True followed the development of the House of Spirituality keenly. It bothered her that women weren't allowed to serve on the body. She didn't protest, but instead made a commitment to try to change the membership to include women. Though Corinne knew that women were disenfranchised in America, and were forced to play an inferior role in the administration of Christendom's hundreds of sects, she was sure that Bahá'u'lláh had inaugurated a new era, in which women would realize equal status with men. But many of the early Bahá'ís, including Thornton Chase, didn't subscribe to Corinne True's beliefs. In fact, he felt that women were too emotional to work effectively on an administrative body. His thinking was understandable, considering the customs and conditions that prevailed in America during the early 1900s.

Altering customs and uprooting biases required patience and wisdom. Reconditioning was needed; without that, discord would break out, ancient prejudices would flare into conflagrations between groups. Because of the way the House of Spirituality was organized – and the body originated the structure, not the Master – reconditioning inevitably took place. While the House of Spirituality made decisions, those decisions had to be ratified by the community at the weekly community meeting. In those days, anyone who attended, Bahá'í or non-Bahá'í, was eligible to express his or her views and vote. A number of women, including Corinne True, weren't shy about stating their opinions. To most of the men, including the House of Spirituality members, this was a test. But it was also a learning experience for them, even though at the time they didn't recognize it as such. Certainly 'Abdu'l-Bahá was aware of what was happening. The House of Spirituality sent Him weekly reports, and Mírzá Asadu'lláh was in contact with Him. The Master not only refused to end ratification by the community of their decisions, but urged the House of Spirituality to encourage women to be more involved in community activities.

The Women's Assembly of Teaching was formed after 'Abdu'l-Bahá, in a Tablet to Corinne, not only stated the equal station of women but encouraged them to organize the teaching work:

> Know thou, O handmaid, that in the sight of Bahá, women are accounted the same as men . . . from the spiritual viewpoint there is no difference between them . . .
>
> As to you, O ye other handmaids who are enamoured of the heavenly fragrances, arrange ye holy gatherings, and found ye Spiritual Assemblies, for these are the basis for spreading the sweet savours of God, exalting His Word, promulgating His religion and promoting His Teachings, and what bounty is there greater than this? . . .[2]

It organized meetings in homes, study groups and public meetings. Though it reported to the House of Spirituality, it operated, unwittingly, as a parallel institution. Obviously this was acceptable at that time since no advice came from

Haifa to disband the Women's Assembly of Teaching. Similar organizational arrangements were made in other parts of the Bahá'í world. In Tehran, for example, there was an Assembly for Zoroastrian Bahá'ís, and in Hamadan, an Assembly for Jewish Bahá'ís. In time, as the Bahá'ís matured in their faith, they would integrate into one local spiritual governing body, regardless of ethnic or religious heritage and sex, as prescribed by the Founder of their Faith. And that happened shortly after Shoghi Effendi became Guardian in 1921.

Corinne True was the first president of the Women's Assembly of Teaching, and was so addressed by 'Abdu'l-Bahá in September 1902.[3] She was holding that position when the Women's Assembly and the House of Spirituality had a serious disagreement about a year later.

Though eager to impart the Revelation to her family, Corinne was careful not to overwhelm them with it. At the appropriate time she would share a Tablet from 'Abdu'l-Bahá or a newly-translated excerpt from the Writings of Bahá'u'lláh with her children, who were impressed with her dedication to her Faith. In the long run, that had a profound effect on them.

Arna, the free spirit, the one who had difficulty accepting discipline, was the child who, at first, showed the most interest in the Bahá'í Faith. Laurence was away at Stanford University. Davis was preoccupied with athletics, developing into a champion pole vaulter and baseball and football player. Basketball, dancing and school work took up most of Edna's time. Katherine was busy pursuing her education.

Corinne realized that caring for and training one's children was more than parental duty. It was an essential Bahá'í act. She turned to 'Abdu'l-Bahá for advice, which He gave in this reply:

> . . . it behoveth thee to nurture them at the breast of the love of God, and urge them onward to the things of the spirit, that they may turn their faces unto God; that their

ways may conform to the rules of good conduct and their character be second to none; that they make their own all the graces and praiseworthy qualities of humankind; acquire a sound knowledge of the various branches of learning, so that from the very beginning of life they may become spiritual beings, dwellers in the Kingdom, enamoured of the sweet breaths of holiness, and may receive an education religious, spiritual, and of the Heavenly Realm. Verily will I call upon God to grant them a happy outcome in this.[4]

Corinne True found some time to become involved in her children's interests, even if she understood little about them. She knew it meant a lot to Davis that she attend his sporting games; so she went to them. 'Poller vaulting', as she called it, was Davis's best sport. But seeing him hurl his body over a wooden bar high above the ground terrified her, although it pleased her to see him enjoy what he did. She encouraged Edna to play basketball, a game she excelled in. The encouragement came forth despite the fact that many people in those days viewed basketball as a man's sport. Edna went on to star in and captain the Smith College basketball team.

Nine months after Kenneth's passing, Corinne True learned that her mother had died unexpectedly while vacationing in the South. She was 62. Most people who knew the Knights thought that her husband would pass on before she did. After all, she was twenty years younger, and basically healthy, while he was confined to a wheelchair.

Corinne's father was stunned. He was one of those who had believed he would die before his wife. Since he had planned on that, he seemed lost, helpless. He was financially able to live and go wherever he wished, but he had simple tastes, and had grown accustomed to having a loyal companion. Also, it was through Martha that he had been able to survive the nine trying years when he had refused to speak to Corinne. His wife had done for his daughter during that period of time what he couldn't bring himself to do. He couldn't wait for Martha to return from her visits with Corinne and the children, to find out how they were faring. She had kept the family together. She had carefully, and with great sensitivity and tact, conditioned him to welcome his daughter 'back home'. And he was aware of his wife's disappointment over his refusal to speak to his son-in-law.

Martha Knight was buried in the South. Her husband knew that she would have preferred that. But what was he to do? He was in his eighties, bound to a wheelchair. He wanted to be close to his children. Corinne and Thomas decided that each would write to him, inviting him to stay with them. Corinne thought her father would choose to stay with his son; after all, Thomas had only one child and she had five, and her father wasn't speaking to her husband.

Moses Greene Knight decided to live with his daughter. When his train arrived at the Chicago railroad station, his daughter and son-in-law were there and Moses went aboard to greet him. As the two men were shaking hands, Moses said, 'Happy to see you, Mr Knight. We are so glad that you chose to stay with us. The children are so excited that you are going to be with us.' And he meant it.

The Trues insisted that Mr Knight occupy their bedroom, which had a bathroom. An adjoining bedroom was used by his personal nurse.

The two men became close friends, never speaking of the past. As for Corinne, the sadness she had felt in earlier years, because her father would not meet Moses, was gone; for her, those years once over were, in Edna's words, 'all over'.[5]

So much of Corinne's time and energy were devoted to serving the Faith. Gone a lot, especially while the children were at school, she wondered if her father resented her absences. Mr Knight didn't complain. Whenever she could, she would talk to her father, usually about subjects in which he was interested. Always she had felt close to him and, basically, was much like him.

To the children, Grandfather Knight was fun and often played table games with them. At such times he would grow extremely competitive, sometimes startling and amusing the youngsters by cheating in small ways. Their father, recognizing an old man's foible, counseled them to allow their grandfather to win. 'Since he is old,' he said, 'why deny him such a simple pleasure?' They enjoyed watching their grandfather react to 'Dixie', the Confederacy's anthem, sung or played on an instrument. He would become quiet, teary-eyed, and his face would grow red. Laurence and Davis took turns shaving him, an exercise that would usually lead to a silver dollar tip. Whenever a new friend of one of the children visited the house, Mr Knight would inquire about the child's background, for he wanted his grandchildren to have good playmates. And the children vied in taking his supper tray to him, for he often didn't eat his dessert.

Moses Greene Knight died while visiting his son Tom and his family on Chicago's South side, two years after his wife's passing. He was 83.

5

'Abdu'l-Bahá's Call for the Temple

The Women's Assembly of Teaching was an energetic group, maybe too energetic for most of the members of the House of Spirituality. Assertiveness, men had been schooled to believe, was a male characteristic. The Assembly was particularly vigorous in promulgating the Faith. Divine knowledge, they felt, must be spread. The women wanted to wage a crusade; while most of the men, especially the majority of the House of Spirituality, were more cautious. Since one of their goals was to legitimize their fledgling Faith in the eyes of the public, people like Thornton Chase were afraid that radical action could undo whatever public relations gains they might achieve for the Faith in the Chicago area. To its credit, the House of Spirituality was run on a sound basis. Consultation was mature; community unity was maintained; the Fund was managed meticulously. The House of Spirituality, composed of successful businessmen and other professionals, frowned on deficit spending. Indebtedness was viewed as a cardinal sin.

So when the Women's Assembly of Teaching, with Corinne True as its president, pushed for renting a downtown hall for weekly public meetings, the House of Spirituality rejected the idea, claiming it couldn't afford to do that. They continued to hold meetings in a large house on the west side of the city. The Women's Assembly of Teaching, on the other hand, felt that a more prestigious place, in a centrally located area, was needed to spread the

Faith more effectively. Both groups sincerely believed their positions would best serve the Cause.

In May 1902, the Women's Assembly of Teaching rented a hall, financing it themselves. A rift broke out between the two groups. Worse than that. Some of the House of Spirituality members sided with the women, refusing to attend meetings. Stable members like Charles Ioas and Byron Lane were among them. Thornton Chase, Arthur Agnew, Ralph Butler, Albert Windust and Dr Thacher carried on while fervently praying for the House of Spirituality. Thornton Chase boycotted the women's downtown gatherings. He believed the women were causing discord.

The dissension troubled Corinne. Could she be to blame, she wondered? She appealed to 'Abdu'l-Bahá for guidance. A month after the downtown meetings were started, Corinne received a Tablet from the Master, addressing her as 'O thou yearning flame, thou who art afire with the Love of God'. In the Tablet, 'Abdu'l-Bahá pointed out that trials and tests can divert even the famous and most learned from the path of God. He cited Judas Iscariot as an example. He went on to say:

> Convey thou unto the handmaids of the Merciful the message that when a test turneth violent they must stand unmoved, and faithful to their love for Bahá. In winter come the storms, and the great winds blow, but then will follow spring in all its beauty, adorning hill and plain with perfumed plants and red anemones, fair to see. Then will the birds trill out upon the branches their songs of joy, and sermonize in lilting tones from the pulpits of the trees . . .
>
> As to thee, blessed art thou, for thou art steadfast in the Cause of God, firm in His Covenant. I beg of Him to bestow upon thee a spiritual soul, and the life of the Kingdom, and to make thee a leaf verdant and flourishing on the Tree of Life, that thou mayest serve the handmaids of the Merciful with spirituality and good cheer.
>
> Thy generous Lord will assist thee to labour in His vineyard and will cause thee to be the means of spreading

the spirit of unity among His handmaids. He will make thine inner eye to see with the light of knowledge, He will forgive thy sins and transform them into goodly deeds.[1]

Receiving a Tablet from the Master always renewed Corinne's spirit. The guidance He gave was much more than met the eye. It had to be studied. He provided perspective; He didn't issue commandments. 'Abdu'l-Bahá knew how immature the believers were, that mistakes were going to be made, even by the most knowledgeable and best intentioned believers. He didn't take sides in the male–female conflict. In pondering His words, Corinne sensed that if all involved in the dispute remained firm in the Covenant, the differences between the groups would eventually vanish, and spiritual growth and unity would result.

In September 1902, the Women's Assembly of Teaching had to abandon their hall. It was too expensive to maintain. Soon those members who were staying away from the House of Spirituality meetings started coming back. It wasn't a victory for the men. The Faith had won out. Not only was the Cause intact, but lessons were learned by all. The women realized how important it was to obey a ruling of the House of Spirituality. The men, in turn, grew more sensitive to the need of being more audacious in teaching. In fact, five months after the women gave up the hall, the House of Spirituality rented a hall downtown for regular Sunday meetings, open to the public. To reinforce the unity that was developing between the men and women, the House of Spirituality sent a letter to the Women's Assembly of Teaching, asking if it would prepare the refreshments for the meetings. The women's response was an enthusiastic 'Yes'. So concerned was the House of Spirituality with maintaining equal participation in the Sunday meetings, it made certain there were women readers. The one time that didn't happen, it sent a letter of apology to the Women's Assembly of Teaching.

Involvement in the early growth of the Faith in America was a time-consuming and energy-sapping undertaking. Many nights Corinne returned home from meetings exhausted and troubled. She wanted so to do the right thing, especially to please the Master, but wasn't always sure she had. There was no one at home to share her spiritual battles with. She could only turn to Bahá'u'lláh and 'Abdu'l-Bahá for solace, peace of mind and guidance. News of disunity in the Bahá'í community was kept from her husband, because Corinne wanted to attract him to the Faith. Besides, she couldn't burden him with her spiritual problems, because the Master had urged her to keep him happy.

> As to thy respected husband: it is incumbent upon thee to treat him with great kindness, to consider his wishes and be conciliatory with him at all times . . .[2]

For Corinne, life couldn't be complete unless Moses could share with her the most meaningful thing. She loved him; yet it hurt that, in some respects, they lived in different worlds. He was kind, thoughtful, generous, a wonderful parent and friend. But how much more they could do for the Faith if Moses were a Bahá'í, she thought. Corinne knew that her Bahá'í involvement must be a test for him, even if he didn't complain. She was away so much of the time, and he must be lonely. They used to do so many things together. Now it was he and the children who were drawing closer, going to the theater, sporting events and picnics. To the children he always defended their mother's Bahá'í work. She was grateful to him for being so understanding and for encouraging her to carry out her Bahá'í duties. In many ways he was leading a Bahá'í life, but that wasn't really enough for Corinne. 'Abdu'l-Bahá realized her concern and revealed a prayer for her to recite on behalf of her husband:

> O my Lord! Make the eyes of my husband to see. Rejoice Thou his heart with the light of the knowledge of Thee,

draw Thou his mind unto Thy luminous beauty, cheer Thou his spirit by revealing unto him Thy manifest splendours.
O my Lord! Lift Thou the veil from before his sight. Rain down Thy plenteous bounties upon him, intoxicate him with the wine of love for Thee, make him one of Thy angels whose feet walk upon this earth even as their souls are soaring through the high heavens. Cause him to become a brilliant lamp, shining out with the light of Thy wisdom in the midst of Thy people.
Verily Thou art the Precious, the Ever-Bestowing, the Open of Hand.[3]

In 1903, with the early disunity stabilized and the Faith being taught vigorously, the House of Spirituality, inspired by news of the Ashkhabad ('Ishqábád) Temple project, felt ready to build a house of worship. They asked the Master for permission. He sent them two Tablets, approving the idea. Eight days after the second Tablet arrived, Corinne True also received one about the Temple to be erected in America. Its contents startled her:

> Now the day has arrived in which the edifice of God, the divine sanctuary, the spiritual temple, shall be erected in America! I entreat God to assist the confirmed believers in accomplishing this great service and with entire zeal to rear this mighty structure which shall be renowned throughout the world. The support of God will be with those believers in that district that they may be successful in their undertaking, for the Cause is great and great; because this is the first Mashrak-el-Azcar in that country and from it the praise of God shall ascend to the Kingdom of Mystery and the tumult of His exaltation and greetings from the whole world shall be heard!
>
> Whosoever arises for the service of this building shall be assisted with a great power from His Supreme Kingdom and upon him spiritual and heavenly blessings shall descend, which shall fill his heart with wonderful consolation and enlighten his eyes by beholding the glorious and eternal God![4]

Although 'Abdu'l-Bahá had not singled her out from 'the confirmed believers', it was clear to Corinne that He wanted her to become involved in 'the service of this building'. '. . .He wrote me instructions about the Temple to my utter astonishment that placed a great responsibility on my shoulders,' she wrote to a friend.[5] But how? she wondered. She wasn't an architect or a builder. Men dominated the real estate business. What could a housewife and mother of five children do to construct a temple? The fact that 'Abdu'l-Bahá had chosen to write to her required her to become involved. Nothing else could have persuaded her to accept the challenge. But what to do first? As president of the Women's Assembly of Teaching, she took the problem to the group. They raised a small amount of money, banked it and named a treasurer.

The next four years saw little progress on the Temple project, either by the House of Spirituality or by Corinne and the Women's Assembly of Teaching. They were confused over several of 'Abdu'l-Bahá's messages concerning the Temple. In fact, there was a strong minority of believers, led by John Sykes and Honoré J. Jaxon, who felt that 'Abdu'l-Bahá wanted a spiritual temple built in each Bahá'í's heart, and that He wasn't calling for the construction of a physical house of worship. The press of other responsibilities such as teaching and fostering community unity detracted from the Temple effort. Besides, it was natural for the believers to gravitate to what they knew and liked best. At that time, they weren't aware of the significance of the House of Worship to the American community. In 1903, how could they be? Corinne, like many others, viewed it simply as a gathering center for prayer, a place where the local friends could meet. The fact that it would rise as a mighty teaching and unifying instrument in America wasn't envisioned.

Corinne didn't, however, forget her obligation to the Temple project. She thought about it almost daily. But there wasn't much she could do. While she carried on her

Assembly duties, and taught the Faith, she longed for the kind of guidance that would help her to grow stronger spiritually, and more detached from the material world. She turned to the One she believed, with all her heart and soul, could fulfill her dearest wish. When she received from 'Abdu'l-Bahá what she sought, she used it as a code for living for the rest of her life:

> Believe thou in God, and keep thine eyes fixed upon the exalted Kingdom; be thou enamoured of the Abhá Beauty; stand thou firm in the Covenant: yearn thou to ascend into the Heaven of the Universal Light. Be thou severed from this world, and reborn through the sweet scents of holiness that blow from the realm of the All-Highest. Be thou a summoner to love, and be thou kind to all the human race. Love thou the children of men and share in their sorrows. Be thou of those who foster peace. Offer thy friendship, be worthy of trust. Be thou a balm to every sore, be thou a medicine for every ill. Bind thou the souls together. Recite thou the verses of guidance. Be engaged in the worship of thy Lord, and rise up to lead the people aright. Loose thy tongue and teach, and let thy face be bright with the fire of God's love. Rest thou not for a moment, seek thou to draw no easeful breath. Thus mayest thou become a sign and symbol of God's love, and a banner of His grace.[6]

In her first four years as a Bahá'í, Corinne True received fifteen Tablets from 'Abdu'l-Bahá. Often unaware of their effect, she grew like a flower that's fed by rain. The Master's exhortations were taken to heart. She knew He knew her weaknesses. Not to heed His messages would be foolish. For over two years, November 1904 to December 1906, no further Tablets reached her. But in that 1904 message He had given her both priceless advice and promise for her future:

> The humbler one is, the more will one advance and the greater will be one's progress.
>
> A musk-like fragrance emanated from the spiritual rose garden of thy letter. This is an evidence that, if it be God's Will, thou shalt in the future make progress, increasingly

exerting thyself day by day in the pathway of self-sacrifice, uttering the praises of God and His glorification, guiding the people, and lighting a lamp that will shed its light through the ages and centuries to come.[7]

During the two years Corinne didn't hear directly from 'Abdu'l-Bahá she intensified her teaching, although she shied away from giving public talks. The thought of facing a large crowd frightened her. Most of the teaching was done in her home, whether in Chicago or on vacation in Fruitport, Michigan. There were times when she would visit cities in Wisconsin to share the Message with gatherings in local homes. Her children remembered that almost every afternoon their mother would be in the parlor telling someone about the Faith, or waiting for the natural opportunity to share the message of Bahá'u'lláh with the guest. She did it calmly, using her knowledge of the Bible and stressing the 'Latter Day' theme. There was nothing she enjoyed more, for she was immersed in the Faith. She wanted to talk about it all the time.

Her children helped her to control her yearning and she appreciated their requests to restrain herself among their friends and among strangers. Though she did this, it wasn't easy. For knowing Who Bahá'u'lláh was, what His message could do for a failing society, she wanted to share the 'good news' with everyone. There was so much unhappiness, so much aimlessness, so much fear all around her, everywhere. She wanted so to help.

In time, Corinne True would master control. But that didn't prevent her dynamic personality from creating the atmosphere in their home. It was a Bahá'í home, where Bahá'í standards were upheld. Whenever a principle was circumvented by the children, Corinne would lovingly remind them of it. When emphasis was needed she would tap her forefinger on the palm of her other hand. To the children that was a sign to heed what was being said.

Corinne surrendered her home to Bahá'u'lláh. And it didn't matter where she was living. To the children, especially the daughters, their home was like a Bahá'í hotel. People from different parts of the world would spend time with them, and for various reasons. Some were traveling teachers; some needed a place to recuperate after surgery; others couldn't afford a hotel. At times, the children had to give up their beds to accommodate the guests. That usually meant Katherine and Arna sharing Edna's bed with her, with Katherine sandwiched between her older sisters. Despite that inconvenience, the girls found a house full of people – many of whom they didn't know – exciting. It widened their experience and helped them break out of the social mold their mother had been brought up in. They knew they were living in a Bahá'í home, because unlike most other Bahá'ís in the early 1900s Corinne had severed all connections with the church. Edna, Arna and Katherine grew up in a home where it was understood that Christ had returned.

Growing up under those conditions was bound to be a factor in Corinne's daughters becoming Bahá'ís. None of them could recall when they accepted Bahá'u'lláh. Their faith was absorbed over the years, little by little. As early as 1903 they were concerned with becoming better Bahá'ís and, like their mother, they knew Whom to turn to for help.[8] Edna was 15 when she wrote to the Master:

Allah'u'Abha

To the Beloved Master, Abdul Baha:
    I have been able to study and learn a great deal of these wonderful words of the Manifestation, through my mother, who is one of Thy maid-servants. My greatest longing and desire is to be able to comprehend the meaning of these words and adjust my life to them. Therefore I ask you please to supplicate to God to clean my heart from all selfish longings and unkind feelings towards others and to fill me with pure desires, kind thoughts, loving deeds and the great knowledge of Thy Teachings.
Your loving maid-servant,
Edna M. True

Katherine, who was only 9, wrote to the Master on the same day as her older sister:

> Allah'u'Abha
> To the Dear Master, Abdul Baha:
> Haji Mirza Hassan promised to take me to the Holy City, Acca, in his robe to see the Beloved Master.
> I am learning the Hidden Words of the Blessed Perfection and desire to live according to His commands. I supplicate to you to pray to God for me to fill me with His Holy Spirit.
> I ask you, won't you please send me a Tablet in your own handwriting. Give my love to all your Household and dear Mirza Assad'Ullah.
> Your little maid-servant,
> Katherine True
> Chicago, Illinois, April 11th, 1903

Both girls received a response from 'Abdu'l-Bahá. These were His Tablets:

> To the Servant of God, Edna True.
> Oh thou who art turning unto God.
> Thy letter was an inheritance of joy and happiness unto me, for its significance was a supplication and an entreaty unto God to make thee a pure servant, exempt from all material desires, sanctified and severed from all save God, that thou mayest be characterized with the attributes of the heavenly angels, cleansed from all desires and earthly wishes, with thy heart severed from all save the knowledge of the divine teachings. Verily, I pray God to nourish thee upon the breast of bounty and rear thee in such a manner that all men of learning shall be amazed, and to make thee a miracle of guidance among the servants.
> Upon thee be greetings and praise.
> (signed) Abbas Abdul Baha
> Acca, June 9th 1903, per Lua M. Getsinger.[9]

To Katherine He wrote:

> To Katherine True.
> Oh thou who art attracted to God! I send this letter

written by my own hand, that thou mayest thank God, thy Lord, the Supreme, grow in happiness in the Love of God and be kindled by the fire of His love, chanting verses of greetings and thanks, and be quickened by the breezes of life blown from the garden of the knowledge of God.

Abbas Abdul Baha

Acca June 9th 1903, per Lua M. Getsinger.[10]

6

Six Days in Akka

While deeply involved in the affairs of the Faith locally and nationally, Corinne True found some time for her family. In fact, 1906 looked like a good year. She was thrilled at the prospect of her eldest son's college graduation and marriage. Laurence had transferred from Stanford to the University of Michigan and was engaged to a young lady from Chicago. Because he had a job waiting for him in the fall, he decided to go to summer school so he could start work immediately after graduation. Laurence was the apple of his mother's eye. He was healthy, considerate and a devoted son. His father adored him. That summer Laurence would try to be with the family at their summer home whenever possible. Ann Arbor was some distance from Fruitport, but it wasn't his studies that kept him from being with the family every weekend. A strong athlete, he was part of a sailing team that competed on weekends.

But Laurence found time to go to Fruitport on 4 August, a Saturday, so that he could celebrate his fiancée's and sister Edna's birthdays. Leaving his family that day was difficult, but he had to be at Saginaw Bay, the site of the biggest race of the season next day; he couldn't disappoint his teammates.

Laurence was never seen again. Halfway through the race, he moved forward on the deck to adjust the sailboat's jib. A sudden gust whipped the sail across the deck, knocking Laurence into the water, apparently unconscious. His teammates tried valiantly to find him. The fierce winds and rough water hampered the rescue effort.

News of the tragedy reached Fruitport that evening. The family was shocked. Moses True sobbed. He sat in his chair for days, grieving. The only time he would perk up was when news from Saginaw would arrive. Perhaps – he and some of the other members of the family felt – Laurence would miraculously show up. A week after the reported drowning, Laurence's body was washed ashore. Moses suffered a heart attack; though he recovered, it took weeks before he could return to work.

The fact that Corinne knew that what had happened to Laurence must be God's will didn't remove the deep, painful ache in her heart. He was such a wonderful person – thoughtful, fun-loving, a young man of sterling integrity, and so happy the day before he died. His future had seemed so bright. The children took the loss of Laurence hard, especially Edna. She and Laurence had a special relationship, maybe because they were so much alike. They were so close that when he gave his fiancée his Delta Kappa Epsilon fraternity pin, he gave a similar one to his sister. And when Edna went off to Smith College, Laurence insisted on accompanying his mother and sister to Northampton, Massachusetts.

Four children left. There was the impulse to protect them from death's untimely reach. But life had to be lived; Davis and Edna were in college, Arna would soon start college and Katherine, a brilliant student, was about to begin high school. They needed to be comforted during this trying time, as well as their father, who was so devoted to his children and loved them so. He was deeply involved in their lives, experiencing their defeats and triumphs, be they at school, at play or on the athletic field. His involvement with them seemed to intensify as his wife grew more and more active in the Faith. Corinne appreciated the arrangement, especially his loving explanations to the children as to why their mother was away so much.

With Laurence's death, Corinne's husband needed more than consoling and emotional support. It wasn't only the loss of Laurence that crushed him. The Saginaw Bay incident opened old wounds; the deaths of Harriet, Nathanael and Kenneth were relived. But Laurence's drowning hurt the most, for he had reached adulthood and was ready to embark on his own life. Moses was so proud of his eldest son. What happened to him made no sense; life seemed meaningless to Moses. His brooding, Corinne knew, could further damage his weak heart. They had talked about returning to Grand Rapids, where the pace of life was slower. Corinne sensed that Moses preferred leaving Chicago. He didn't press the issue because he realized how much his wife's Assembly work meant to her, although a less hectic lifestyle would be less of a strain on his heart. They both knew that, but didn't raise the point. Moving to Michigan, she reasoned, wouldn't mean an end to Bahá'í work. There were lots of people there who needed to know about the Faith. They made plans to move.

Once again, Corinne True drew the family together, trying to provide some perspective, some insight into the latest tragedy. It wasn't what she said to her husband and children, but her attitude and faith that helped them recover from Laurence's sudden death. Her children never saw her shed a tear. She organized the funeral arrangements and comforted her family, all the time giving the impression that whatever happens is for the best. In time, her children would grow to appreciate that quality in their mother, manifesting calm during times of crisis.

For Corinne True, comfort came from 'Abdu'l-Bahá:

> Do not grieve on account of the death of thy son, neither sigh nor lament. That nightingale soared upward to the divine rose-garden; that drop returned to the most great ocean of Truth; that foreigner hastened to his native abode; and that ill one found salvation and life eternal.

> Why shouldst thou be sad and heartbroken? This separation is temporal; this remoteness and sorrow is counted only by days. Thou shalt find him in the Kingdom of God and thou wilt attain to the everlasting union. Physical companionship is ephemeral, but heavenly association is eternal. Whenever thou rememberest the eternal and never ending union, thou wilt be comforted and blissful.[1]

Laurence's death sparked an inescapable urge in Corinne True to see the Master. It didn't matter that He was 6,000 miles away, in a strange land and still a prisoner of the Ottoman Empire; and that she feared travel. With encouragement from her husband, she wrote for permission to visit Akka, with daughter Arna.

The fact that Mr and Mrs Arthur Agnew, also of Chicago, were making the same pilgrimage, relieved some of Corinne's fear of venturing overseas. They booked passage on the same ship.

During the time between deciding to try to see the Master and setting sail, Corinne was busy organizing a Women's Assembly of Teaching petition, calling for Temple construction to start. Nearly eight hundred signatures were collected from believers across the country, an enterprise carried out by Corinne. It was Moses True who sorted the sheets of paper that flowed into the True home. He glued them together, creating a large scroll which he placed into a metal cylinder. The House of Spirituality had instructed Arthur Agnew to deliver the scroll to the Master.

Corinne was to give 'Abdu'l-Bahá other things, things she hadn't planned to carry. When the believers learned of her impending pilgrimage, many of them called on her, asking to present Him with gifts – all sorts of things: pictures of their families to bless, as well as letters with questions and requests for Persian names for their children, even a fruitcake. By the time she left, she had one large suitcase filled with their gifts. Corinne had to deliver them all because she knew that most of the Chicago believers would never get to the Holy Land. Whatever they asked her to give the Master was a part of them; in a sense, it was their way of making the pilgrimage.

Then came news that the Agnews couldn't make the pilgrimage; their son had been taken ill. So the House of Spirituality turned to Corinne to deliver the scroll. Nothing, other than a directive from 'Abdu'l-Bahá, could keep her from Akka. She had to meet Him. It also helped to be swept up by Arna's spirit of adventure. Arna seemed to be more excited about the trip than its purpose. Her curiosity, exuberance and earthy wit helped Corinne blunt the edge of her fear of long-distance travel. She was actually afraid to board the steamer. At one point Arna told Corinne, 'Oh Mother, I can speak French and we will get along alright.'[2] In some respects, having Arna along was like being accompanied by her husband, who stayed at home with Katherine. He was always so reassuring. (Caring for the unpredictable Arna would have been too great a challenge for Moses, who had to work most of the week.)

Arna's enthusiasm and fascination with everything new also kept her mother from thinking too much about home, the place she enjoyed being the most. But there were also thoughts of what was in store for her and Arna. Each minute on the sea brought her that much closer to Akka, and to the One who had liberated her.

When Corinne, with Arna, set sail from Boston on the SS *Republic*, she was under the impression that the Master wasn't being harassed by the Turkish authorities, though He was officially a prisoner of the Ottoman Empire and, since 1901, had been strictly confined within the prison-city of Akka. During 1905 and 1906, however, He had enjoyed better relations with the officials. But by 1907 the Ottoman Sultan had become thoroughly alarmed by the successes of Persian revolutionaries in Iran, and the enemies of 'Abdu'l-Bahá saw in this situation a chance to renew their accusations against Him, which had partially succeeded in 1901. This time they hoped to accomplish either His execution or deportation to some remote place. Among their charges were that 'Abdu'l-Bahá was conspiring to overthrow the rulers of Palestine, was building a fortress on Mt Carmel – the Tomb of the Báb – and that English and American pilgrims were supporting His plans. Rumours and even danger surrounded 'Abdu'l-Bahá in Akka as Corinne and her daughter were steaming toward the Holy Land.[3]

In 1907, the only way to reach Akka was by sea. The railroad linking Cairo with Akka hadn't been built yet. The train connection which would be instituted twelve years later would turn out to be a more comfortable travel arrangement than the one Corinne and Arna experienced. The steamer which they had boarded in Alexandria anchored about a mile from Haifa, a sleepy village across the bay from Akka. It was early evening of 25 February, with the sun still shining on the point of Mt Carmel. Springtime in Palestine was well on its way. An incredible sight for Corinne, who knew that Bahá'u'lláh had visited that mountain several times, and that 'Abdu'l-Bahá had spent considerable time there.

Because Haifa didn't have port facilities then, several large rowboats, manned by eight to ten sturdy Arab oarsmen, approached the side of the ship. All passengers would be lowered onto a little hanging platform, one at a time. Getting into the rowboat was tricky. The transfer had to take place when the smaller vessel was being lifted by a wave. At that point one or two of the Arab sailors would grab the passenger and haul him or her into the rowboat, not the most graceful way of entering a new place. It was something Corinne True had never experienced before. The process was repeated in reverse when the rowboats reached the small dock.

To Corinne, Haifa was as she had envisioned it being 1900 years ago: men and women wearing the kind of clothing worn during Jesus' time; camels, donkeys and horse-drawn wagons on the narrow, often unpaved roads. There were no automobiles. But the quiet was appreciated, and so was the fresh air. A welcome difference from the hustle-bustle of Chicago.

It was a perfect setting for waiting to meet the Master. Interestingly, Corinne and Arna were housed at the Hospice of the Little Child in the German Templer colony; many of the Templers had left their homeland and come to Haifa in 1868 to await the return of Christ.

Corinne didn't know how long she would have to stay in Haifa and it is unknown whether she realized, at the time, the full extent of the Master's problems; but she had received instructions before leaving home to stay in the inn until contacted. Being so close to Him and yet unable to see Him wasn't easy, though 'Abdu'l-Bahá took care to make her stay in Haifa an enriching experience. That day the Master's wife had come to Haifa, and His two sons-in-law, driving His carriage, called the first evening to take her and Arna to see her and His beautiful daughter, Rúhá Khánum, who was living in the Master's new house on Haparsim Street. While meeting them drew her closer to her Beloved, it also heightened her anticipation of going to Akka. When they returned to their hotel, the night air was balmy and the moon was practically full. In bed, she stared at the sky, thrilled that she was at heaven's threshold. For eight years she had waited to be where she was now. Both she and Arna slept well.

The next morning Madame Scaramucci, a Bahá'í who had accompanied the Trues from Port Said, Egypt, to Palestine, came by to take Arna on a sight-seeing trip, an experience Corinne didn't dare deny her exuberant daughter. Actually, she looked forward to being alone. There were packages and letters to sort out for the Haifa friends. But Corinne didn't have time to do much sorting because she was soon called for to be taken to Mírzá Asadu'lláh's home. Should she go without her daughter, she wondered? It seemed that she had no choice, because the caller wasn't going to leave without her.

Corinne was greeted warmly by Mírzá Asadu'lláh, his wife, two sons and a daughter. Having spent time in Chicago, helping to organize the Bahá'í community, Mírzá Asadu'lláh wanted to hear about the friends he knew and what progress the Faith was making in America. He was thrilled by the news Corinne shared with him. Soon the Master's wife and daughter arrived, and after coffee and cookies, Corinne returned to the inn. As she expected, Arna was back from her trip, concerned at not finding her mother there.

The afternoon was glorious. Rúhá Khánum took Corinne and Arna, in her Father's carriage, up Mt Carmel to the Tomb of the Báb. The idea of sitting in the spot where the Master might have sat nearly took Corinne's breath away. Though unfinished, the Tomb was a commanding structure built on solid rock, high above the sea and the village below. At the time Corinne couldn't know what the brownish stone Tomb would look like fifty years later, encased in white and crowned in gold, one of the wonders of the Holy Land. Yet what she experienced that afternoon was a wonder to her. The custodian's wife greeted Corinne and Arna with a handful of freshly-picked red roses. After Rúhá had taken them inside the building and explained the inner rooms, she led Corinne and Arna to the edge of the flower garden in front of the Tomb, where chairs had been placed. As they sat down, the custodian's wife approached with violets for her American Bahá'í sisters and served them Persian tea. The only sounds were those that belonged naturally to that blessed spot: bird songs from time to time. The sun shone brightly and the sweet scent of spring flowers freshened the air. There wasn't much one could say, for the eager heart wanted only to drink in the sacred beauty that permeated everything.

The vista was more than beautiful, for nearby was

Elijah's Cave, close to where Bahá'u'lláh had proclaimed His mission; and down below were the houses the German Templers had built to await Christ's return. Undoubtedly there were those among them who had seen the Blessed Beauty on the Mountain, or walking by their homes. And across the blue Bay of Haifa was Akka.

Corinne awoke the next morning, wondering when she would see 'Abdu'l-Bahá. She and Arna had been in Haifa for two nights and a day; and not a hint of when they would take that twelve-mile trip to Akka. Corinne was like a child who hadn't seen her much-loved father for a long time.

As they were dressing for breakfast, someone knocked on their door. It was a messenger with word that they were to proceed to Akka. At 10 o'clock they boarded the Cook Travel agency's carriage with Mme Scaramucci. It was a plain wagon, with a cloth roof, hard wooden seats, and three horses leading the way.

As the carriage rumbled through Haifa's cobblestone streets, the Bible, which she knew so well, seemed to come alive. Christ and some of His disciples had probably walked along the way, as well as some of Israel's ancient prophets, including Elijah.

After Haifa, the carriage rushed onto the seashore, and followed it until reaching the gates of Akka. It was a better route than the interior roads. And they must have been bad, because the drive along the sand wasn't easy. At one point the carriage had to swerve out to sea, in order to avoid the mouths of two streams emptying into it. The wagon wheels were completely immersed in the water, and Corinne felt the horses struggling. Though travel wasn't something she relished, and the trek into the sea seemed ominous, Corinne remained calm. Focusing on what the Master had told an earlier pilgrim helped: 'Love knows no fear.'[4]

Akka was different from Haifa, right from the start. Accustomed to open cities, seeing a centuries-old high weatherbeaten wall encircling the city disturbed Corinne. What a gruesome sight! Not a tree; a parched and barren place. Truly a prison. Yet, she thought, within those grim walls dwelt a precious Prisoner.

The carriage drove through the gates and to the House of 'Abdu'lláh Páshá, where the Master had lived since 1897, and where Shoghi Effendi was born. It was an expansive building with courtyards and red brick archways. From the outside it reflected the character of the prison-city, worn and old. But inside, the captors and enemies of the Faith had no control over the spirit. Light, that emanates from a divine Source, encompassed every room.

In its simplicity there was a rare eloquence about the household. Corinne was certain that even the meanhearted would be touched by the atmosphere in 'Abdu'l-Bahá's home. To her it was the place she had always longed to be. She had finally found her true home. Peace and calm prevailed; but it was unlike any other tranquil spot she had been to. The room she and Arna shared was simple: there were two small beds, straw matting on the concrete floor, a vase with fresh flowers on a table and a wooden bench. From the window they could see the battered sea wall and the Mediterranean. Corinne now understood the meaning of a Tablet the Master had sent her in 1903 in regard to His confinement:

> . . . This prison is sweeter to me and more to be desired than a garden of flowers; to me, this bondage is better than the freedom to go my way, and I find this narrow place more spacious than wide and open plains. Do not grieve over me . . .[5]

To Corinne it was more than being 6,000 miles from Chicago. She was in a different world. Since becoming a Bahá'í she had learned, little by little, that this new world does exist and humans can reach it. Soon after she and Arna had settled into the room, Munavvar Khánum, the

Master's youngest daughter, came to the door bearing a gift of three roses from her Father for them and their fellow-pilgrim, Mme Scaramucci. A few moments later, they heard the Master's steps in the hall and 'Abdu'l-Bahá appeared with a handful of hyacinths, pink and purple, which He divided into three parts. They were the first hyacinths of the season, gathered early that morning by the gardener. Such an outpouring of love, they felt, as He greeted them. Corinne had never been exposed to such a pure expression of caring. She felt completely loved and assured, for her a brand new experience. Without thinking, she bent a knee and kissed the Master's hand. (Obviously she wasn't aware of Bahá'u'lláh's prohibition of hand-kissing. In 1907 Western Bahá'ís were unfamiliar with that law.) She did what her heart commanded her to do. Certainly the Master understood. As she stepped back, she realized that what was unfolding before her had been experienced before – in a dream, shortly after becoming a Bahá'í. In that dream a grown daughter was with her. Sixteen-year-old Arna was standing beside Corinne, also swept up by the majesty of 'Abdu'l-Bahá. Meeting the Master was different from anything Corinne had expected: 'I really was not prepared for such a Manifestation of Power. I expected the Love but pictured Abdul Baha as the Christian does the meek, humble Nazareen. I found Him to be a powerful Dynamo – A Lion – as well as the Most Majestic Personage I ever hope to see.'[6]

He spoke briefly, welcoming them to His home, and stating how happy he was that people from the East and West were uniting. Through the power of the Word of God, He added, hatred between orientals and occidentals was diminishing and, eventually, that Word would be the cause of uniting their hearts. Soon after He left, they were joined by Munavvar Khánum and another Bahá'í lady, bringing Corinne and Arna each a tangerine, and also a gift from the Master. While they talked until dinner time, Corinne thought of the friends back home. If only she could preserve the flowers and fruit to share with them. Though they were simple gifts, the spirit in which they were given moved Corinne. What a lesson! To give wholeheartedly; to serve lovingly.

When Corinne and Arna entered the small dining-room for midday dinner, the Master took them by the hand and led them to the table. He seated Arna to His right, as His guest of honor. A Burmese believer served them and the food was Persian and tasty, but that wasn't what interested her. It was the serenity in which the meal was being eaten that intrigued her. What could she say on the first day with 'Abdu'l-Bahá? She was an open receptacle. The Master, after eating a bite or two would talk. Not as a preacher. Not even as a teacher. More like a healer, a healer of the soul. He talked about tests and how necessary they are. He was reaching the very core of Corinne's being where deep sorrow lay. She knew He knew her better than she knew herself. He likened tests to a ship laden with food, headed to a people dependent on the cargo, being tossed about by fierce winds and high waves. Those aboard were uncomfortable. Yet the ship must proceed, for it carried food which would be the cause of life. So man must suffer the winds and waves of tests to bring life to the people. At one point He referred to Jesus' time when people tested Him; in reality, He said, Jesus was testing them.

Late that afternoon the Master came to see them in their room, as He could not have tea (the evening meal) with them because some officials of Akka had come to call on Him. Corinne asked His daughter at tea if she would give the gifts from the American believers to 'Abdu'l-Bahá, but Munavvar Khánum declined, saying that He wanted Corinne to do this.

Next morning Corinne was disappointed that Arna didn't join her to go to early morning prayers at 7:30 with 'Abdu'l-Bahá and His family, but the youngster was exhausted from the trip.

It was a thrilling experience being with the Master and

His family, which included His sister, Bahíyyih Khánum, His wife and daughters, and their husbands and children. It was their daily meeting for prayer, where the Creative Word and prayers were chanted, and tea was served. Corinne had never witnessed before such an expression of reverence, even among the children. With that kind of atmosphere it was easier to attain a prayerful mood. The love of God took on a deeper meaning.

One little boy of six came in quietly, kneeling near the door with folded arms. He listened intently until 'Abdu'l-Bahá asked him to chant. Though Corinne didn't understand the words, the spirit radiating from that little heart transported her into a dimension beyond anything she had ever hoped for. The Master praised the child and then gave him a handful of flowers.

After the prayers, and a visit of a half hour or so with the ladies of the household and two Russian pilgrims from 'Ishqábád, His daughter took them to breakfast.

About an hour later, when Corinne and Arna were in their room, they didn't have long to think about what would follow, for one of the Master's daughters came to the door to take them to meet the Master, and to bring the suitcase of gifts they had carried from America. 'Abdu'l-Bahá was waiting for them as they entered a room they had not seen before. Soon they were seated with the case nearby on the floor, except for that precious scroll that Moses had carefully packed. Corinne held on to it, placing it behind her on the divan. The Master was sitting across the room as she began to present the gifts, for which he thanked her, showing special interest in the pictures of the Chicago friends. But before she could present the scroll, He got up, came over to her, picked it up and raising it high exclaimed, 'Mashriqu'l-Adhkár! This . . . this is what gives me great joy. Go back . . . go back and work for the Temple; it is a great work, the best thing you could do, Mrs True.' He patted Corinne on the back, praised her work on behalf of the Temple and said she was to be His own daughter. Declaring her His daughter was an event she would never forget. It wasn't the words alone she would remember, but the expression of His total acceptance.

Though moved by what the Master had said to her, Corinne had the presence of mind to inquire about the kind of Temple He envisioned. She asked where it should be built. Away from shopping and business sites, He said. She described the lay-out of the city, and asked if it should be near the lake's shore. He approved of that idea, also pointing out that it should be on a large piece of land. Then 'Abdu'l-Bahá went into the next room and returned quickly with a ground plan, describing what the Temple should look like. It would have nine sides, nine avenues, radiating from the building. Between each avenue there would be a garden with a fountain in its center.

The Master's exuberance inspired her. At that point she knew what she had to do. But could she do what was asked of her? There were also the plans she and Moses had made to move back to Grand Rapids, to a simpler, calmer way of life.

The Master laid down his pencil and gazed into Corinne's eyes. It was as if no one else was in the room. Just the two of them. With great intensity, He explained how important it was for her to stay in Chicago and help build the Temple. Accomplishing that, He said, would do more for the Faith than anything else at the time. 'Devote yourself to this project – make a beginning, and all will come right.' But He warned that doing the work wouldn't be easy; that she would suffer and be misunderstood. 'Pray for the strength you will need to achieve your goal,' He said. Corinne would view that advice as a life-long order.

At the time Corinne didn't realize that her destiny was being shaped before her eyes. All she knew was that she was receiving direction, divine direction that had to be followed, as the sincere student follows the wise teacher.

The next morning Corinne gained some understanding

of what the Master meant about teaching and deeds. Standing at her open window, she watched 'Abdu'l-Bahá, in the courtyard below, helping over two hundred of the neediest in Akka. It was something He did every Friday. Corinne had never seen such a wretched group of people: the downtrodden of the area, men and women and children, some blind, others crippled, their children dressed in rags, a man in a patched quilt and an old woman cloaked in a gunny-sack. With the guidance of two or three Bahá'ís, they stood in an orderly way on two sides of the courtyard while the Master went from one to another, pressing into each one's palm a coin or two and speaking some word of encouragement or praise, asking about the health of some or patting others on the back. For most of them, meeting 'Abdu'l-Bahá may have been the only act of kindness they had experienced during the week. But not everyone was deserving of help. Two men didn't receive anything from the Master. They had tried twice, and both times were refused. Later, Corinne learned from 'Abdu'l-Bahá why He did that. He had told them where they could find employment and they hadn't gone. But most of those who came to the Master each week were truly helpless souls, many too feeble to work or unable to find employment. Fishing and carrying heavy loads were about the only kinds of work available, the Master told her.

As Corinne watched 'Abdu'l-Bahá, she was reminded of the spirit of Jesus, 'the humble Nazarene of 1900 years ago'. Nowhere else in Akka was this kind of giving going on, not even among the most influential clerics. What truly amazed her was that this wholehearted expression of generosity she was witnessing was being offered by a Prisoner.

When the crowd had departed from the courtyard, Corinne chanced to pass by the Master's door. He was resting on His bed, very tired, but He noticed her and asked His daughter to bring her in. Evidently, He knew she had been watching Him with Akka's poor, because He talked about them, calling them His friends, even those few who harbored ill-will toward Him. One must love all, friends and enemies alike, He said. Human beings should live in harmony with each other just as the heavenly bodies in the universe do.

Corinne was moved to share with the Master how the Women's Assembly of Teaching had bought a home for three orphaned children and their grandmother.

'Beautiful!' He said in English and in a powerful voice. 'Beautiful!' Bahá'ís, He went on to say, have the responsibility to care for orphans. They should open their homes to them, train and educate them and teach them the Faith. Orphans are God's children and a great test to people. God blesses those who do good works, He added.

Then He excused Himself to attend to a large pile of Tablets He had been writing – those precious epistles of hope and guidance. Corinne knew how important they were to her. At times, a Tablet from 'Abdu'l-Bahá had brought light into her life when darkness was encroaching. She was convinced that whatever He wrote was what she needed. It didn't matter that she couldn't understand some points. Understanding would come, she believed, if she did what He prescribed. That pile of Tablets on the simple table would soon be posted to believers all over the world, lighting up their lives, too. In the future she would derive pleasure from closing her eyes and recalling that heavenly room, where so much love and wisdom were generated and shared with friends everywhere.

Today we can only wonder that 'Abdu'l-Bahá found time to write those thousands of Tablets, each one specially phrased to treat a particular problem, strengthen the faith of a certain believer, guide a stumbling community, mediate disputes without offending anyone, and always finding a way of preserving unity among the friends. Somehow He found the time, squeezing the writing in between the demands of the household, attending to the pilgrims, directing the construction of the

Shrine of the Báb, providing counsel to Druse, Muslim and governmental leaders, serving Akka's poor and ailing, directing the affairs of a fledgling world faith, and caring for His family. He worked every day, even on Friday – a day of rest for Akka's citizens when shops and schools were closed. But there was no rest for Him, even at the dinner table, for He was attending to the secret needs of the friends by addressing questions they hesitated to share openly with anyone, even with Him. His ability to do so much wasn't due to extraordinary physical health. When Corinne was on pilgrimage in 1907, 'Abdu'l-Bahá was suffering from rheumatism, acquired from sleeping on the cold, damp floor of Akka's prison morgue for more than two years.

That same afternoon Bahíyyih Khánum, the Master's sister, came with His oldest daughter to call on the pilgrims in their room. For Corinne, coming to know her was an experience she would treasure forever. Like her Brother, the Greatest Holy Leaf (as she was known) was always busy from early morning to midnight, managing the Master's household, seeing to the needs of the family and those with them, and caring for the pilgrims. All who met her felt her quiet strength, experienced her wisdom and compassion, and turned to her when 'Abdu'l-Bahá was away. She understood the reality of her Father's Covenant as centered in the Master, knew what she had to do, and carried out her duties with unfailing devotion.

During her visit, Corinne asked Bahíyyih Khánum to share some of her experiences during her Father's lifetime and this she did, from their exile from Iran when she was only six to their arrival in Akka some fifteen years later. She spoke particularly of her mother's suffering, with small children to care for, and of the rigors of the last journey by ship and sailing boat, which brought them to the dreadful prison. Although they were left without food or water in dusty cells unoccupied for a long time, when

6. *The True family at home, 711 West Adams Street, Chicago, circa 1896, with all their children except Harriet who had died in 1892. (Left to right) Laurence, Corinne with Nathanael, Arna, Edna, Moses True, Davis, Kenneth and Katherine*

7. The House of 'Abdu'lláh Páshá, with its arched red-brick entrance through which pilgrims entered the courtyard. The two windows on the upper floor (right) are of the room of the Greatest Holy Leaf.

8. The room in the House of 'Abdu'lláh Páshá in which 'Abdu'l-Bahá received His guests (as recently restored)

9. The main hall in the House of 'Abdu'lláh Páshá. The door at the back (right) leads to the room of the Greatest Holy Leaf, and that on the side wall (right) to the room in which the Holy Family would gather for morning prayers and tea.

10. Arna, at about the age (sixteen) of her pilgrimage with Corinne in 1907

11. Corinne at Fruitport in the grounds of their summer home; the child may be Nathanael.

the large key turned in the lock they were full of joy because they would not be separated from Bahá'u'lláh. The Master had to send word to them not to chant so loudly their prayers of thanks. 'It was thrilling to have her tell of this,' Corinne recalled many decades later. When Bahíyyih <u>Kh</u>ánum left them after her short visit, she said she would come often if only she could speak English with them. Moments later she sent a small bottle of attar of rose as a parting gift.

Corinne's pilgrimage was more than she had expected. But was her daughter benefiting from her visit to the Holy Land? The first three days Arna seemed restless, even bored. Evidently 'Abdu'l-Bahá sensed Corinne's concern and the needs of Arna. At lunch one day, He turned to her and asked if she was happy. When she responded, 'Yes, but not very,' Corinne cringed. But her embarrassment soon vanished when 'Abdu'l-Bahá smiled, obviously pleased with Arna's candor, and asked if she would like to be with the Persian children in the other part of the house.

The Master's solution worked well. It didn't matter that the children couldn't understand English, and Arna didn't know Persian or Arabic. Her natural love for them was a language the youngsters understood. She taught the boys and girls, including 10-year-old Shoghi Effendi who had come for the weekend from his school in Haifa, all the American games she knew. One afternoon the Master entered the courtyard and stopped to watch Arna with an excited group of Persian children playing jump-rope. Impressed, He took a turn, turning the rope.

Arna settled well into the Holy household. In fact, so well that one of 'Abdu'l-Bahá's daughters dressed her in a Persian woman's clothing, including the veil. They roamed Akka's streets, even went to the mosque where the men prayed and chanted. All of this was done, of course, without Corinne's awareness.

One afternoon while in her room writing letters, Corinne heard a knock on her door. When she opened it, she found a veiled Persian girl standing there. Corinne motioned her to come in. As the two sat facing each other, unable to say anything, Corinne grew anxious. The difference between the East and West was apparent. She couldn't tell her guest to leave; that would be discourteous. On the other hand, what did she want? Who was she? With every passing minute, Corinne grew more unsettled. She had never liked being away from home. And now she was in a strange land with a strange culture, 6,000 miles from Chicago, and uncertain what was going to result from this visit.

Corinne's anxiety suddenly exploded into anger when the girl burst into uproarious laughter and removed her veil. How could a daughter play such an awful trick on her mother? Corinne thought. But then she realized that Arna was being herself, and feeling at home in Akka.

Corinne learned something from almost everything that happened on her pilgrimage. Attending the early morning prayers with the Holy Family was a special experience. Not only was she inspired by the chanting of the verses of God; some of the people she met inspired her too. She would never forget, for example, the 'beautiful, happy-faced young woman, sitting on the floor with the samovar, making and serving tea'. The story of her husband's martyrdom greatly moved Corinne.

Her name was Sakínih Sulṭán. She had been married only a year, living in Yazd in Persia, when her husband and his brother were arrested with five others for being Bahá'ís. For days there was no news of their whereabouts. One day a howling mob of religious fanatics paraded in front of their mother's home where the young wife was living, carrying on long poles their decapitated heads. In an undated Tablet written for Sakínih Sulṭán, 'Abdu'l-Bahá was to describe what happened to her husband's head:

> . . . to make them waver in their faith . . . they flung it into the courtyard of their spacious home . . . They [the

mother and his wife] took that noble head, and set it down outside the house, . . . and told them: 'God forbid! The head that we have offered up on the path of God, we will not take back.'⁷

Since the young widow had no means of support and would not contemplate remarriage, the Master took her and her young daughter into His household. And what a household! To Corinne it was what the world ought to be like: over forty people living together in unity, some black, some white, Arabic, Persian, Burmese, Italian, Russian, English and American. The Master's home was a blessed spot, a point of light that for the sake of humanity needed to be extended to homes everywhere. By observing the way things were done, Corinne learned what teaching was. Later, in describing 'Abdu'l-Bahá's home to a friend, Corinne wrote, 'The life lived and not preached is what creates the wonderful atmosphere of that Home. It is natural and normal and easy. No one ever criticizes or finds fault with anyone – they only see the good in everyone . . .'⁸

For Corinne her short stay in Akka was an experience of rebirth. Exposed to so much of value, it was difficult to appreciate everything that happened at the time. Later, upon reflection, understanding would come of experiences with the Master. For example, while on pilgrimage the Bahá'í period of fasting began. About a year later she described to a friend what the Master had taught her about its significance:

. . . It [the Fast] is a time of cleansing outwardly and inwardly – polishing both the lamp and the niche it stands in. A spring house cleaning time out and in . . .

Since Abdul Baha made me understand why at this particular time we are commanded to keep the Fast, it has become a living, exhilarating ordinance to me and I long for it. He showed me that it celebrates the time the Great Laws and Revelations were pouring out from God upon Baha'o'llah in such torrents that he was filled with the

Heavenly meat and drink and needed not the material. So as we keep the Commemoration of this Mighty Outflow, we come closer into realization and our spirits are advanced.[9]

It was difficult for Corinne to consider 'Abdu'l-Bahá a prisoner, because there was no one she had ever met who was freer, or who could liberate others the way He could. She knew that from personal experience. Yet there were reminders of His restrictions in the Holy Land, limitations worse than being confined to a prison cell. Corinne became privy to one of those restrictions, and it nearly broke her heart.

When 'Abdu'l-Bahá learned that his wife was going to take Corinne to the Tomb of Bahá'u'lláh, He appeared at the entrance of Corinne's room and asked her for a favor: would she kiss the threshold of His Father's Tomb? The Master had been prevented from visiting that sacred spot for three or four years because of His confinement within the walls of Akka.[10]

In Akka, Corinne True took little notice of time. In fact, it was as if time didn't exist. There was a dream-like quality to the pilgrimage experience; yet it was real, but not in an ordinary sense. For what happened during her six-day stay in the Master's household would never be forgotten. How could the explorer on the mountain-top forget the magnificent rainbow arching the verdant valley?

When, that Saturday evening, the Master came to call on them, Mme Scaramucci asked if she might stay until Monday. He agreed, and advised Corinne and Arna to travel with her as they had come together from Egypt. The present Governor was not friendly, He explained, and it was best to shorten their stay. He also asked Corinne to visit the believers in Paris and London. It was unexpected for she had planned to go directly home. But because He wished it, she did not hesitate to alter her plans.

When their pilgrimage came to an end and Corinne was ready to leave, the Master sent for her. It would be her last interview with Him. 'I asked Him what He wished me to do,' she recalled many years later. 'I wish you to live in Chicago. I wish you to work for the Mashriqu'l-Adhkár, and if you do that you must live in Chicago.' As she sat beside Him, He took her hand. It was as though, she has said, a great power was pulsing through her – a 'most unusual thing'.

Most difficult of all was saying goodbye just before leaving for Haifa. 'Oh, it was terrible,' she remembered. And the Family felt the same way – as though they had known each other all their lives.

Because He knew her better than she knew herself, without being told the Master realized the fear and distaste she had felt in Naples where she remained on the boat when others went ashore; how in Alexandria, when they had to change ship, she was so frightened of the Arabs who swarmed aboard; and how the experience of disembarking in Haifa had alarmed her. And so He spoke to her inmost being when, holding her hand, He spoke to her of love, universal love, and the importance of loving everyone, even the seemingly unlovable. Above all, He gave her the key.

'Mrs True,' He said, 'when you go back I want you to look at every human being and say to yourself, "You are a letter from my Beloved, and I must love you because of the Beloved Who wrote you. The letter may be torn, it may be blurred – but because the Beloved wrote the letter, you must *love* it."'

Those who met Mother True in after years came to hear and ponder the Master's counsel so simply stated. He had planted a seed in fertile soil, and though it meant overcoming attitudes and behavior fashioned by her early experience, because her heart relied on 'Abdu'l-Bahá, she tried to obey Him. His words were the theme to which she would always refer, and share with others, throughout her life.

When Corinne and Arna reached Naples, a letter was

awaiting her from her husband. The Agnew family were on their way to visit the Master and would be arriving in Naples shortly. Deciding to wait for them, two days later Corinne and Arna were at the dock to greet the Agnews; to their surprise they found two other Chicagoans with them, Carl Scheffler and Thornton Chase. Corinne described that meeting in a letter to a friend:

> None of them knew we were in town either, so the surprise was equally great to both sides. After a few delays all secured rooms at our hotel and we were one happy family. I tell you . . . we see each other's faults tremendously when working closely together; but after a little separation these faults fade away and the noble qualities shine brighter and brighter. It was just as if the members of the party were one soul that we met that Easter Sunday . . . We fulfilled literally Jesus' injunction: 'Ye must become as little children.' We ate cake and drank lemonade like a lot of boys and girls, some going to the Blessed Master and some returning from the Holy Visit! You can picture the feelings of us all.[11]

As it turned out, the Master's request that Corinne visit Paris and London had great significance for the Temple project, as she conveyed the Master's love and vision and began new friendships of lasting importance to the work she was about to undertake.

7

The Struggle for Unity

While Corinne True and her daughter were on their way home via Paris and London, Thornton Chase, Carl Scheffler and the Agnews were on pilgrimage, experiencing, at one point, something they hadn't expected. It was the Master's response to Mr Chase's questions regarding the Temple. 'When you return consult with Mrs True – I have given her complete instructions.'[1]

Mr Chase was startled. He simply wasn't prepared for what 'Abdu'l-Bahá had said. The Master had upset his notions about the role of women in the Faith. Had the Master doubted Thornton Chase's firmness in the Faith, He wouldn't have been so direct with him. What was said was obviously meant to broaden and deepen the American pilgrims' understanding of a certain aspect of the Bahá'í teachings.

Since the Master's statement concerning the Temple had been addressed to three members of Chicago's House of Spirituality, that body's deliberations on the proposed House of Worship would have to take into account Corinne True's connection with the project.

When she returned home, her husband sensed that the pilgrimage had greatly reinforced Corinne's commitment to 'Abdu'l-Bahá. Moving to Grand Rapids, and whatever that represented to him, was out of the question. Moses True agreed to look for a bigger house. It had to be bigger, even though most of the children were grown, because Corinne's involvement with the Faith, especially her work on the Temple, would grow. Two years after her pilgrimage, 5338 Kenmore Avenue became the Trues' new address, a house where a number of historic events would take place.

Corinne attacked the challenge of building the Temple with a vigor that seemed endless. She had understood and completely accepted what the Master had told her while on pilgrimage: 'Devote yourself to this project – make a beginning, and all will come right.'

Now she knew that the Temple was not going to house simply a Chicago Bahá'í congregation. It would be, in a sense, a national cathedral, a sign of God's latest revelation on earth, a force uniting the American believers, and a mighty teacher.

Since it would be an American spiritual center, Corinne reasoned, all of the Bahá'ís in North America should play a role in building it. She waged a campaign to solicit contributions from every believer in North America. Of course, this effort was endorsed by the Women's Assembly of Teaching. All money received was placed in the Assembly's bank account. But that soon changed when Corinne was named Temple Fund secretary by the House of Spirituality.

She was careful in the way she solicited funds. It wasn't the traditional direct approach. No passing of the plate, or direct mail appeals. She never asked for contributions. Rather she tried to inspire and educate the Bahá'ís. Writing to them about her pilgrimage was one way. Scores of letters were sent out. Five, six, sometimes ten a day. And when contributions were received, she would respond with another letter; not a simple thank-you note, but a genuine letter – all handwritten by her. In many ways they were epistles of enlightenment. Some examples:

> It is an American Temple and not a Chicago Temple alone and therefore the responsibility rests at the door of every Bahai in this land to Arise with all the powers of his or her being to further this Work.
>
> What an honor the Master has bestowed upon the

Bahais of America to encourage us to Arise for the accomplishment of the Greatest Work ever accomplished in any Dispensation namely the building of a House of Worship during the Day of the Manifestation of the Spirit upon the earth . . . Will you express to the Beloved of God the deep gratitude of the Chicago Assembly for this great help and encouragement.

In some recent notes from Acca it was said that Jesus told His Disciples to build His Church and from that Word has come the outward manifestation of the multitudes of churches erected in His Name. Today Abdul Baha says build a Mashrak-el-Ascar in Chicago and it is coming most beautifully.[2]

Since her return to Chicago Corinne had been consumed by a desire to share her pilgrimage with others. It didn't matter that it had been a deeply personal experience. Others should benefit from it, she felt, because many would never get to Akka. For her, it had been six days of heaven.

In 'Abdu'l-Bahá's house, people worked hard, often on practical, even mundane, matters, although no one came close to working as hard as the Master. Heaven, Corinne realized, was an attitude. And 'Abdu'l-Bahá demonstrated it every moment of His life regardless of the circumstances. In His presence she sensed someone completely content with God's will, happy and serene although not unaware of the tests and problems of the world; He focused on life's potentialities, always striving to release and develop them, and drawing strength and knowledge from the Divine Source. A group of people with such an attitude, or striving to attain it, creates a heavenly atmosphere, like the one in the Master's home. And sincere visitors like Corinne were so affected by it that they didn't want to revert to their former outlook. They dedicated themselves to attaining such an attitude, and helping others attain it. To share her pilgrimage with others, Corinne decided to write a booklet.

It took her several weeks to write *Notes Taken at Acca*, which was published by the newly-formed Bahai Publishing Society based in Chicago. In it she successfully conveyed the spirit of the Holy household and the power and majesty of the Master, as well as 'Abdu'l-Bahá's keen enthusiasm for the American Temple project.

Actually, the pages on the Temple were the other reason for writing the booklet. She hoped that those who read it would be inspired to become more involved in the building of the House of Worship.

Besides writing the booklet, working daily in encouraging Temple Fund contributions, serving on the Women's Assembly of Teaching, and holding two offices on it, Corinne managed to fit in regular teaching efforts, mostly in her new home. Everyone who called on the Trues was viewed as a potential Bahá'í.

Because she knew how hard the Master worked, Corinne was compelled to do as much as she could for the Cause. Others marveled at her work capacity. To her it was doing what had to be done. She didn't dwell on what others considered chores. What she did were tasks for Bahá'u'lláh; and she was confident that if it was God's will, the work would get done.

'Abdu'l-Bahá knew Corinne True was a doer, who would willingly sacrifice her life for the Faith if she had to. But He also knew that in fulfilling her responsibilities, she could grow overzealous and bypass the House of Spirituality in dealing with critical community issues. As a natural leader, she had an instinct for quickly zeroing in on problems and devising solutions on the spot.

Corinne's insatiable drive to achieve wasn't motivated by a need for recognition. Her strong intuition and desire to fulfill the Master's wishes fueled her desire to achieve. Whatever she thought was right she would defend or promote with wholehearted determination. But she wasn't always right: in 1903, for example, she had insisted that the Temple be built right away so the Chicago friends would have a place to worship. She had envisioned a local temple. Later, her pilgrimage gave her the right focus on the matter.

It was understandable why some of the early Bahá'ís clashed with her, especially some of the more assertive men, who felt she craved power. They were unfamiliar with such a display of drive in a woman, not realizing that Corinne's all-consuming love for the Master was what drove her. She wasn't an egotistical person. In fact, she was modest by nature. In her written account of the early days of the Faith which she prepared several years after her first pilgrimage, she never once mentioned her association with the Temple project.

For Corinne patience was hard to develop. So much had to be done by so few. Getting things done in the Bahá'í community in the early 1900s was difficult. Not only were the resources meager, but there were philosophical differences among the Bahá'ís. Though they didn't lead to schism, unofficial camps evolved. There were the organizers vs. the non-organizers; the intellectuals vs. the spiritual perfectionists. People like Thornton Chase spearheaded the drive for strong organization; without it, they felt, the Faith would grow chaotic. On the other hand, the non-organizers believed structure would impede the flow of Divine Guidance. The intellectuals and spiritual perfectionists feuded over interpretation of the Creative Word. The intellectuals took a liberal view of the Holy Writings, while the spiritual perfectionists were the fundamentalists. Corinne's natural inclination was to side with the non-organizers, but she knew it was wrong to take a position. So did many of the other believers; nevertheless, their feelings would unwittingly manifest themselves, causing, at times, heated disputes.[3]

This condition troubled Corinne. Deep down she viewed it as a stumbling block to the Faith's progress. Later in life she would understand that in 1907 the Faith was in its infancy, that the first believers would be less mature than future generations of Bahá'ís. She and her contemporaries possessed many cultural characteristics that were counter to Bahá'í principles. It would take more than a lifetime to divest oneself of them. Consequently the early American Bahá'ís were bound to clash. Corinne had little patience with the intra-community battling in 1907. Her natural inclination was to shortcut it, and take on projects alone, sometimes circumventing the House of Spirituality. But 'Abdu'l-Bahá wouldn't let her do that. In Tablets, He often reminded her of the importance of working with the Faith's institutions. For example:

> . . . consult with the House of Spirituality of Chicago. Ye must all be perfectly united and harmonious, until, through this harmony, ye may perpetually receive help from the Kingdom of God.[4]

Corinne viewed the Master's reminders as loving guidance, not as chastisement. She knew she could easily get carried away with something she wholeheartedly believed in. 'Abdu'l-Bahá's advice was always welcomed, and it led her to greater understanding. Through 'Abdu'l-Bahá's patient and fatherly guidance, Corinne True learned that obeying the Faith's institutions was like obeying Him. But this understanding came about gradually. A lifetime of doing things a certain way wasn't going to be altered immediately, even if she wanted that to happen.

She didn't want to be the cause of conflict among the believers. Yet in the eyes of some Bahá'ís she was viewed as such. That hurt deeply. But what could she do? Compromising with the Master's directions was out of the question. She preferred being disliked even to thinking of not fulfilling what she believed were 'Abdu'l-Bahá's instructions.

Corinne's ideas regarding the site for the Temple sparked controversy. She felt compelled to secure land that was near a large body of water, away from the blight and noise that commerce usually generates. It should be a spot pleasing to the eye and soul; a place comparable to the location of the Tomb of the Báb. Her notion was based on her pilgrimage talks with the Master. Consequently she felt absolutely certain that what she was looking for was right. Shortly after returning from Akka, she waged an independent search for a suitable site. For weeks – usually on Saturdays – she headed north of Chicago, along the Lake front, often accompanied by Cecilia Harrison, the widow of an Anglican priest. The trek required heavy work shoes. After taking a horse-drawn trolley to 'the end of the line', she often walked through fields, where she climbed fences and waded across streams. After many forays into what many Chicagoans felt was the wilderness, Corinne found what she called 'the chosen place'. It was 'a thickly-wooded tract' of land on 'a bluff overlooking Lake Michigan in what is now the village of Wilmette . . .'[5]

The House of Spirituality had sent out its own search teams, concentrating mostly on Chicago's south side. Two places near Jackson Park were popular, mainly because they were centrally located. The House of Spirituality had to take that into consideration because the site discovered by Corinne True would be out of reach for many city-dwelling Bahá'ís. It would take them nearly two hours to get there and another two to return home. But Corinne True wouldn't budge from her stand; and that annoyed many believers, including some who were close to her.

Her frenetic pace led to a physical breakdown, forcing her to go south to recuperate. When she returned to Chicago she plunged back into the same routine. One of the first things she did was to try to persuade the House of Spirituality to sponsor a national Temple Project conference. It was something that was desperately needed, she felt. Deep down, Corinne sensed that Chicago's House of Spirituality would be unable, by itself, to accomplish the building of the Temple. It was something she hadn't shared publicly. But having other Bahá'í communities in the country involved in the Temple's development would increase the available resources, and maybe then some meaningful progress would be made.

At the invitation of the House of Spirituality to about two dozen Bahá'í communities, nine delegates, joined by about ten from the Chicago area, attended the one-day conference on 26 November 1907, the 'Fête Day of 'Abdu'l-Bahá'. It was the first national conference to be held in America. Some who couldn't be there sent letters and telegrams expressing their views on a Temple site. The letters from Philadelphia and Seattle contained money for purchasing land. First, the delegates inspected the proposed sites, including a favored spot near Jackson Park in the heart of Chicago, and several sites north of the city.

Selecting a suitable site dominated the conference discussion that evening, which was held in the Trues' West Adams Street home. There were those who preferred a rustic setting where believers could worship in serenity, while others felt it should be in the heart of the city's poor, becoming a tower of strength and hope for them.

Thornton Chase believed that such discussion was meaningless when the Faith didn't have enough money to buy a decent site. Ways of securing funds, he felt, should be addressed first. It wasn't only Mr Chase's conservative financial policy that influenced his position. He was aware of the Master's appeal not to incur any debt in erecting a Temple.

A Persian believer challenged Thornton Chase's reasoning, pointing out that with unity and faith the money would be found and the House of Worship built.

According to the incomplete minutes of the conference, Corinne True didn't enter into the Temple site discussion. What she had to say was shared after an opening prayer for unity read by Thornton Chase. In a prepared statement she made an appeal for unity, mostly quoting from 'Abdu'l-Bahá. That was a test for some of her critics. For she was often accused of hiding behind the Master's words, making it difficult to refute her.

Although the conference plans called for a decision to be made on what site to purchase, none was made. The delegates left, however, leaning toward some site north of Chicago, not necessarily Corinne's spot.

From the day she returned from her pilgrimage, Corinne hadn't had time to dwell on the past. And that was a blessing, since her son Laurence had been dead for only seven months. Her Temple and teaching projects dominated her life, especially since they were being developed in a highly-charged atmosphere of clashing viewpoints. Her children remembered their mother coming home from Bahá'í meetings exhausted, lying down on the parlor couch and sometimes crying quietly. Because she wouldn't share what went on at the meetings with anyone, it was difficult for her husband and children to comfort her. They learned that the best thing to do when she was upset was not to disturb her. Perhaps one of the reasons she wrote so frequently to 'Abdu'l-Bahá was a need to share her burdens with someone.

But during the turbulent year of 1907 there were some moments of relief. One in particular stood out. It was a letter from 10-year-old Shoghi Effendi to Arna, written in French, thanking her for the writing-paper she and her mother had sent him. Corinne sensed something special about the boy.

8

A Wonderful Coincidence

1908 was another frustrating year for Corinne True for very little progress was being made in carrying out the Master's urgent appeal to raise up a Temple in America. As the new year began, a site hadn't been purchased. Corinne persuaded the Women's Assembly of Teaching to urge the House of Spirituality to buy at least a small portion of the Wilmette property overlooking Lake Michigan.

Two lots were bought in April with an option to obtain twelve adjoining lots, which comprise the land where the Temple now stands. Whether the House of Spirituality would have approved the purchase had Thornton Chase been at the meeting when the women's appeal was made – that we'll never know.

But what is certain was Thornton Chase's displeasure with the House of Spirituality's action. In fact, he sensed Corinne's involvement in what he believed to be a carefully manipulated womanly plot. He shared his feeling with Hooper Harris of New York.

> Personally I have no desire except to see the real desire of Abdul-Baha carried out, and yet it does seem to me rather lacking in wisdom to place the Temple away out in the country, where it not only requires from one and a half hours to two hours with the very best transportation to reach it, to say nothing of a long walk at the further end, rather [than] within at least 'reaching' distance of the city center.

If I had been there at the time, I do not think I should have assented to that location. But I understand there was a regular 'lobby' of about five women that beset the H. of S. to not only do something, but to get that particular piece. I just tell you this *privately*. Mrs True was, and always is, the leader in such things. I feel exactly as you express yourself about messages from Abdul-Baha. In fact all the statements you have made in these letters agree perfectly with my personal ideas.

Will try to write you something about the Temple matters for the Bulletin, but don't know what it can be.[1]

To Corinne, the House of Spirituality's action was a beginning, nothing else. But at least a beginning had been made. The rest of the acreage should be secured, she felt. Considering the House of Spirituality's past performance on such matters, Corinne decided to share with 'Abdu'l-Bahá a plan that would quicken the Temple's development.

Her plan called for relieving Chicago's House of Spirituality of the responsibility of building the House of Worship. A national organization representing a cross-section of America's Bahá'í communities would take over the responsibility.

The Master enthusiastically approved Corinne's plan, while urging consultation with the House of Spirituality and perfect unity and harmony with them. And in that same Tablet, He declared that women should be members of the organization.[2] He sent a letter to Chicago's House of Spirituality urging it to organize a nationwide meeting that would represent all of America's believers.

Now, Corinne felt, meaningful progress was going to be made. She was confident that with a national body directing the Temple project, building could start in the foreseeable future. It didn't matter that no architectural design had been selected, nor the rest of the property purchased.

Elated, Corinne and Cecilia Harrison sanctified the two

lots by placing nine stones on the ground and anointing them with attar of rose, water and olive oil; then they read some prayers.[3]

Corinne was certain that a Bahá'í Temple would be built, for the Master wanted one erected. Because it meant so much to Him, she committed herself wholeheartedly to making sure that His wish would be fulfilled. In the fall of 1908, she received a Tablet from 'Abdu'l-Bahá. Like many of His others to Corinne, it intensified her already passionate yearning to carry out the Master's wish:

'Surely', He wrote, 'the beloved of God and the maidservants of the Merciful in all the cities of America must put forth the utmost of effort in order that the Mashrak-el-Azcar be raised in that land.'[4]

To her the Master's statement was clear. It was the number one priority. All that had to be done was to take His appeal to heart and all would be achieved. She took what He wrote personally, and had difficulty understanding why others didn't. 'Abdu'l-Bahá's appeals energized her, endowing her with a force that kept the Temple project alive.

From the beginning of her work as a Bahá'í it was apparent to Moses True that Corinne's greatest happiness came from her experiences in the Faith. It was something she couldn't hide, especially from him. So he tried valiantly through the years to help her as much as possible in what she obviously believed was the most important thing in her life. He loved her and it made him happy to see her happy.

At the start of 1909 they were in their new, big house on Kenmore Avenue, and Corinne was buoyant and optimistic. Moses was swept up by her enthusiasm over the impending nationwide convention of 20–23 March that would organize a national body to coordinate the Temple project. Thirty-nine delegates attended. Thornton Chase, the House of Spirituality's chairman, greeted them with a moving appeal for unity. Corinne followed by reading 'Abdu'l-

Bahá's Tablet to the delegates. The Master's message stressed the importance of the American Mashriqu'l-Adhkár to the Faith's future; that what they were about to undertake was more than building another Temple in the world. '. . . the founding of this Mashrek-el-Azkar is to be the inception of the organization of the Kingdom.'[5]

The delegates approved unanimously of Corinne's 'chosen place' as the site for the Temple and within days work began on purchasing the twelve remaining lots.

The most moving event of the convention took place on the last day, on the third floor of the Trues' home, a large room where Moses played billiards. It was there that the Bahai Temple Unity was formed, an organization that would eventually do more than try to construct the House of Worship. From it would spring the first American National Spiritual Assembly (benefiting from thirteen years of its predecessor's experience).

Three women were elected to the nine-member Executive Board, including Corinne True, who assumed the familiar post of financial secretary. In a sense, being elected to that office was a vote of confidence for the work she had been doing for Chicago's House of Spirituality during the past two years.

After adopting the organization's constitution, which had been drafted the previous day, the delegates arose, holding hands and facing east. A prayer of thanksgiving was given; and after reciting the Greatest Name nine times, they stood in silence for a moment. To Corinne that expression of unity was a sign of a new day in the struggle to fulfill the Master's desire of raising up a Temple in America. The convention had been a success. Aside from her pilgrimage, she had never experienced such 'eternal joy'. It had been a love feast, a gathering that would have made 'Abdu'l-Bahá happy. For nothing made Him happier than learning about real unity among the friends. She had to share with Him her joy over the convention He had called.

None of the delegates had any inkling of what the Bahai Temple Unity would evolve into. Nor were they aware of another historic event that was taking place during their convention, 6,000 miles away on Mt Carmel.

On 21 March 'Abdu'l-Bahá had the marble coffin (sarcophagus) 'designed to receive the body of the Báb' transported to the vault on Mt Carmel where it was to be interred. That evening, by the light of a single lamp and in the presence of friends from East and West, the Master Himself placed within that coffin the wooden casket containing His sacred remains.

> 'When all was finished,' Shoghi Effendi writes, 'and the earthly remains of the Martyr-Prophet of S̲h̲íráz were, at long last, safely deposited for their everlasting rest in the bosom of God's holy mountain, 'Abdu'l-Bahá, Who had cast aside His turban, removed His shoes and thrown off His cloak, bent low over the still open sarcophagus, His silver hair waving about His head and His face transfigured and luminous, rested His forehead on the border of the wooden casket, and, sobbing aloud, wept with such a weeping that all those who were present wept with Him. That night He could not sleep, so overwhelmed was He with emotion.'[6]

News of the national convention had brought joy to 'Abdu'l-Bahá. In His reply to Corinne's latest letter, He wrote:

> In reality a wonderful coincidence hath taken place! On that blessed day, 'Abdu'l-Bahá hastened to Haifa . . . The sacred remains of His Holiness the Exalted One (the Báb) after sixty years of being moved from one place to another . . . were finally laid to rest on Mount Carmel, the mountain of the Lord, and in Chicago there was held at the same time the convention of the delegates of the Mas̲h̲riqu'l-Ad̲h̲kár . . .
>   . . . if possible, commence the building of the Mas̲h̲riqu'l-Ad̲h̲kár. Do not delay.[7]

Before His reply could have reached Chicago, a com-

12. Delegates to the first nationwide Bahá'í Convention, 20–23 March 1909, which established the Bahá'í Temple Unity for construction of the Mashriqu'l-Adhkár. This photograph shows them at the entrance of the Trues' new home, 5338 Kenmore Avenue, Chicago. Corinne stands in the back row (centre) with Thornton Chase just below to her right.

13. *Corinne Knight True (1861–1961)*

14. *Moses Adams True (1857–1909)*

15. The committee of fifteen gathered at the Trues' home, 1 August 1909, to consider architects' plans for the Mashriqu'l-Adhkár. Standing, left to right: Mr Windust, Mr Remey, Mrs True, Mr Lesch, Mrs Brush, Mr Hall, Mr Brush, Mr Chase, Mr Jacobsen, Mr Currier. Seated, left to right: Mr Scheffler, Mr Struven, Mr Agnew, Mr Woodworth, Mr Fuller. (Names from Bahai News, vol. 1, no. 6, p. 1)

mittee of fifteen had gathered in the True home on 1 August 1909 to consider plans submitted by architects for the Temple. (See illustration opposite page.)

Considering her personality, the Master's appeal to the term, 'do not delay', must have heightened her burning commitment to carry out immediately whatever He asked. The fact that His appeal was prefaced with the words 'if possible' probably took second place. Corinne understood the spirit of the Message. She seemed to sense what He really wanted and felt a deep need to help fulfill His wish. The Master wanted Temple construction to start, she felt, and no delays. To her it was all so simple. In her mind, she probably reasoned that if 'Abdu'l-Bahá made such an appeal then somehow that would quicken the completion of the project. She actually believed that by 1912, and no later than 1914, American Bahá'ís would be worshipping in their own House of Worship.

But most of the Bahá'ís didn't share her optimism, including her fellow Bahai Temple Unity members. Not that there was friction between them three months after the organization was formed, although some must have interpreted her eagerness to 'forge ahead' as impatience, perhaps even a lack of reasonableness.

In a letter to Helen Goodall, Corinne exhibited her passion to serve the Master. It was a passion that seemed to possess her, though she tried hard to control it in public; there were moments when her guard would fall and she would write things like: 'I feel like mounting the housetops and shouting to the people to Arise for the Temple . . .'[8]

As financial secretary of the Bahai Temple Unity her work for the Faith increased. Now contributions were coming from different parts of the world, and that meant sending letters to foreign contributors as well as to the Americans who gave. And American contributions were increasing. Her home became the headquarters of the Bahai Temple Unity. Not only did its Executive Board meet there, but its various committees as well. It was a situation that Corinne probably favored, because she would be in a better position to help hasten the Temple's construction. (In a sense, she was the cox of the Bahá'í crew that was racing against procrastination, doubt, apathy, uncertainty and fear. The Ma<u>sh</u>riqu'l-A<u>dh</u>kár would be the prize awaiting the crew at the end of the race.)

In the middle of the whirlwind of activity was her husband Moses, a strong believer in maintaining family unity. By the fall of 1909 all three daughters were home. He liked that. Edna had graduated from Smith College in May; Arna, who had spent a year at Smith and dropped out, was back home and Katherine was going to high school locally. Davis was the only one away but not very far. He was still at the University of Michigan preoccupied with baseball, track and football.

Though the girls were close to their parents, the kind of togetherness that had dominated the True household when they were younger was naturally missing. The songfests around the piano, the impromptu plays in the parlor seemed gone from Moses' life, undoubtedly leaving a void that was never to be filled. And Laurence's death still haunted him. Though he appeared robust, he wasn't well. His heart had grown weaker, and no physician was treating him. He did, however, get some relief from chest pain from a masseur who would come twice weekly to the house on Kenmore Avenue.

Towards his wife's deep involvement in the Faith Moses refused to be an onlooker. He actually plunged into the Bahá'í work, especially in what was occurring at home. Often he would package materials for the Bahá'ís, give advice on logistical matters and act as host for Bahá'í meetings. He was drawn to the activity and genuinely wanted to help, for he truly found joy in serving others. Being a gregarious person, Moses didn't mind the different people who came to his house, all kinds of people – black, white, Malay, Indian, Persian, Jew, Catholic, the sophisticated and unschooled. Mail from overseas arrived almost daily. Messages from the Holy Land made the True home into a spiritual nerve center in North America.

Was Moses a Bahá'í? Many of the believers wondered. He hadn't openly declared his belief in Bahá'u'lláh. But on 26 November 1909, at the Day of the Covenant celebration which was taking place in his home, with himself and the three girls having the honor of serving the friends, Moses True shared his feelings about the Faith to Percy Woodcock, a guest from New York. 'If the Revelation is as you say it is, Mr Woodcock, then I am a Bahá'í.'

Fifteen days later Moses True died. Death came unexpectedly, because Corinne and the children were impressed with his high-spirited and joyous demeanor during the period between the celebration of the Day of the Covenant and his passing. Yet they sensed that physically he had been slipping. A hint of his condition came from the masseur; 'Mr True's pulse is much too rapid,' he told Corinne. 'He must avoid exertion of any kind.'

The day he died, he seemed as chipper as ever. After breakfast with Corinne and daughter Edna, he put on his new overcoat, which he was going to wear to work for the first time. As he checked it out in the hall mirror, Edna and Corinne teased him about how elegant he looked. Before he left, his wife begged him not to exert himself.

As he approached the station, he heard the train coming. He hurried up the stairs. When the doors opened, he fell into a seat, seized by a massive heart attack. Two stops later his body was removed from the train and Corinne was advised what had happened to her husband, who was 52 when he died.

Moses and Corinne had been devoted to each other for twenty-nine years. For the majority of their lives they had lived together, confided in each other, helped each other. When she was weary, he was usually nearby to cheer her up. It had been a good marriage. The children had certainly benefited from his compassion, love and fun-filled spirit. He had brought sparkle to the family, and provided companionship to the children when Corinne had to attend to Bahá'í tasks. Corinne knew that had she married someone like herself, perhaps a man like her father, life would have been a constant clash of wills. Not that Moses always capitulated to his wife's wishes. It's just that he recognized her genuine love of God, and no one of good conscience, he believed, could stand in the way of anyone expressing that emotion in the form of service. He was Corinne's greatest supporter.

Corinne would miss him, especially his sense of humor, even his pranks which at times were directed at her. Corinne was an easy target for him, because she usually took everything at face value. For example: one afternoon he boarded a trolley-car in downtown Chicago. He noticed Corinne absorbed in the evening newspaper, no doubt checking out the miserable condition of the world. There was space for another passenger next to her. He moved down the aisle and slipped onto the seat. She never once looked up from the newspaper. When he tried to look over her shoulder to read what she was reading she moved the paper closer to him so he could read more easily. But Moses moved closer, extending his head so that he was blocking her view. That was the limit! With fire in her eyes, she turned to scold the person next to her. But not an angry word was uttered; instead she broke into laughter.

Though an important element in her life was gone and adjustments had to be made, she never wavered from her religious duties. In fact she grew more involved in the Faith. She was certain that Moses was being cared for and was reunited with the children he had missed so much. That thought comforted her. What also comforted her was Percy Woodcock's letter of condolence in which he revealed what Moses had told him at her home on the Day of the Covenant. Hundreds of letters of sympathy poured into 5338 Kenmore Avenue. And Corinne tried to answer each one. To a close friend she wrote:

... Really dear Sister, the great wave of sympathy and condolence and grief which sweeps against one at such a crisis is almost enough to take you off your feet, but the Presence of the Great Spirit of Abdul Baha holds one fast.

As this is the Springtime in the Cause great thunderstorms must attend to its establishment and each soul will be able to find just how deep down into the Work it has thrust the tendrils of his or her heart, and if they are deeply, firmly rooted, the storms will only make them stronger. Pray dear Sister that I may not be shaken by this catastrophe. God was very present and merciful and I was able to be very calm. If we are too calm the people feel we are inhuman, therefore it is really best for them to see us express tenderness of heart. Before these four children I am trying to hold up the banner of the Immortality of the Soul and I tell them constantly to think of the great progress and gain of the soul of their father instead of dwelling on their own loss. They are doing remarkably well and such a peace and calm reigns in the home. If one feels the loss he or she quietly sheds a few tears and soon the sun is shining again brightly.[9]

Corinne's dedication to the Cause frightened some of the Bahá'ís. To continue at the vigorous pace she set prior to Moses' death seemed heartless to some people. But she was not about to endure a period of mourning. Death had come to mean to her a natural step in the process called life, the heartache caused by Moses' sudden passing a natural phenomenon; but God's work had to be done. With that understanding she didn't allow his death to impede, in any way, her Bahá'í responsibilities. Corinne forged ahead in a climate of optimism. She was confident that the Bahai Temple Unity would achieve what the Master wanted, as well as alter the believers' focus on Bahá'í administration, something she felt sure was desperately needed.

With the emergence of the Bahai Temple Unity, Chicago's House of Spirituality slipped more and more out of the national Bahá'í limelight. The process was reinforced with Thornton Chase's move to Los Angeles to head his firm's West Coast operations. His deep understanding of the Faith and firmness in the Covenant would be missed by the Chicago friends.

Corinne was aware of Thornton Chase's contributions to the Cause, and the Master's love for him. But she was, in a sense, a fatalist. To her, there was a divine reason for everything.

Was Corinne's hard work for the Faith a way of escaping from the sorrows she had encountered in recent years? Some Bahá'ís felt it was. And no matter what she said or did to dissuade such thinking few minds were changed. She wanted desperately to be with the only one who really understood her – and that was 'Abdu'l-Bahá. Life then would be predictable, calm and fulfilling.

Corinne received two translations of a Tablet from the Master in March 1910. Both fueled her already blazing spirit. It no longer mattered what people were saying about her unorthodox reaction to her husband's passing. In the later translation these were 'Abdu'l-Bahá's words:

> Although this calamity hath been great and intense, thou shouldst, at the time of adversity and misfortune, be patient, zealous, calm, firm and long-suffering. These are the qualities that befit such as thee.[10]

Corinne looked forward to the Bahá'í national convention during the Riḍván period. The gathering of the believers from different parts of America always thrilled her because it demonstrated the expansion and universality of the Faith. She prayed for unity, because she knew how much the Master wanted the friends to remain unified. That, she knew, was more important to Him than anything else, even the development of the Temple.

The singing of the Vaheed Choral Society helped to lift the convention to new spiritual heights. By holding concerts, the choral society proved to be a means of raising funds for the Mashriqu'l-Adhkár. Other fund-raising schemes were revealed at the convention, including a Widow's Quilt Fund, the use of 3,000 Blessing Boxes, and promoting the sale of Bahá'í hymn books.

Corinne encouraged those endeavors with supportive letters to individuals and communities, and in her reports that appeared each Bahá'í month in the *Star of the West*.[11]

Corinne was reelected to the Bahai Temple Unity's Executive Board, serving again as its financial secretary. But there was some relief for her. Perhaps Chicago's women sensed the burden she was carrying and so didn't elect her to its Assembly of Teaching.

Shortly after the convention, Corinne received distressing news from Ann Arbor, where her son Davis was attending the University of Michigan. He had damaged his knee in a pole-vaulting accident. Corinne was more upset than Davis, and his assurance to her that the doctor felt the knee would heal soon didn't help. All he needed, he told his mother, was some time to relax.

Davis and a classmate spent the summer at a logging camp in Oregon. Instead of staying with his friend's family, the two young men lived in one of the worker's cabins. They cut timber, hiked, swam, climbed mountains. All of that activity seemed to strengthen his knee.

Corinne's summer in Fruitport was not a two-month romp in the country. The pace of Bahá'í activity was as swift as in Chicago. The only difference was the setting. She wouldn't take the time off from her duties as the Bahai Temple Unity's financial secretary. Letters flowed from Fruitport to Fund contributors worldwide. There were also the teaching responsibilities. She felt compelled to support the Grand Rapids, Muskegon and Fruitport Bahá'í communities – communities she had helped to raise during previous vacation periods. She attended and spoke at their meetings. Her summer home was as busy as the one in Chicago. Different guests were there almost every week, and some stayed much longer. Since most of them were Bahá'ís, she put them to work for the Cause. Special gatherings were set up. In the summer of 1910, for example, she invited Carl Scheffler to speak on 'Why I am a Bahá'í'. Louise Waite shared her pilgrimage notes with the Bahá'ís and their friends. Elizabeth Greenleaf, who spent the entire summer in Fruitport, gave several talks. And Corinne hosted an area-wide Unity Feast that summer which scores of people attended. The event thrilled her, because many of the Michigan Bahá'ís had firm roots in Christianity. They weren't the professional truth-seekers, the utopians, the social idealists and the adventists the Faith attracted in Chicago. For the most part the Michigan Bahá'ís she knew and taught the Faith to were from rural or small-town America. It proved to her that such people could be moved by Bahá'u'lláh's Message, and their diversity, she felt, was needed in the Faith.

That summer Corinne returned to Chicago for a few days when news of the arrival of a prominent French Bahá'í reached her. She opened up her home for Hippolyte Dreyfus, who spoke on the teachings of the *Kitáb-i-Aqdas*. But soon she was back in Fruitport holding 'teaching dinners' and public meetings at her home.

In the fall of 1910 news of 'Abdu'l-Bahá's trip to Egypt ignited hope among the American believers that He would travel further west and eventually come to America. He was no longer a prisoner, having been freed during the 'Young Turk' rebellion in 1908. There wasn't anyone who wanted the Master to be in the United States more than Corinne. His presence, she felt, would strengthen the unity of the friends and would inspire them to greater commitment to complete the Temple project. And she also needed to see Him. It was the kind of need a person has who longs to see the sun after days and days of gray skies.

Corinne took advantage of His possible coming with an appeal in her monthly financial report in a November issue of *Star of the West*:

This Mashrak-el-Azkar will, perhaps, be the only one built in America during the remaining years of Abdul-Baha's earthly mission and it behooves us to bring this project to a point of completion that its corner stone may be laid in the event of his coming to America next spring. If we do not awake to this golden opportunity, future generations will point to us and say: 'Why did the early Bahais of America sleep so long and let this, one of the most glorious privileges of the ages, slip by unheeded?' Stop and meditate, friends, upon the necessary part a Mashrak-el-Azkar, dedicated by his holy presence, will play in the future history and development of the world. Will it not become a visiting point for all nations and people throughout centuries and cycles? The inflow thus produced will return an outflow of vitalizing spiritual influence and its accessories will shed the light of the highest sciences, arts and crafts and the most magnanimous works of charity and hospitality .[12]

Though the possibility of the Master's visit cheered Corinne's heart, there was distressing news concerning Davis. And it wasn't about his knee, which had healed. He complained of feeling weak shortly after returning to the University. This was strange since he had eaten and exercised well in a part of the country known for its clean air. Doctors diagnosed Davis's rundown condition as tuberculosis, the dreaded disease that had taken Corinne's sisters' lives. She had always feared that her family had a predisposition to tuberculosis, and perhaps Davis had inherited a tendency toward it. Certainly it didn't help to know that the cabin in Oregon where Davis stayed had been occupied by a worker who died from tuberculosis shortly after Davis moved in.

But his doctors were encouraging. They considered Davis's case was only 'slight'. To prevent complications Corinne sent her son to an outstanding sanitorium in New York's Adirondack mountains. Six months there, she thought, should clear up whatever trace he had of the disease.

9

The Master's Protection and Guidance

If Corinne's enthusiasm for the Temple project was waning in early 1911 because of her son's illness, nothing she did or said indicated that that was the case. Mercifully, she received a Tablet from the Master around that time. If she had been entertaining the thought of slowing down, that thought quickly evaporated when she read His appeal:

> ... endeavor ye with all your power and generosity so that ye may raise this first foundation in the Name of Baha in the continent of America. I supplicate God to pour upon thee heavenly blessings and that thy family be protected from every sadness and sorrow in this world.[1]

The Master's message couldn't have come at a better time. Knowing that 'Abdu'l-Bahá was praying for her family was reassuring. Davis was in God's hands.

When word of his relapse in April reached her, she personally took him to the Oakes Home, a sanitorium in Denver, Colorado, where the doctors felt he had a better chance of recovering. She spent two weeks with him, and planned to take her three daughters to see him in the summer. Would her last remaining son be taken from her? It was a thought she couldn't escape. Though it hurt to think about such a grim prospect, she knew that his fate was to be determined in a realm beyond her puny powers. In a letter to a friend, Helen Goodall, Corinne laid bare her soul: 'It is a fiery ordeal to fight that awful disease tuberculosis. For almost a year now I have tried doing the things advised by the most skilled physicians and nurses.

THE MASTER'S PROTECTION AND GUIDANCE 95

God alone knows how the battle will result. Through these hot fires our souls are to be refined.'[2]

News of the Master's presence in Europe fired the American believers' hopes that He would soon grace their shores. Corinne prayed that He would come. Maybe she prayed, in part, for personal reasons. Perhaps 'Abdu'l-Bahá would see her son and heal him.

There were many disappointed American Bahá'ís when 'Abdu'l-Bahá returned to Egypt after His European tour. Of course, the optimists clung to a section of a Tablet He had sent to the American believers that year, in which He wrote, 'If it pleases God next year I will take a journey towards the West . . .'[3]

Others sensed they didn't deserve a visit from the Master. The discord among the Americans troubled Him greatly. There was too much backbiting and fault-finding. His Tablet to them in the spring of 1911 had stated frankly what must be done in order for Him to come to America:

> If ye are yearning for my meeting, and if in reality ye are seeking my visit, ye must close the doors of difference and open the gates of affection, love and friendship. Ye must pulsate as one heart, and throb as one spirit.[4]

Corinne wished she could do more to strengthen the bonds of unity among the friends, for she wanted to please the Master. Yet at times, when she addressed the subject, some of the friends would bristle, causing the opposite effect. She didn't know what she was doing wrong. There were times she would say nothing lest what she said would set off bad feelings. Often her appeals for unity were viewed as sermons: an anathema, especially to those who had broken away from religious orthodoxy. At times she felt helpless in trying to strengthen community unity. It was a frustration equal to the one concerning the Temple project, about which the Master continued to remind her. In the spring of 1911, there was another reminder from Him in His own handwriting:

O thou daughter of the Kingdom! Today in America no matter is greater for the elevation of the Word of God than the Mashrak-el-Azkar. Surely give it the utmost importance. I am always waiting that a good report regarding the Mashrak-el-Azkar should come.[5]

If only she could report good news more often. She tried, but didn't dare exaggerate the American friends' efforts. What she reported to Him had to be totally accurate. For to her, communicating with the Master was, in a sense, like communicating with God.

While the Bahá'ís waited in hope of 'Abdu'l-Bahá's visit to the United States, Corinne grew more and more convinced that the building of the Temple would be a major factor in unifying the American Bahá'í community. And the Master's presence in the United States and Canada would surely speed up the Temple project.

Because 'Abdu'l-Bahá kept underscoring the importance of the Temple work in His Tablets to Corinne, she viewed them as a sign to channel most of her energy into it. In her mind everything else was less important. In earlier years, when her children were young, she had been the heart of the family, ever busy with her basket of mending as they played around her. But now the children were grown, and by April 1912 only three daughters would be left, all occupied with their own pursuits. By wholeheartedly serving the Cause of God, she truly believed, the right things would happen in all aspects of her life.

In the summer of 1911, Corinne learned that Davis had rallied. He seemed more like his old self. Moving him to Colorado was proving to be a wise decision. And it was nice having Edna at home. She had returned from Italy where she had been with Katherine, who was studying there. But Edna didn't stay home for long. She wanted desperately to be with her brother, an idea Corinne found difficult to approve. On the one hand she wanted someone from the family to be with Davis; on the other hand, there was the likelihood that Edna could catch the disease. After consulting with a physician, who prescribed ways of preventing infection, Edna left for Colorado.

Seeing his sister lifted Davis's spirit. And he had already been feeling better. His condition seemed to improve even more when Edna rented a house, where she and Davis would live. She knew how much he detested living in an institutional environment. In their home he could entertain some of his friends; and some of hers could visit. Edna tried to attend to Davis's spiritual needs. Though he respected the Bahá'í Teachings, he remained a Christian Scientist. She found a local Christian Science reader who came frequently, giving him considerable comfort.

Serving her brother brought joy to Edna. Certainly she did it to help him recover, but there was another reason: something inside her – a feeling she couldn't explain – that drove her to serve others. After graduating from Smith College in 1909, she had spent almost a year in a poor Chicago neighborhood teaching girls to play basketball and other games. She did it without pay. Arna volunteered her services too, working with preschoolers. Incidentally, Arna wasn't going to be kept from seeing Davis either. After all, she had always been close to Davis, closer to him than any of the other children. She didn't stay as long as Edna, however, because she was being courted by Leo Perron, whom she was planning to marry.

In the fall there was wonderful news from the East: 'Abdu'l-Bahá was coming to America. Just the knowledge of His impending arrival generated more activity in the Bahá'í communities; the believers drew closer; and Corinne noticed a marked increase in contributions to the Temple Fund. The fact that He was going to address the Bahai Temple Unity Convention during Riḍván thrilled her. Now she was certain He would be in Chicago. If only He could stay in her home. She sent Him a letter, asking if He would be her guest during one of His visits to Chicago. After all, she reasoned, she and Arna had been His guests when they were in Akka.

Edna tried hard to make Davis's Christmas cheerful. It wasn't her fault that he couldn't enjoy what she had prepared. Davis had grown weaker and was coughing more. In fact, his doctor told Edna that her brother's situation was hopeless. Though she didn't share the doctor's prognosis with Davis, she sensed he was aware that death was near. He never panicked. It was obvious to all who called on him that he believed in an afterlife. Edna did too; but there were moments when basic human feelings welled up in her and she was overcome with sadness and anger. Those moments came when she watched her brother sleep. Davis was only 24. To Edna her brother's exploits on the athletics field were still vivid; so were his prankish antics during the parlor games he and his brothers and sisters used to play with their father after dinner. Such a generous and free spirit. Davis and Edna heeded the doctor's suggestion to go home to be with their mother and the rest of the family. By March they were back in Chicago. And in a few weeks 'Abdu'l-Bahá was to arrive in America.

On 11 April 1912 the SS *Cedric*, carrying the Master, stopped in the bay approaching New York's port. Quarantine and customs officers came aboard, followed by journalists trying to find the most celebrated passenger on the ship; they found Him on the upper deck clothed in oriental robes and wearing a white turban. To many of the reporters 'Abdu'l-Bahá was a world peace leader. Little did they know that the majestic figure before them had never gone to school, and never held a news conference or given a public talk prior to His visit to Europe the previous year. Nor could they fully appreciate what the Master truly represented. Some, however, experienced a sense of His majesty and a glimpse of His vision. Reporter Wendell Phillips Dodge of the New York City News Association was among them:

> When the ship was abreast the Statue of Liberty, standing erect and facing it, Abdul-Baha held his arms wide apart in

salutation and said:
'There is the new world's symbol of liberty and freedom. After being forty years a prisoner I can tell you that freedom is not a matter of place. It is a condition. Unless one accept dire vicissitudes he will not attain. When one is released from the prison of self, that is indeed a release.'[6]

Waiting at the pier were several hundred Bahá'ís from many American communities. They had been there since early morning, and the *Cedric* didn't dock until noon. Corinne wanted to be there. She had planned on it. But she couldn't leave Davis. Even though the Master was to be in Chicago in two weeks, there was no guarantee she would see Him, let alone meet with Him. It all hinged on Davis's condition.

'Abdu'l-Bahá arrived in Chicago on the night of 29 April. On the following day, He met with journalists and a few local believers in His Plaza Hotel suite. When He learned of Corinne's latest crisis, the Master, accompanied by Dr Zia Bagdadi, left immediately for the True home. He arrived shortly after noon. Seeing Him, being close to Him, hearing His voice, and being the object of her Lord's love and compassion, transformed her home into His home.

He wanted to see Davis. And how she had wished He would do that. 'Abdu'l-Bahá spent a long time with her son. When He emerged from Davis's room, He walked across the hall and entered another room with Dr Bagdadi behind Him. Inside, He began pacing back and forth and in a voice that seemed to spring from the depths of His soul, He cried out repeatedly: 'The calamities in this house must cease.'

The Master came downstairs and told an eager Corinne that her son was a wonderful young man and that He found him much better than expected. Overjoyed, she felt as though a great weight had been lifted from her heart. Davis would recover; she was convinced of that.

'Abdu'l-Bahá couldn't stay long. He had three lectures to make that day and suggested that Corinne come too. Her daughters urged her to go. After all, Davis was bound to recover and they could care for his needs.

For Corinne it was an exciting afternoon and evening. It was like being with a mighty king. And there was no doubt in her mind what kingdom He ruled on earth. Those officials at Hull House and the Fourth Annual Conference of the NAACP sensed that someone special was in their midst when He spoke to the large audiences about the importance of promoting racial unity.

That night more than 1,000 people gathered at the final public session of the Bahai Temple Unity Convention to hear the Master speak on the significance of the Mashriqu'l-Adhkár. Predictably, what He said was taken personally by Corinne. Once again He was reinforcing her already heroic commitment to the Temple project. His words also broadened her understanding of the purpose of the Mashriqu'l-Adhkár. It was to be an instrument not only for unifying the American believers, but for unifying all of mankind.

What a day it had been! The Master had led her into the world of the spirit, where He dwelt. No words could describe the experience.

Only later did she realize that by being with 'Abdu'l-Bahá that day, He was protecting her from what was taking place at home. He knew all along that Davis would die. When the Master told her that her son was better than He expected, He was really referring to his spiritual condition. Apparently 'Abdu'l-Bahá had been impressed with Davis's understanding of life's journey to the spiritual kingdom.

Learning that Davis's passing was peaceful comforted Corinne. What moved her, however, were his last words. He had expressed happiness that 'Abdu'l-Bahá was with his mother during his final moments.

16. 'Abdu'l-Bahá, the Center of the Covenant of Bahá'u'lláh

17. 'Abdu'l-Bahá at the dedication of the Mashriqu'l-Adhkár grounds, Wilmette, 1 May 1912

18. 'Abdu'l-Bahá in Lincoln Park, Chicago, 5 May 1912, after His meeting with children at the Plaza Hotel

19. Laurence Knight True (1885–1906), who died when 21 in a sailing accident on Saginaw Bay

20. Charles Gilbert Davis True (1886–1912), who died during 'Abdu'l-Bahá's first day in Chicago. No men were left in Corinne's family.

THE MASTER'S PROTECTION AND GUIDANCE

The day after Davis's death Corinne was present at the Temple site at the corner of Linden Avenue and Sheridan Road in Wilmette. Being there was difficult. Her last son – gone. Would the human tragedy that seemed to stalk her ever cease, she wondered. But Corinne had to be there for the dedication ceremony, not because of its historical significance, but because 'Abdu'l-Bahá was coming. It was a cool, cloudy and windy day, not the kind of day one expects on the first day of May. Nearly 400 people were waiting for 'Abdu'l-Bahá's arrival. He was to dedicate the Temple site in the tent behind the crowd. Some in attendance were surprised to see Corinne, for Davis had died the previous day. It simply wasn't customary to do something like that. But those who knew Corinne well weren't surprised. Certainly the Master wasn't. When His taxi drove up, a Persian stepped out of the vehicle, asking for Mrs True. In a few minutes she appeared and was ushered into the car, the guest of her Beloved. The car didn't go far, only to the bridge on Sheridan Road that spans the canal bordering the Bahá'í property. Why the Master singled her out isn't officially known. Was it because He wanted to see the new bridge and canal locks at the end of Wilmette harbor? Or to inspect the Temple site's boundaries? He didn't need Corinne with Him to do that. Surely it was an act of compassion considering her loss of Davis the previous day. But was it more than that? Was it also a demonstration of faith in Corinne True, directed at those who questioned, even openly criticized, her ability to work on the Temple project? Though the trees on the site prevented the crowd from seeing what was happening on the bridge, a group of children playing behind the gathering spotted 'Abdu'l-Bahá and Corinne walking toward the back entrance of the tent. He greeted them warmly, gently patting all of them.

Inside the tent were about 300 people seated in a circle. There wasn't an empty seat. In fact, people were outside trying to catch a glimpse of the Master and straining to hear His voice.

In His talk He cast His vision into the future, stating that there would be many other temples in America and elsewhere in the world; but the Mashriqu'l-Adhkár in the Chicago area would have special significance as the first one erected in the West.

There were snags in carrying out the dedication ceremony. The golden trowel given to the Master to dig a hole for the dedication stone wasn't strong enough to break through the ground. An ax, borrowed from someone across the street, was handed to 'Abdu'l-Bahá, who swung it powerfully, again and again, until He broke into the earth below. Finally, a shovel was produced by a young man who had borrowed it from a work crew near the village center. When the shovel was handed to the Master, Corinne True reportedly suggested to Him to have women participate in the ceremony. 'Abdu'l-Bahá called on Lua Getsinger to come forward. It required a second urging by the Master to draw Lua to Him. Corinne was the second one to dig up a shovelful of earth. Following her, representatives from different races and nationalities took their turn with the shovel. After placing the stone in the hole, the Master pushed the earth around it and declared that 'The Temple is already built'.[7]

To Corinne the Master's declaration meant that there was no question about whether the Temple would ever be built. It was simply a matter of the believers focusing faithfully on the vision He had shared with them that chilly, gray, windy day in Wilmette. To her the burning question was when the Temple would be completed. It didn't matter that no foundation had been dug or design approved. She remained optimistic that the Temple would be built in a few years.

Davis's funeral was the following day. It was a Bahá'í funeral: a strange thing to do some people must have felt, considering that her son had never embraced the Faith. But Corinne knew her son, loved him deeply and, through the Master, had strong faith in the existence of life after death. In her mind she undoubtedly felt certain that when Davis passed over, the validity of Bahá'u'lláh's Message would become clear to him.

After the funeral the True family received a message from 'Abdu'l-Bahá, urging them to meet with Him at His Plaza Hotel room. Corinne, Edna, Arna and Katherine hastened to go. He spent some time with them, directing most of his talk to Corinne. She was moved to learn that the Master had taken time from His hectic schedule to visit Davis's grave and pray not only for him but for Moses and the other children buried nearby. He assured her that there would come a time when she would be reunited with them. Her children, He said, had been transplanted into a beautiful garden. He also spoke of the nearness of the spiritual world, while still in this world – that each of us is helped by souls who have passed on. To make the point He looked out the window, calling attention to the gardeners who were caring for the plants in Lincoln Park across the street. The plants, He added, aren't conscious of the gardener. Yet the gardeners are pruning, watering, feeding the flowers, as well as transplanting them, helping them grow. 'This family will be together,' He repeatedly promised her, 'and you are together right now.' Once again 'Abdu'l-Bahá had drawn Corinne into His world, comforting her and spiritually fortifying her.

Corinne didn't have to wait until 'Abdu'l-Bahá returned to Chicago over four months later to see Him again. While visiting New York City, she was asked by the Master to look after His household during a five-day stay there. There was no need to think about what she should do. Her decision was instantaneous. No thought was given as to whether she was capable of caring for a group of people, especially people from a different culture. The fact that she had always had a maid and a cook didn't escape her. But the prospect of being with the Master, and serving the One who continuously served others with such exuberance and joy, overcame her doubts.

What happened in New York turned out to be an unforgettable experience and an important lesson in how faith is to be expressed. She shared what she learned with her friend, Albert Windust:

> ... Through this experience I was given to know the reality of the truth Jesus taught about the station of the one who is the servant. As Abdul Baha said, the servant is always with his Master and being a servant in this household I found many times a day we heard the most wonderful lessons given by Abdul Baha which could not have been ours had we not been serving in the capacity we were. Where else could one be an invited guest and crave the privilege of washing dishes, sweeping, dusting and making beds but in this Sacred Household?[8]

She was also privileged to witness, in the home and in the presence of 'Abdu'l-Bahá, the marriage of Harlan and Grace Ober which Howard Colby Ives performed. Standing with Mr Ives, the Master gave His blessing with hands upraised, as the bride and groom knelt. 'It was indeed a heavenly marriage,' she wrote many years later. 'Would not a moving picture of this event not be wonderful for future generations and help poor wayward humanity return to the knowledge of true matrimony ... The Glorious Master was clad in pure white and His marvelous white hair made His Divinity more striking. I heard Him tell them they must be together in all the worlds ...'[9]

Little did Corinne expect that her New York visit would see an event of historical significance for Bahá'í women. While there, the Master told her that the Chicago community must now allow women to serve on its House of Spirituality. He dissolved the existing one and sent Howard MacNutt of Brooklyn, NY, to Chicago to oversee the new election. Corinne was elected to the House of Spirituality, which 'Abdu'l-Bahá charged with teaching the Cause and caring for the welfare of the community.[10] At the time she wasn't aware of what the

THE MASTER'S PROTECTION AND GUIDANCE 105

new duty would mean in her life, because she was overcome with elation over the Master's removal of an administrative barrier against women. It was a new day for the Faith in America. What 'Abdu'l-Bahá did was a confirmation of Corinne's personal belief that with His presence in America the Faith would grow stronger and more unified, and needed changes would be made.

Shortly after Corinne returned to Chicago, her community was privileged to see a silent motion picture film of 'Abdu'l-Bahá, taken at the home of Mr and Mrs MacNutt. When the believers in Western Michigan pressed to see the film, Corinne rented the *Star of the West*'s copy and held a showing in Muskegon, not far from her summer home.[11]

Corinne was ecstatic when the Master accepted her invitation to stay in her home from 12 to 16 September. During those four days 5338 Kenmore Avenue became a magnet in the American Bahá'í community. All kinds of people were attracted to the True home. At every meeting the large downstairs rooms were filled to capacity. Some sat on the floor. Others perched themselves wherever they could on the staircase. But even when there weren't any formal meetings, people streamed in and out of Corinne's home, seeking interviews with the Master. Often those private events turned into opportunities to share the healing Message of Bahá'u'lláh. Albert Windust remembered what happened when Mrs Ida Boulter Slater, who had known of the Faith for ten years without becoming a Bahá'í, finally met the Master in the True home.

She and her husband went upstairs to the room where 'Abdu'l-Bahá was holding interviews. After five minutes they came out and descended the stairs, obviously moved. In fact, Mrs Slater was crying. Albert Windust later learned from her what the Master had told her: 'You have sought the kingdom of God in many ways and have journeyed far and it was good; but now, you have come home.'

'I knew I had come home,' she told Albert, 'when I entered the presence of 'Abdu'l-Bahá. Those were not tears of sorrow; they were tears of spiritual joy.'[12]

While the Master was at the True home, Corinne and her daughters learned much about His power and how the Faith is to be lived. In retrospect, they agreed that everything 'Abdu'l-Bahá did during those few days was a lesson on how to be a real human being.

The day He arrived, Corinne served tea to the Master and the Persians accompanying Him. In fact, it was the kind of tea that Persians normally don't like and His translators urged Him not to drink it. He drank it anyway, replying to them, 'This is the best tea of all, because it has been prepared with love.'[13]

Arna had a problem, and the Master sensed what it was. She had developed a fever that kept fluctuating, plus a slight cough. Corinne feared that Arna had contracted tuberculosis. And the chances were good that she had caught the disease from her brother, because like Edna she had spent considerable time with Davis during his last days. Arna shared her mother's fear, a fear that caused a personal dilemma. She was in love with a young man, Leo Perron, and they were planning to marry. If she had tuberculosis, she felt, it wouldn't be fair to Leo to go ahead with the marriage. Strangely, while she harbored these thoughts, the Master kept touching her shoulder. One morning 'Abdu'l-Bahá noticed Arna holding a thermometer; she had apparently just taken her temperature. He took the instrument from her, snapped it in two and told her to throw it away. He assured her that she would be well and to go ahead with her marriage plans. She and Leo were married in Chicago, 2 October 1912. Arna never contracted tuberculosis.

Arna also saw another side of 'Abdu'l-Bahá. One day, while sharing with the Master the contents of her hope chest, she showed Him a picture of her fiancé. At that point He asked with a twinkle in His eye, 'Which one is

THE MASTER'S PROTECTION AND GUIDANCE

my present?'

'You can have anything you want,' Arna replied. 'Abdu'l-Bahá picked up the picture of her fiancé, smiled and pressed it to His chest, saying, 'This is the one I'll take.' Waiting a few moments, he handed it back to her.

On a more serious note, Corinne witnessed how the Master and those around Him were protected. While in Chicago, He and several believers, including Corinne, were scheduled to journey to Kenosha, Wisconsin, where He was to give a talk. They were in the True home, and the Master was speaking to a group of believers. One of His secretaries tried to remind Him that He would miss His train to Kenosha if they didn't leave right away. But 'Abdu'l-Bahá continued talking.

Everyone but the Master seemed disappointed when they reached the railroad station and discovered their train had left. Only 'Abdu'l-Bahá took it in stride. Later, during the journey when their train slowed down, the believers noticed that they were passing the wreckage of the earlier train. It had collided with a southbound train, injuring many people.

For Corinne it was another lesson that one of the major aims of life is to learn to rely on Divine protection in all aspects of life. She knew the Master did. She also knew that whatever He did was for the benefit of those with Him. A great concern of hers was whether she would be able to acquire just a fraction of the kind of faith the Master always displayed.

Her faith would soon be tested by 'Abdu'l-Bahá. It took place on the railroad station platform on the last day of His Chicago visit. While waiting for His train to St Paul, Minnesota, the Master turned to Corinne and said, 'Mrs True, I want you to speak in public. I want you to tell the people about the Faith.'

Stunned, she replied, 'But Master, I can't do it; I have no training, no experience . . . I'm too frank.' Corinne had always been reserved. Public speaking wasn't her forte.

There were so many gifted orators among the Bahá'ís, especially the men. She was in a dilemma, because the Master had made this request. She wouldn't know how to begin to become an able speaker; but she knew she had to make a beginning. And 'Abdu'l-Bahá, as if reading her mind, provided her with guidelines to follow. 'Forget what you can't do,' He said. 'Stand up and turn your heart wholly toward me. Look over the heads of the audience and I'll never fail you.'

Though the prospect of having to give a public talk frightened her, her fear of failing to heed the Master's appeal drove her to speak as He urged her to do. From then on she was able to speak easily and fluently to all audiences.

One of Corinne's closest friends, Albert Windust, was also at the railroad station. 'Abdu'l-Bahá beckoned Albert to sit next to Him. Of course, the young printer and *Star of the West* editor eagerly complied. No sooner had he sat down than the Master slapped his left thigh hard three times and, with each blow, He said, 'There are many wolves in Chicago!'[14] He was referring to Bahá'ís who lusted for power and status in the Faith – the potential Covenant-breakers. 'Abdu'l-Bahá didn't mention names. Nor did he try to frighten the friends. Those with whom the Master shared His concern over Covenant-breaking were fairly enlightened believers. He wanted them to be vigilant but not paranoid. The Faith was in its infancy; and so many of the early American believers were in such a lofty state of consciousness that they would be easy prey for some crafty person seeking a special following. Preserving the Faith's unity was the Master's primary concern. Some of the Persians in America had to be watched. To Corinne, 'Abdu'l-Bahá said, 'You can trust Dr Zia Bagdadi.'[15] And she did, becoming a close friend of his and often working with him on Bahá'í projects, even during the most trying times.

Before 'Abdu'l-Bahá left Chicago during His September

THE MASTER'S PROTECTION AND GUIDANCE 109

visit, Corinne had experiences with Him that clarified questions she had tried to bury. They were tear-stained questions that during weaker moments in her life would surface, causing feelings of grief; and usually this pain and heartache she experienced alone. But she never allowed those sad thoughts to restrict her strong attraction toward the spiritual world. From then on, through 'Abdu'l-Bahá's help, she would be able to bear them. She was sure of that.

There was her husband, Moses. 'Abdu'l-Bahá answered the questions she feared to ask, assuring her that they would be reunited in the next world and that Moses had accepted Bahá'u'lláh.

Another time when alone with the Master, Corinne, uncharacteristically, unburdened herself; 'I have had a great many sorrows, 'Abdu'l-Bahá,' she said. 'I have had a sad life – sad things to bear.'

'I know, I know, Mrs True, because I have sent them to you,' the Master replied.

Corinne didn't flinch. In fact, 'Abdu'l-Bahá's response brought peace to her heart. Those terrible questions had been answered. They had been put to rest forever. The Master knew the measure of Corinne True's spiritual strength. She could withstand the truth and in time understand the wisdom related to her suffering.

She became stronger. After a while, friends who had lost someone dear to them would contact her, seeking support. And she would always give it, usually drawing upon the support the Master had given her during her personal crises. Her letters contained quotations from 'Abdu'l-Bahá's Tablets or Shoghi Effendi's letters to her. During her life she received nearly fifty Tablets and cablegrams from the Master and many letters from the Guardian.

10

'The Money Came . . . Rolling In'

'Abdu'l-Bahá's departure from North America in December 1912 seemed to cast a spell of sadness over the Chicago community. With His presence there was so much more vitality. He evoked a sense of hope that whatever goals had to be won would be won. And the American community, as a whole, seemed more unified. There wasn't time for bickering and fault-finding. All thoughts seemed to focus on wherever the Master traveled on the continent. News of His activities was sought eagerly.

Certainly Corinne missed Him. She felt that with the Master in America the Faith would grow in numbers and maturity, and that swifter progress would be made in building the Temple. During His eight-months tour of the United States and Canada there had been a marked increase in donations to the Temple project. Her hope that He would return (in the near future) eventually grew into a belief.

With the Master gone, Corinne's impatience grew more apparent. Progress on the Mashriqu'l-Adhkár was moving too slowly. She wished the Bahai Temple Unity's Executive Board, of which she was a member, would get more things done. But there was a bright spot – New York City. Corinne noticed that New Yorkers were contributing generously to the Temple Fund. So many of them were giving that she went through two receipt books in a few months.[1]

The Chicago community, on the other hand, was in a slump. The House of Spirituality was unable to generate any enthusiasm among the believers. As a member of the institution the condition concerned Corinne, who had conceived of what she felt was an appealing teaching campaign. Women, she believed, were ripe for the Faith. All that was necessary was to inform them of the Revelation's liberating teachings on women's rights. The fact that women were serving on the highest administrative body in America, as well as locally, should motivate the emancipation-minded women to at least investigate the Faith. Corinne printed 3,500 leaflets on the state of women in the Cause, and mailed them to people she felt would be impressed with what the Bahá'ís had achieved in the struggle to win equal rights for women. Corinne was certain the leaflets would have great appeal. After all, American women were relegated to inferior roles in churches, government, and industry.[2] In 1914 they still were denied the right to vote in federal elections. Finding a woman doctor, lawyer, engineer or business executive was rare. And there certainly weren't any female ministers, priests and rabbis.

Though Corinne was committed to teaching the Faith, her commitment to the Temple project was greater. It was greater because the Master felt it should be at that time. Corinne was tested. Some of the members of the Bahai Temple Unity, spearheaded by Dr Frederick W. D'Evelyn, wanted to borrow $6,000 from the Temple Fund to wage a national teaching campaign. Her immediate response as financial secretary was to resist the effort. She wired the Master, saying: 'SHOULD ANY OF TEMPLE FUND BE USED FOR TEACHING FRIENDS?' His quick response was: '. . . USE TEMPLE FUNDS FOR TEMPLE ONLY.'[3]

There were times when it was difficult to make payments on the bank loan that helped to acquire Temple land. Though the Bahai Temple Unity's Executive Board was proud of the fact that it was never late with a payment, there had been some near misses. On one occasion it appeared that making the monthly installment would be impossible. There simply wasn't enough money in the Fund. Corinne besought Bahá'u'lláh's help. Bernard Jacobsen, the Bahai Temple Unity's treasurer at the time, came down from Kenosha to confer with Corinne. They decided that they would go to the bank to appeal for an extension of time. Because the Faith had gained a fine credit record, they felt the extension would be granted. But then bankers are not predictable, and also there was the Master's concern that all bills be paid when due.

Not long after Corinne and Bernard sat down before a Northern Trust Company bank official, a foreign exchange clerk called out, 'Is Mrs True there?'

'Yes, I am here,' she replied.

'Well,' said the clerk, 'we have just received a draft from the Persian Bahá'í community and deposited it into the Bahai Temple Unity account.' It was enough money to pay that month's installment. To Corinne and Bernard, it was a miracle.

Corinne's instinct to protect the Temple Fund was prompted by an earlier Tablet from 'Abdu'l-Bahá in which He had advised avoidance of contracting any debt in building the Temple.[4] The plan was for paying off one developmental phase of the Mashriqu'l-Adhkár project before starting another. Six thousand dollars had to be raised to complete payment of the last bit of Temple land. Corinne hoped that the money would flow in by the end of 1913.

But she wasn't going to rely only on hope. In her letters to the believers she emphasized the importance of wiping out the debt by the end of the year so that the Faith in America could channel its energies into the next phase of the Temple project.

Corinne was looking beyond the acquisition of land. If only something could be built on the site, she thought, it would be an incentive to speed up construction. She wrote the Master, pleading with Him to send her the specifications for the dome. With that, she believed the foundation could be built. It's doubtful that 'Abdu'l-Bahá sent her the specifications. But her appeal to the friends worked. At the end of 1913 'the money came literally rolling in'; on 24 December 1913, the Bahai Temple Unity had enough money to pay off the remaining $6,000 debt.[5]

Shortly after the Master left America, the Trues had another person living with them. Saichiro Fujita, a Japanese young man who had embraced the Faith in California, grew close to Edna and Katherine who were living at home. Arna had already married Leo Perron when Fujita moved into 5338 Kenmore Avenue. To Edna and Katherine he was like a brother, someone they could confide in. To Corinne, Fujita was like a son. She asked him to live with her family because 'Abdu'l-Bahá had asked her to look after him. Fujita had wanted desperately to return to Haifa with the Master. Serving 'Abdu'l-Bahá was his fondest wish. He also dreamed of installing electricity in the Holy Shrines and the Master's home. Though 'Abdu'l-Bahá promised Fujita that one day he would serve at the World Center, he was to remain in America to complete his education. Corinne helped him enroll at an electronics institute in Chicago and secure a part-time job at Marshall Fields department store, repairing toys. At times he acted as Corinne's unofficial chauffeur, driving her from place to place. He loved cars.

To Fujita, being with the Trues was like being home. He felt at ease, totally accepted. Usually wherever the Trues went, he came along as a member of the family. When Corinne went to Fruitport during the summer, Fujita often accompanied her. They liked being together. Their affinity for each other probably sprang from their all-consuming love for the Master. Those who possessed such an intense feeling for 'Abdu'l-Bahá formed an imperishable bond that transcended words. Their distinguishing characteristic was their wholehearted desire to serve the Cause as 'Abdu'l-Bahá wished them to serve it.

The first summer Fujita visited Fruitport, he met Wyatt Cooper while swimming at a local lake. They grew to be lifelong friends. Wyatt's parents and aunt, Mary Frazier, had been attracted to the Faith by Corinne. Their farm, which had been in their family for over 150 years, was not far from her summer home.

Though Fujita was about fourteen years older, the two had much in common. They liked swimming and riding horses and each had an enterprising spirit. They ventured into business together, growing vegetables on a patch of land on the Coopers' farm. Fujita bought a horse and wagon to haul their yield six miles to Muskegon every Saturday in summer, leaving at 5:30 a.m. sharp. Wyatt never forgot his experiences with Fujita, maybe because his friend manifested the same spirit as Corinne and her daughters. He was warm, generous and dignified, and it was apparent how deeply he loved the Cause. The mention of 'Abdu'l-Bahá would evoke an expression of love and reverence in him that could only stream from a celestial source. By knowing Fujita, Wyatt's faith strengthened.[6]

When Wyatt was born in 1902, his mother was already a Bahá'í. There was even a Bahá'í group in Fruitport. Corinne had started teaching there in 1899. While walking away from the local post office one day, she told a summer resident from nearby Grand Rapids about Bahá'u'lláh and 'Abdu'l-Bahá. This was Delina Perry, who eventually became a Bahá'í. But Fruitport's first Bahá'í was Mrs Petersen, whose whole family soon accepted the Faith. Through Corinne's efforts communities were established in Grand Haven, Grand Rapids, Muskegon, as well as Fruitport, which became a Local Spiritual Assembly in 1909. In later years, when Wyatt was married, all of his immediate family – his wife and two sons, Clarke and Lawrence – accepted Bahá'u'lláh.

An experience in the local Congregational church helped Wyatt turn to Bahá'u'lláh. When he asked his Sunday School teacher why he hadn't lived during the

'THE MONEY CAME . . . ROLLING IN'

time of Jesus, she said, 'You simply didn't live at time.' Dissatisfied with her answer, he posed the s̲a̲ question to his mother who sat him down in the parlor a̲. said, 'Wyatt, we are living in a new day', and proceeded to tell him about Bahá'u'lláh, as well as 'Abdu'l-Bahá who was living across the sea. The next Sunday Wyatt went to the Bahá'í Sunday School at the Petersens, which more than ten Bahá'í youngsters from the area attended regularly.

The Coopers, especially Wyatt's mother, were close to the Trues. In later years Wyatt spoke of Arna pushing him about in a carriage. He also remembered Corinne's generosity and warmth. At 17, Wyatt was invited to live with Corinne in Chicago. She enrolled him in a printing school where he studied for two years.

The communities raised in Western Michigan were strong. When news of 'Abdu'l-Bahá's presence in Chicago reached them, Mrs Mary Frazier, Wyatt's aunt, was delegated by the other Bahá'ís to go to Chicago with an invitation for the Master to visit their area.

Undaunted, Mary Frazier somehow got to 'Abdu'l-Bahá's suite at the Plaza Hotel. When she presented the invitation to the Master, He took her hand and urged her to have the friends come to see Him in Chicago. Rushing to the Michigan Avenue dock to catch the last boat home, Mary found it was starting to pull out. She felt she had to return home as soon as possible to share the Master's invitation with the other believers; she had to get aboard that boat. She made such a fuss that the dock master called the ship back, something the shipping line rarely did.

Mary arrived in Michigan early in the morning. During the remainder of the day she traveled to Grand Haven, Grand Rapids, Muskegon and Fruitport, contacting the Bahá'ís in all of those communities. That same night about fifteen believers boarded the ship for Chicago. The next day they were in the presence of the Master, who took Mary Frazier's hand and commended her: 'Sacrifice! Sacrifice! in the name of Bahá!'

Mary Frazier had always loved the Faith and sacrificed for it. Despite her husband's opposition, she found time to teach and wash neighbors' clothes in order to contribute more to the Bahá'í Fund.

As for Wyatt, he had to give up printing; his allergy to printer's ink forced him to turn to cooking as a vocation. He did well at it, both in restaurants and schools, including the Bahá'í schools in Geyserville and Green Acre. But Wyatt was to make his mark in a different career. In a way, his involvement in it wasn't his choice. When early in 1953 the National Spiritual Assembly was looking for someone to create the gardens for the May 1953 dedication of the House of Worship in Wilmette, Edna, Katherine, and Borrah Kavelin suggested that Wyatt be employed. As a boy he had worked on his family's farm and later on a flower farm in Michigan, but he had had no formal training. For the grounds of a building like the House of Worship, it might have been thought that a qualified horticulturist was required. But their recommendation turned out to be right. Wyatt Cooper not only became the Temple's chief gardener, but his designs won many awards at International Flower and Garden Shows in Chicago. He was also made Superintendent of Buildings and Grounds for the Temple, a position he held for some nineteen years until his retirement in 1969. He died in 1977.

To Wyatt, a humble, loving man, Corinne True was his guardian angel. She saw in him what he couldn't recognize himself. Her faith in him helped him gain confidence, and grow spiritually and mentally. When serious problems would plague him, he would turn to the Trues for advice.[7]

11

Two Kinds of War

There were some disappointments in 1914. Contributions dropped 50% from the previous year's level. Progress on the Temple project was lagging far behind the schedule Corinne had in mind. With the formation of the Bahai Temple Unity in 1909, she had expressed confidence that believers would be worshipping in the Ma<u>sh</u>riqu'l-A<u>dh</u>kár certainly by 1914. But not even 'Abdu'l-Bahá's presence in America had fired the friends, she felt, to the kind of dedication required to complete the Temple project. Though the Temple site had been acquired, there wasn't a sign of construction on the land. And there wasn't going to be before $200,000 was raised, a sum the Executive Board felt was needed before construction could start. That was the way the Master wanted to proceed. Although Corinne accepted 'Abdu'l-Bahá's guidance without question, she remained frustrated. There were all the letters she had written imploring the friends to help raise up the Ma<u>sh</u>riqu'l-A<u>dh</u>kár; and there were the talks she had given, heartfelt appeals laced with appropriate quotations from Bahá'u'lláh and 'Abdu'l-Bahá. For example, in a letter to the American Bahá'ís she had written:

> ... The followers of Baha'o'llah should not pause a moment in the great endeavor to complete the Mashrakel-Azkar. Abdul-Baha says, 'the most important thing in this day is the SPEEDY ERECTION of the Edifice. Its mystery is great and cannot be unveiled as yet. In the future it will be made plain ...'
> A stated amount as a building fund has been named. Is

not this in itself a call to the Bahais, singly and collectively, to make every effort possible to raise the fund? It is a call to activity. Work, work, work! — so that the 'Greatest Branch' of God may dedicate the foundation and lay the corner-stone of this Edifice and pronounce a blessing upon it that will give it a superlative degree of importance throughout countless ages.[1]

Of course, she knew that 'Abdu'l-Bahá had predicted a dramatic decrease in contributions, and that a marked increase would follow.[2] But it was about two years since He had made His prediction. To Corinne the prognosis seemed gloomy.

Earlier in the year exhaustion forced her to take a break from her duties as financial secretary. She traveled west, visiting Los Angeles, San Francisco, Portland, Seattle and other West Coast communities. It wasn't what the trip was intended to be — a vacation. It turned out to be a teaching trip instead and an opportunity to share the Fund's condition with the friends. She returned to Chicago as exhausted as when she had gone. A few months later, Arna, noticing her mother's condition, wrote to the Master asking if He would permit Corinne to visit Him. Arna felt that only the Master could regenerate her mother.

The Master's response was surprising:

> . . . it would be much better if for the present she could travel in the United States to places wherein the air is pure, and the weather temperate. In this way she will have simultaneously a change of weather and opportunities to guide the people. When she hath found strength enough to journey to the East I will specially send for her.[3]

Obviously Corinne was disappointed. But she would heed His suggestion, undoubtedly pregnant with a wisdom she was unable to fathom at the time. Perhaps the Master felt that Corinne was too embroiled in the daily demands of the Faith, that balance was required; she needed to unwind, a change of pace. Perhaps, knowing her attachment to Him and that the impending World War would interrupt His communications for a long time, He wished to turn her attention to a wider field at home. He knew her nature and her devotion to the Covenant. Going on vacation must have been a test for her, especially after reading His moving appeal of the previous spring, which appeared in *Star of The West*, a journal she read from cover to cover:[4]

> Friends! The time is coming when I shall be no longer with you. I have done all that could be done. I have served the Cause of Baha'u'llah to the utmost of my ability. I have laboured night and day, all the years of my life. O how I long to see the loved ones taking upon themselves the responsibilities of the Cause! Now is the time to proclaim the Kingdom of Baha! Now is the hour of love and union! This is the day of the spiritual harmony of the loved ones of God! All the resources of my physical strength I have exhausted, and the spirit of my life is the welcome tidings of the unity of the people of Baha. I am straining my ears toward the East and toward the West, toward the North and toward the South that haply I may hear the songs of love and fellowship chanted in the meetings of the faithful. My days are numbered, and, but for this, there is no joy left unto me. O how I yearn to see the friends united even as a string of gleaming pearls, as the brilliant Pleiades, as the rays of the sun, as the gazelles of one meadow!
>
> The mystic Nightingale is warbling for them all; will they not listen? The Bird of Paradise is singing; will they not heed? The Angel of Abha is calling to them; will they not hearken? The Herald of the Covenant is pleading; will they not obey?
>
> Ah me I am waiting, waiting, to hear the joyful tidings that the believers are the very embodiment of sincerity and truthfulness, the incarnation of love and amity, the living symbols of unity and concord. Will they not gladden my heart? Will they not satisfy my yearning? Will they not manifest my wish? Will they not fulfil my heart's desire? Will they not give ear to my call?
>
> I am waiting, I am patiently waiting.

Before going west Corinne had a scare. Another personal calamity was looming: Arna and her husband had gone to Berlin, Germany, to visit his parents – and World War One had erupted. Getting out of that city seemed impossible. Corinne wouldn't leave until she knew Arna and Leo were safe. After several weeks of trying, they managed to escape to Rotterdam, where they booked passage for home. The good news was a relief. But the time spent worrying had aggravated her already poor physical condition. There would be other scares, but none would result in the kinds of tragedy that had occurred earlier in her life. Edna, Arna and Katherine would outlive their mother.

Edna and Katherine accompanied Corinne to the West, mainly to make sure she experienced a real vacation. They knew that given any chance to do Bahá'í work, she would enthusiastically tackle it. But her daughters felt she needed a period of recreation. Such an experience would refresh her spirit and make her more effective in the future. They chose to go to Hawaii for six weeks, where there were no known Bahá'ís, although two prominent believers, George Latimer and Charles Mason Remey, would be in Hawaii at the same time.

The Trues stayed at the only hotel on Waikiki Beach. Though there were many hours of gazing at the blue-green ocean and clear skies, a far cry from snow-laden Chicago, Corinne managed to teach the Faith, especially among the hotel guests. Her daughters couldn't prevent her from doing that.

One of the highlights of her Hawaiian visit was meeting the Island Queen. The audience was arranged through a Hawaiian friend of Mason Remey, whose father was close to the royal family. Corinne was accompanied by George Latimer and Mason Remey, who stated they were in Hawaii on behalf of a great religious movement promoting universal peace and brotherhood. After the Queen was given a Bahá'í leaflet, which she asked to be autographed,

TWO KINDS OF WAR

Corinne promised to send her a photograph of 'Abdu'l-Bahá, and did this later.[5]

The purpose of the stay in Hawaii was accomplished. Certainly Edna and Katherine were satisfied with the results. The sun and rest had made their mother more relaxed. The Master's wisdom in directing Corinne to go to places in the United States where 'the air is pure and the weather temperate' became apparent to Corinne. Had she been able to go to the Holy Land as she wished, her already high intensity concerning the Faith would have been greatly, maybe dangerously, reinforced. But by 1915 war was raging in Europe, and communication with 'Abdu'l-Bahá was cut off. No Tablets were reaching the United States.

A rejuvenated Corinne True arrived in San Francisco fit and thrilled at attending not only the National Bahai Temple Unity Convention but the first International Bahai Congress which was held as part of the Panama-Pacific International Exposition, 19–25 April 1915. A year preceding this major event in the proclamation of the Faith in America, 'Abdu'l-Bahá had encouraged the San Francisco Bahá'ís who had arisen to organize 'a Congress for universal peace', and in another Tablet at that time had called on the believers to 'think about going' to the Exposition, describing their central purpose in these words:

> Everyone goes to the Exposition either for amusement or recreation, or in hope of obtaining commercial benefits. But you, who are the believers of God, enter the Exposition with the desire to summon the people to the divine Kingdom . . .[6]

Undoubtedly, the Congress would be a unique opportunity to legitimize the Faith in America, to acquaint some of the leaders of thought with Bahá'u'lláh's teachings, to make influential friends for the Faith. The Congress was considered so important by 'Abdu'l-Bahá that He instructed

American Bahá'ís to hold it even if the Exposition organizers refused to allow religious societies to participate. Rent a nearby hall, He advised. The Master also advised that a cross section of eloquent speakers be chosen to address the Congress.[7]

Not only were the Bahá'ís allowed to hold their Congress at the Exposition, but its Directorate, in an official reception given to the International Bahai Congress, presented a bronze medallion as a symbol of appreciation and recognition of their 'universal efforts', 'whose sole purpose and aim . . . is the unification and solidarity of the people of the world . . .'[8]

San Francisco was in a festive mood at that time. There were parades, bands playing in parks, and cheer and joy in the streets. San Franciscans were celebrating the ninth anniversary of the recovery from the earthquake and fire that had practically demolished their city in 1906.

Within the Bahai Congress, meanwhile, a divine blaze enkindled every heart in the hall, and a sense of belonging to a providential movement whose charge was the spiritual conquest of the planet prevailed. The memory of the Master in America was imprinted in their consciousness, images and feelings they would cherish forever. He had come, late in age and ailing, to plough the hard but fertile soil of America and plant spiritual seeds. It was done, and people like Corinne True saw growth in the Master's American garden; but more nourishment was needed and only He could give it. She knew He knew that, and that's why she was sure He would return.

Everyone at the Congress was aware of what was missing: a message from 'Abdu'l-Bahá. At every other convention He had cabled a message to the delegates, but now communications with Haifa were closed. It was a time when the delegates and some other Bahá'ís across the country might have wondered privately if they would ever hear from the Master again. But in San Francisco the believers were together, more than one hundred of them, each drawing strength from the other.

It was the Riḍván Feast, held in Mrs Helen Goodall's spacious Oakland home across the Bay, which set the tone of the Congress. Her opening remarks, a word-picture of the Master's visit to her home, seemed to draw Him into the Congress before every delegate's eye. In her description, she mentioned how 'Abdu'l-Bahá walked through her home, smiling and repeating, 'This is *my* house, this is *my* house!' Mrs Ella Cooper, her daughter, read words 'Abdu'l-Bahá had spoken there in 1912. A number of speakers followed: Roy Wilhelm as toastmaster, Hooper Harris, Albert Windust, William Hoar, Joseph Hannen and Mary Hanford Ford. Corinne was also 'called for and made a brief but impressive talk', and Dr D'Evelyn concluded with an account of the Master's arrival in San Francisco.

What stirred the delegates most was not the oratory. It was a cablegram from Persia, revealing the martyrdom of a noted Bahá'í teacher and the danger to the believers there. It also appealed to the delegates to seek help from their government to protect the four American Bahá'í women working in Tehran.[9] The realization that members of their Faith were being murdered for their beliefs drew the delegates closer together, breaking down for the moment whatever barriers existed between them.

Yes, there were barriers, and Mrs Ford, a noted art historian and writer, and like Corinne independent and strong-minded, drew attention to one of them in the article she wrote about the Riḍván Feast for *Star of the West*. With the other believers, she had been inspired and illumined, but she also felt compelled to train a journalist's light on the problem, a deed Corinne probably hailed. '. . . the addresses of women were not a feature of this congress,' she wrote, 'and in fact one would hardly have surmised from scanning the program of the Congress how warmly the equality of women is advocated by Bahá'ís everywhere. Perhaps the marked absence of women from the list of speakers will ensure their presence in the congresses of the future, for certainly the work of women in the Bahá'í Cause is of supreme importance.'[10]

The fact that more than two-thirds of the Congress participants were women, many of them dedicated and effective Bahá'í teachers, gave credence to Mrs Ford's observation.

As for the Bahai Temple Unity's Convention in San Francisco, history was made there. The Executive Board was charged by the delegates to 'select teachers, and . . . circulate this Message throughout the world . . .'[11] A special fund was to be set up to finance the effort. The action has particular interest, since the Master's first five Divine Plan Tablets did not reach the believers until 1916, and also because the Bahai Temple Unity's duties had been officially expanded. It was evolving into what would eventually be known as the National Spiritual Assembly.

The establishment of another fund, many Bahá'ís feared, would cut into the contributions to the Temple project. The optimists, however, felt that a successful teaching program would produce more contributors to both funds. Corinne wanted to believe the optimists. But several months later in Chicago, she noticed that the rate of giving in 1915 was even lower than the previous year, which had been poor. Only the Master's promise in 1912 that an increase in contributions would follow a period of decreased giving gave Corinne hope for the future.[12]

Being unable to hear from 'Abdu'l-Bahá was a test – though Corinne had received a letter from one of His secretaries, assuring her of His 'good health' and that He had returned to Haifa after spending several months in a Druse village. Also reassuring was mention of His prayers 'for the spiritual success and prosperity of the believers and hopes they will embody in their lives the ideal principles of Truth.'[13] 'Abdu'l-Bahá hadn't received a letter from America in ten months.

To an observer it might have seemed that the fledgling

Faith of Bahá'u'lláh was leaderless. But in the United States and Canada institutions of authority were developing. How would the American Bahá'í Community have fared without the Bahai Temple Unity, especially when access to 'Abdu'l-Bahá had been cut off? The friends seemed to rally around the institution during the uncertain days of 1915 and early 1916. Teaching activity increased. An Executive Board appeal – via mail – to all American Bahá'ís generated greater giving to the Temple Fund. When the Board announced a plan of raising $200,000 by 12 November 1917, the hundredth anniversary of Bahá'u'lláh's birth, donations increased even more, as the Master had predicted. The American Bahá'í Community was maturing. Its dependence on 'Abdu'l-Bahá wasn't as all-consuming as it had been prior to the war.

Somehow five Tablets from the Master reached the Executive Board in 1916. They were on teaching. Nine more were to follow. The fourteen Tablets were a plan on how to spread Bahá'u'lláh's Message throughout the world. The North American Bahá'ís were responsible for taking the Faith to 120 territories and islands. To Corinne and other Bahá'ís the Tablets of the Divine Plan were the kind of guidance that was desperately needed. They provided the direction the Board's teaching plan lacked. The teachers called for would know where to concentrate their efforts. Certainly the Master knew where in the world they would be most effective. His trip to America had been a scouting mission as well as a consolidation, proclamation and teaching effort. During His eight-month stay, He had been able to sense the American believers' teaching potential. Based on His findings, His intuition, and undoubtedly His celestial assistance, He drew up a systematic plan. It was more than a list of places. It provided the believers with insights on how to teach and what an effective teacher can achieve. Corinne viewed the Divine Plan as God's blueprint for the establishment of His Kingdom on earth. Nothing else was needed, for whatever teaching plans would evolve in the future would be influenced by the Tablets of the Divine Plan. That's what she believed.

Corinne's enthusiasm for the Plan was tempered to a degree, when she finally heard directly from 'Abdu'l-Bahá. It had been two years since she had received a Tablet from Him. What had sustained her was the Creative Word and the Master's previous Tablets. They were reread and pondered many times. And the memories of her pilgrimage and meetings with the Master in America were also sources of comfort. His latest message, like so many of the others, was a reminder of her responsibility to the Temple project:

> O thou my daughter of the Kingdom:
> Praise be to God, that thou art assisted and confirmed in the service of the Mashrak-el-Azkar and art spending thy effort in the erection of this edifice. The construction of this great building is the first divine foundation of the people of Unity in America and it will be like unto [a] Mother unto the temples of God. All the temples which will be built in the future are born from this great Temple.[14]

In 1916 Corinne True was 55. There was no doubt in most people's minds that she had surrendered her life to Bahá'u'lláh. Her brother Tom knew it, as did his wife Helen and son Duerson. He was close to his sister and he knew she cared for him and his family, but it was apparent what possessed her heart. Though tolerant, Tom couldn't fathom how his sister could be so committed to a particular religion. He had left the Presbyterian Church. After a bout with agnosticism in college, he rediscovered God and believed in the immortality of the soul. But Tom never joined a church. Most of his energy was channeled into his law practice, which grew to be successful. He knew his sister wanted him to become a Bahá'í. But he never seriously studied it, which was a source of disappointment to her. Nevertheless, they tried to remain close.

TWO KINDS OF WAR

Every Thanksgiving and Christmas both families would come together.

For Corinne such affairs were journeys into a world she had left behind. The talk of high society, of exotic vacations, of profitable financial transactions, were for her remnants of a collapsing society. Though she knew that and also knew that Tom and his family wouldn't accept such an assessment – certainly not while they lived in elegant comfort – Corinne managed to fit in well, for she had grown up in the same privileged class. What really protected her from being critical or condescending was the Master's exhortation to make all whom you meet feel at ease and accepted.

On 6 April 1917 the United States was at war, siding with the Allies. It was a colossal conflict, spanning two continents. Among the American Bahá'ís there was talk of Armageddon, that the cataclysm Bahá'u'lláh referred to was at hand. It isn't certain whether Corinne felt that way, but in a letter to a friend she expressed her views on the war: 'It is all so dreadful to contemplate on one hand but so glorious on the other hand because it marks the Rise of the Sun of Truth. Universal Peace will come out of all of this destruction although the birth pains are most severe.'[15]

The United States War Department was drafting young men into the army. Davis would have been eligible. So would Laurence. But knowing them, Corinne felt, they would have volunteered. Corinne considered herself a soldier – a soldier in Bahá'u'lláh's army. Certainly the aims were different from those of the armies locked in battle in Europe and the Near East, as 'Abdu'l-Bahá had explained, shortly after watching a regiment of soldiers march by His window while visiting Stuttgart, Germany, in 1913:

> They are ready to fight for their fatherland. How barbarous it seems to send men who do not even know each other to the battlefield in order to shoot each other down. The Bahai Grand Army consists of the invisible

angels of the Supreme Concourse. Our swords are the words of love and life. Our armaments are the invisible armaments of Heaven. We are fighting against the forces of darkness. O my soldiers, my beloved soldiers! Forward! Forward! Have no fear of defeat; do not have failing hearts. Our supreme commander is Baha'o'llah. From the heights of glory he is directing this dramatic engagement. He commands us! Rush forward! Rush forward! Show the strength of your arms. Ye shall scatter the forces of ignorance. Your war confers life; their war brings death. Your war is the cause of the illumination of all mankind. Your war means victory upon victory. Their war is defeat upon defeat. Their war is the origin of destruction. There are no dangers before you. Push forward! Fire! Fire! Attack the enemy. Your efforts should be crowned with the diadem of eternal peace and brotherhood.

'His holiness the Christ was fighting even upon the cross and his triumphs have continued through ages and cycles.'[16]

In Chicago, the Bahá'í army's campaign wasn't going well. Ever since 1910 or 1911, undercurrents of disunity had been festering which erupted in 1917–18. The Master had noted the situation during His visits to Chicago in 1912 and had privately warned both Corinne True and Dr Bagdadi to be alert to signs of disobedience to the Covenant of Bahá'u'lláh, of which He was the appointed Center. The episode became known as the 'Chicago Reading Room Affair', named after the Reading Room which Luella Kirchner opened in 1913, with the approval of 'Abdu'l-Bahá. The study classes and teaching events held there attracted about a hundred Chicagoans and at first contributed to renewing the vitality of the community, once the hub of Bahá'í activity in America. While the Bahá'í communities of the East Coast – Boston, Montreal, New York and Washington – were progressing, the Chicago community was feeling the crippling influence of disunity, the very condition the Master detested most. The extent of the disaffection emanating from the Reading

Room became apparent when its members proclaimed it the Chicago Bahai Assembly, 'as distinct from the House of Spirituality or Spiritual Assembly, established by the command of Abdul Baha'. In addition, loyal and knowledgeable Bahá'ís became aware that 'ideas . . . very foreign to the teachings of Abdul Baha'[17] were being taught in the Reading Room.

The fact that the Master wasn't reachable for much of that time, due to the interruption of communications during the War, didn't help. Corinne was certain He would have put an end to it. Dealing with the problem created an agony that, in some respects, was more painful than losing a child. Trying to resolve the problem was difficult. There was just so much time Corinne could devote to her national and local Bahá'í work. As it was, she did little else. Being financial secretary of the Executive Board of the Bahai Temple Unity was a full-time responsibility. Along with that duty was considerable worry. Would the funds meet the Faith's financial goals? $200,000 had to be raised by 12 November 1917. And the prospects of meeting that goal appeared dim, despite the valiant attempts by many believers to raise the money necessary to begin building the Temple. Some friends contributed their favorite jewelry. Stocks and Liberty Bonds were donated. One Bahá'í's inheritance of $14,000 was given to the Faith. Nickels, dimes and quarters were donated as well. Each contribution was acknowledged by Corinne with a loving letter. Yet there were the local problems.

In the words of one student of the Reading Room affair, which by then was spreading its negative influence to other Bahá'í communities in America: 'The local conflict came to a head in April 1917 at the Boston convention, to which both the House of Spirituality and the Reading Room sent delegates. In the summer the newly elected House of Spirituality determined to expunge the by now rebel Reading Room; and in November, during the Chicago-held Centenary celebrations [12 November 1917] of Bahá'u'lláh's birth, representatives of the national community took up the affair and appointed an investigative committee.' On 9 December the committee, whose four members were among the most outstanding Bahá'ís, 'reported in favor of the House of Spirituality to a special meeting' of forty-eight believers from nineteen communities. The committee also charged that the Reading Room members 'were violators [of the Covenant], creating disunity and spreading false teachings . . .'[18] At the 1918 Convention in Chicago, to which the Reading Room group had been denied representation, the committee's report was unanimously approved, not only by the assembled delegates but by all those attending.[19]

Unhappily for Corinne, much of the opposition of the Reading Room members had been directed at her and Zia Bagdadi, who had taken an active role in the affair. Specific charges had been made against Corinne's work as financial secretary for the Temple Fund and as member of the House of Spirituality. She had been vindicated, both by the Committee of Investigation and the Bahá'ís in their support of its findings. But for her there was nothing to gloat about. It was a battle the Faith had won. Lots of people had been hurt, some good people. And it had generated an ongoing deep ache in her heart. The long, unhappy conflict with the Reading Room group had been an ordeal for her. It had been emotionally draining. At first glance, most of her friends never noticed the agony she was experiencing. It wasn't her nature to display emotion, especially anything negative affecting her. It was especially difficult because the lack of access to the Master meant she couldn't share her feelings with Him. Albert Windust, a sensitive man and a good friend of Corinne's, sensed her torment. There were times when he would come over to the True home to comfort her. He didn't give much advice, just listened, mostly with the heart. As for Zia Bagdadi, she couldn't imagine how she could have withstood the conflict without his help. She had heeded the Master's instruction 'to trust him and work with him'.[20]

Despite her painful ensnarement in the Reading Room ordeal, Corinne was not sidetracked from her chief responsibility. For the special conference in Chicago, commemorating the hundredth anniversary of Bahá'u'lláh's birth, she was asked by the Executive Board to be the last speaker. She didn't relish the assignment for she preferred working in the background. She rarely spoke at the Bahai Temple Unity conventions; when she did, it was only for a few moments and she wouldn't volunteer to speak. She never considered herself an orator. But Corinne was especially radiant when she addressed the conference about the progress being made in erecting the Temple. She seemed happy even though she knew the American Bahá'í community had failed to achieve the goal of raising $200,000 by 12 November. On 10 November, the night of her address, the Temple Fund was short by $67,000. Nevertheless, what she said was positive, with not a hint of rebuke in her voice.

> In this day the Sun of Spiritual Truth has again arisen in the Orient, and its radiance is seen in the Occident as well. Baha'o'llah has said that the human family was once one, dwelling together in the greatest state of harmony. Then differences crept in and racial and religious bias appeared until discord and hatred were found among the children of men. The great purpose of the Bahai Movement is to restore the foundation of human solidarity. The Mashrak-el-Azkar is the outward sign of the inward spiritual Reality which brings to pass this glorious work. Those who join with sincerity in the building of this unique and wonderful edifice share the bounty of God and are under His protection.[21]

Completing the Temple in the Master's lifetime was a personal goal of Corinne's. What joy that would bring Him! Actually, it was a burning desire that she tried hard to hide, because if exposed it might frighten some of the believers. So it must have hurt deeply that it took three more years before work could start in laying the Temple's foundation.

Though her efforts as financial secretary for the Bahai Temple Unity took up most of her waking hours, she always found time to encourage and deepen relatively new or young believers. It was often done in her letters of gratitude to contributors to the Temple Fund. One stands out. It was addressed to a young woman who was part of the only Bahá'í family in Atlanta, Georgia.

> . . . I hope, Madie, God will send you many souls to give the great message to – for the world is so sorely in need of these Teachings. The qualities mankind needs are dependent upon the heat and light from the Sun of Truth to make them grow. The sooner man turns his face to that sun, which today is Abdul Baha, the quicker will these fragrances emanate from his heart and people be to one another brothers and sisters, because all are the creatures of the One Heavenly Father . . . Mankind in reality is so beautiful if the Divine Gardener trains and cultivates the garden of the heart. That is the crying need today. The jungle needs a cultivator to develop luscious flowers and fruits. How grateful we are to know that Abdul Baha is that gardener today and we can put ourselves under His care and know all that comes to us is His love for us even if our limited sight veils the wisdom – we can trust Him.[22]

12

Farewell to the Master

With the United States embroiled in a World War, its citizens were swept up by a patriotism that reached fever pitch. From coast to coast Americans were hailing the greatness of their country. Scores of hastily-composed jingoistic songs blossomed into popular tunes. The 'stars and stripes' were proudly waved. Battle-clad troops on parade drew hordes of cheering admirers. And it didn't take a national holiday to run up the flag.

There were different reasons why people were so patriotic. To some, it was an opportunity to show the world how mighty the United States really was. These people were certain that only the 'Yanks' could end the bitter impasse between the Allies and Germany. And by doing that, the United States would assume the leadership it rightly deserved. It would become the envy of other nations.

The patriotism many other Americans displayed stemmed from a feeling that their country had an opportunity to play a significant role in ending a war that would end all wars.

Within the American Bahá'í community, the believers weren't united on their views regarding their country's involvement in the War. Some felt that since Bahá'ís were supposed to be loyal to their government, they should openly support the United States war effort, while others refused to back it, citing Bahá'u'lláh's opposition to killing as their reason. Because some of the Bahá'ís were passionate about their views, conflict arose in some of the communities. (Some twenty years later, with guidance from the Guardian of the Faith on the Bahá'í attitude to service in time of war, no further conflicts would arise.)

Nevertheless, the Bahai Temple Unity's Executive Board took an official stand by assuring their government of the Bahá'í Community's absolute loyalty to the United States. Corinne didn't share her feelings publicly, but accepted the Board's position. Deep down, she deplored the idea of nations fighting. To her it was an obvious sign of how much humanity needed Bahá'u'lláh's guidance. Considering the heedlessness of the great majority of people, she felt, perhaps extensive destruction is unavoidable. Maybe only from the carnage of a terrible, costly war would the desperate survivors be susceptible to Bahá'u'lláh's healing and unifying Message. In a way, Corinne maintained a detached attitude toward the War. Whatever happens, she believed, would be the will of God.

Evidently her daughter Edna wasn't as detached, because she wanted to serve in the reconstruction effort in France. And there was a way to do that. She had been invited to join the Smith College Relief Unit, composed of fifteen of her former fellow collegians with a doctor and nurse attached. But Corinne was reluctant to let her go. She feared for her daughter's safety. Yet she knew that Edna's motive to go overseas was to serve the needy, certainly a Bahá'í thing to do. But her motherly instinct was strong, much tested over the years. She had already lost five of her children. On the other hand, Edna was an adult, 28 at the time, and she could do what she wished; but Corinne knew that Edna wouldn't go without her mother's blessing. If she gave permission and something disastrous happened to Edna, Corinne wasn't sure whether she could endure that. It was a conflict she seemed incapable of resolving, but reluctantly she gave her consent. So Edna joined the Unit, but with regret at causing her mother such anxiety.

At first, Edna's unit was stationed in the shell of a

bombed-out château close to the front, where they could hear firing constantly. They slept and ate in tents. The château's basement was still intact and was used to store supplies. Certainly a far cry from 5338 Kenmore Avenue, but Smith College took great care of them. Edna rarely thought about the comfort she was missing; there was so much to do for so many who had lost so much. Helping the needy wasn't a new experience for her. She had spent several years working with children and youth in Chicago's slums.

The Smith College Relief Unit had been assigned several villages that had been overrun by the Germans and recaptured by the Allied forces. They had to resettle the original populations, who had fled shortly before the Germans seized the villages. Edna was a truck driver, going to Paris periodically to collect supplies and deliver them to the villagers. At times she would have to load cows aboard her truck.

The resettling work was a gratifying experience. To see people returning to their roots was to watch hope being renewed in the human heart. It was essentially the elderly, the children and women who returned to their homes, most of which had suffered great damage. Most of the young men were in the army.

Later the unit was called upon to establish canteens for the American troops fighting in the Château-Thierry region. They were in close connection with a hospital for the wounded, whom they cared for and sent on to Paris hospitals or to other arrangements made for them. It was a service the US military command had ordered but could get no volunteer organization to undertake. So Edna's unit volunteered.

When the Germans waged a successful counterattack, their canteens turned into makeshift hospitals. It was there that Edna got a close look at the tortured face of war. The suffering on the front lines was etched on the faces of the wounded. When a wounded man was brought in, the first thing they did was to put a pillow under his head and light a cigarette. (They had great piles of pillows.) Though it wasn't Edna's job to be with the wounded soldiers, she found herself in their midst, moving from stretcher to stretcher, dispensing hot chocolate, listening to them, trying to comfort them. Just seeing a kind, gentle-spirited American woman made some of them smile – a real victory, considering the wretched surroundings.

On Armistice Day the roar of cannon ceased. Suddenly, all they could hear was the quiet – an unbelievable quiet – hoping and praying that the War was over, for they had no news at first. Then some of the wounded began to arrive from the front and were examined by doctors who sent some on to Paris. They were all *so* busy. Before long, however, the Smith College Unit returned to its original assignment in the villages, and was welcomed by the villagers with 'We knew you would come back'.

The work of the Smith College Unit had not ended with the Armistice in November 1918, but continued for some time. Communication between the Master and His Western Bahá'í friends was soon restored, and a few Tablets – some having been held in Haifa for a long period after He had revealed them – began to arrive in December. At the end of January 1919, Shoghi Effendi, who was then serving as His secretary, informed Dr Bagdadi in Chicago that 'Abdu'l-Bahá had 'revealed nearly one hundred Tablets for the friends in the United States . . .'[1]

As early as 23 November 1918, Corinne had written to the Master and, in His reply, He referred approvingly to Edna's service in the War, adding that she 'is permitted to present herself whenever she has the opportunity'.[2] Edna herself had addressed Him while still serving in France; His reply at the end of March not only praised her work but advised her to 'continue these services until the end in the same department', continuing, 'whenever it has been made possible for thee to undertake a trip to the Holy Land in the utmost joy and fragrance, thou art permitted to present thyself'.³ Without delay Edna wrote to her mother, in the hope that Corinne could obtain the necessary documents and meet her in Paris for a pilgrimage together.

When Corinne received the news of Edna's Tablet, every doubt regarding her European adventure vanished, and she proudly shared with those believers close to the True family some of Edna's exploits in France.

As to making another pilgrimage, Corinne had not thought of such a venture. After all, she had already been on pilgrimage in 1907, and she had so much important Bahá'í work to do. There was still the drive to amass $200,000 for the Temple. And there was the teaching effort that 'Abdu'l-Bahá had stressed in His last Tablet to her. Going to Haifa would require a month of her time. As much as she loved being with the Master, she realized that doing the work He required was more important. But there was Edna, so enthusiastic about seeing the Master. She couldn't disappoint her. Corinne had to scramble to get a new passport and book passage to Paris where she would rendezvous with her daughter.

Of course getting to Europe was one thing but getting to Haifa was another. She needed permission from the Master to make the pilgrimage. Her close friend, Dr Zia Bagdadi, cabled 'Abdu'l-Bahá on Corinne's behalf: 'TRUE WILL JOIN DAUGHTER TO VISIT YOU IF PERMISSIBLE.' Bagdadi received a quick response: 'PERMITTED ABBAS.'⁴ On 13 August she set sail from New York City, but not before taking care of Fujita's travel arrangements to Haifa. His greatest wish had been granted. He was to go to serve the Master in the Holy Land.

But before describing this most happy pilgrimage let us return briefly to America where, in early 1919, the small national community seemed to be maturing, and Corinne was more active than ever. Certainly the Bahai Temple Unity was stronger. Taking on the coordination of teaching in North America was a factor in its growth, as were its efforts to consolidate the American community. And it was gaining greater respect from the believers.

Corinne was still a member of its Executive Board and still its financial secretary. For ten years she had served in that capacity, while many changes in membership had taken place during that time. And she would continue to serve in the same position for several more years. In the meantime 'Abdu'l-Bahá kept praising her for the work done on behalf of the Mashriqu'l-Adhkár. But with every pat on the back there was an appeal to extend even more effort to complete what He called 'this Universal Edifice'. In this same Tablet, which she received shortly after the Armistice, the Master revealed to her that the time for teaching was exceptionally ripe:

> . . . the friends of God must strive with heart and soul and promulgate heavenly teachings and spread far and wide the Light of the Kingdom; for the world of humanity has acquired, as a result of this great carnage [World War I], a great capacity for the propagation of universal peace. Ears are longing to hearken to the call of the oneness of the world of humanity, to universal reconciliation, and to the abandonment of ignorant prejudices.
>
> In fine, if all the friends of God engage in the promulgation of heavenly teachings, the establishment of universal peace shall be a foregone conclusion.[5]

Reading that excited Corinne. If only there was more time in a day. If only she could generate more energy to do all the things that had to be done, especially in the teaching field. Through her the Master was urging the friends to seize the present-day teaching opportunities, because they might pass, and similar ones might never come again in their lifetime. She tried to share that Tablet with every Bahá'í she knew.

During the Bahá'í Congress held in New York in April 1919, Corinne took the opportunity of an invitation to speak to show the relationship of the Temple to teaching in its widest purpose. Here are a few of her thoughts:

> ... We have been living under the material civilization, but the day has come when the divine civilization must be established – the spiritual brotherhood of man ... We will always have wars until some great power comes into the world and inspires and fills us with one great aim and one great purpose and we sacrifice our lesser aims to this great, this enormous aim ...
>
> The great Mashrekol-Azkar stands for that sacrifice of self, that sacrifice of the personal, so that we may come into this knowledge of the oneness of humanity ...
>
> ... In a temple of the Lord, in the house of God, man must be submissive to God. He must enter into a covenant with his Lord in order that he shall obey his commands and become unified with his fellow man ... he must recognize all as one family, one race, one nativity, all the servants of one God, dwelling beneath the shelter of the mercy of one God.
>
> When we really and truly arise and fulfill the building of such a church as that ... we will not separate our brothers and sisters into these divisions; we will recognize the oneness of all humanity. And so this Mashrekol-Azkar is the universal house of worship because it is the only house of worship in the world except the one at Ishkabad, Russia, that does really carry out these teachings.[6]

Corinne wanted to increase her teaching effort, even though to those who were close to her she seemed to be teaching all the time. From the very moment she awoke in the morning, she was ready to share the Message of Bahá'u'lláh with someone. That consciousness stayed with her throughout each day. Should a salesman appear at her door, Corinne was prepared to teach him the Faith. While shopping in department stores, even during vacations, her awareness continued. Her Fruitport, Michigan, home was really a travel-teaching base of operations and an unofficial deepening center. She was conditioned to seize the slightest opportunity, for to her, teaching was a state of mind, nurtured by the Writings of Bahá'u'lláh and

'Abdu'l-Bahá. With that kind of attitude, along with a powerful intuition, Corinne was able to find true seekers, and eventually penetrate their defenses and move them into Bahá'u'lláh's embrace. Nothing gave her more joy than to witness a soul become illumined. To Corinne, teaching was synonymous with happiness. But her responsibility as a teacher didn't end with leading people into the Faith. She nurtured them, as a parent guides a child. Despite her demanding responsibilities as financial secretary of the Bahai Temple Unity, she was in contact with those Michigan believers she directly or indirectly attracted to the Cause. She wrote to them, always encouraging letters with excerpts from the Master's Tablets to her. She visited them – not only while in Fruitport, and she remembered them in her prayers.

Meeting Edna in France in October 1919 for their pilgrimage was wonderful. Her daughter, who was on furlough from her unit, seemed healthy, and she looked so smart in her blue uniform. It was a delightful reunion. Both wanted to get on to Haifa, but there was some urgent business to attend to first. Fujita was in trouble down in Naples, Italy, about 300 miles from Genoa where they were scheduled to embark for the Near East.

When they reached Naples by train, they found Fujita bewildered and frustrated. He had been there for days trying to get the Japanese consul to obtain permission for him to go to Egypt, the last leg of his journey to Haifa. Every day the consul would cable for permission through the Japanese consul in Cairo. But there was no positive response. Neither the Japanese consul nor Fujita could determine what was wrong. Corinne and Edna assured Fujita that when they reached Cairo they would sort out his problem. And they did. In fact he arrived in the Egyptian capital two days after they did. A long time after, Fujita shared his greatest regret with Edna True and Thelma Jackson: 'I wanted to serve 'Abdu'l-Bahá all my life,' he said sadly, 'but He died.' Fujita reached Haifa in 1919 and the Master passed away two years later.

In getting to Cairo Corinne and Edna had to travel to the other coast of Italy – to Brindisi. There they met someone whom they had heard a lot about – all good things – but had never met. While eating breakfast in the hotel's dining-room, Corinne noticed a distinguished-looking man, sitting alone at a table nearby. She turned to Edna and said, 'I think I know who that man is.'

'Who do you think he is?' Edna asked.

'I believe it is Dr Esslemont.'

'The Scot who is writing a book about the Faith?'

'Yes.'

The stranger glanced their way, as if he sensed he knew them. But there was no communication between them in the dining-room. Soon after returning to their room there was a knock on the door. It was the same man.

'Could you by chance be Mrs True?' he asked.

'Could you possibly be Dr Esslemont?' Corinne responded.

The Trues spent two delightful days with John Esslemont. They were sunny days, rather balmy. Edna found the long walks with him along the Appian Way both delightful and illuminating, as they discussed the Faith and the state of the world. She not only got to know more about the charming physician, but his knowledge of Roman history was extraordinary. He made the area around this ancient city come alive. They sailed in separate ships from Brindisi on 23 October, the Trues in the morning and Esslemont that afternoon. But they would shortly meet again in Haifa where he was to consult with 'Abdu'l-Bahá concerning the book he was writing about the Faith.

Traveling for Corinne was still a test, and as a Bahá'í she seemed to be doing more of it every year. Fortunately Edna was along, who loved to travel. Some of her daughter's enthusiasm shored her up. There was one good thing about this trip to the Holy Land: the entry to Haifa wouldn't be as hair-raising as in 1907, when she was lowered into a small boat on the high seas and rowed to shore through choppy waters.

In 1919 there was a railroad linking Egypt with Haifa. After several days in Cairo, Corinne and Edna took a train from Kantara on the Suez Canal, across the northern tier of the Sinai and then up the coast of Palestine to Haifa. 'It was the most difficult part of the journey,' Corinne wrote at the end of her pilgrimage, 'no comforts whatever on the train, only a bunk to wrap oneself in a steamer rug and stretch out for the night. It was quite thrilling to find oneself riding through that territory which Moses led the children of Israel through in his journey from Egypt to the Promised Land.'[7] It was good that they befriended some British soldiers who were on their way to Palestine. The Englishmen made sure that their compartment was next to the Trues, for the train had a notorious reputation: many people, especially the elderly and women, were preyed upon by thieves. From time to time a soldier would check in with the two American women.

To Corinne, Haifa hadn't changed. In fact, it probably looked much the same as it did in Jesus' time. Mt Carmel was still rocky and barren. The only paved roads were the narrow, twisting, cobblestone ways she had traveled before. Haifa was a sleepy little village. Occasionally, an Arab in the traditional white headdress would come down the main thoroughfare leading a camel or riding a donkey. Some veiled women carried pails of water or bundles on their heads. Curious children stared at the two American women. It was hot and dry and what was supposed to be grass was parched by the torrid Near Eastern sun. It was understandable why shade was considered precious, probably as precious as a glass of cool water.

For Corinne there was much that was familiar, but twelve years after her first pilgrimage there was also much that was different. The Master was no longer a prisoner.

21. 'Abdu'l-Bahá with pilgrims and other Bahá'ís on Mt Carmel beside the Tomb of the Báb, Sunday afternoon, 9 November 1919. Edna and Corinne are standing in the first row (3rd and 4th from left) and Dr Esslemont, also in this row, stands on 'Abdu'l-Bahá's left (2nd person beyond).

22. Dr John E. Esslemont (1874–1925), elevated to the rank of Hand of the Cause of God by the Guardian soon after his death, and subsequently described by him (27 March 1957) as 'one of three luminaries shedding brilliant lustre annals' of Bahá'í communities in the British Isles. (This photograph was taken not later than early 1920.)

23. Edna Miriam True, as she appeared on the passport she used for her 1919 pilgrimage with her mother

24. Five American pilgrims who had met Corinne and Edna in Paris on their outward journeys to Haifa and again in Cairo the day after the Trues were last with 'Abdu'l-Bahá. Shoghi Effendi (2nd from right) had guided Corinne and Edna to the Holy Places in Akka and Haifa, and this photograph captures his happiness which so delighted them. The party is on their way to Akka from Haifa toward the end of November 1919. The five pilgrims were W.H. Randall (4th from right behind Fujita), Mrs Randall (in carriage but not visible), Margaret Randall (taking the photograph; she is now Counsellor Bahiyyih Winckler), George Latimer (1st on right) and Albert Vail (2nd from left). Others include Dr Luṭfu'lláh Hakím, later a member of the first Universal House of Justice (3rd from right) and Saichiro Fujita (to his right).

FAREWELL TO THE MASTER

He was now living in a stone house at the foot of Mt Carmel. There was even a garage to house the large automobile sent to 'Abdu'l-Bahá by Helen Goodall, Corinne's close friend. The vehicle was so wide it could only go down a one-way street. And in 1919 Haifa didn't have such special roads. It was even too big to get through Akka's city gate.

Many of the children whom Arna had looked after in 1907 were grown, including Shoghi Effendi, the one who so loved 'Abdu'l-Bahá and had written that lovely letter to Arna in French when he was 10. As a young man of 22 he seemed to have an excellent grasp of English. Many of the Tablets that Corinne and other Bahá'ís had received in the past year had been translated by the Master's eldest grandson. Several months prior to her second pilgrimage, Corinne had received a letter in English from Shoghi Effendi. It mentioned nothing of his personal achievements or plans. But it did reveal an unusual tenderness and kindness and awareness of his Grandfather's complete sacrifice to the welfare of the Cause.[8]

Corinne and Edna were honored to have Shoghi Effendi guide them to the Holy Places in Haifa, Akka and Bahjí. He was, Edna has said, a 'wonderful person who impressed everyone'[9] – direct, yet kindly, and with an inner strength. He seemed so happy, so pleased with life, and laughter came easily. There was a smile in his eyes even when he talked. Corinne loved to hear him laugh, for it was like the breeze that cools the blistering desert. His love of life didn't detract from his respect for the Holy Places he had been directed to guide Corinne and Edna through; his reverence for the Faith was deep and natural. One reason why he was probably so happy was because he was able to serve the Master, something he had always longed to do, especially as a translator of His Tablets. And he was leaving shortly for Britain to enter Oxford University where, among other things, he hoped to perfect his English and become a more effective translator.

Sitting around the dinner table with the Master at its head – and in the Holy Land – was an occasion that stirred special feelings within Corinne. In a way, it was like participating in the Last Supper. She felt this even though she knew that 'Abdu'l-Bahá was not a Prophet of God. And yet she experienced no restraint in sharing her thoughts with the Master. There was something about His manner that put everyone with Him at ease. Those in His presence always felt that He genuinely cared for them, that He really wanted to help them. It was as if others were doing Him a favor by allowing Him to serve them. His expression of humility was perceived more by the heart than the eye. It was generated by a depth of love and fear of God that others around Him hadn't reached.

'Abdu'l-Bahá talked with Corinne about the Temple project. He didn't seem anxious about its slow progress. In fact, He assured her that the Temple would be built and would be the great teacher it was destined to be. Of course Corinne desperately wanted it to be built in the Master's lifetime.

He was especially pleased with the development of the Bahai Temple Unity as an administrative body, and praised Corinne for her part in this. Evidently in Chicago she was too close to the workings of the Faith to appreciate the amount of growth that had taken place since her first pilgrimage. As a member of the Executive Board for so long she was enmeshed in the daily activities, noticing more of the growing pains than the progress made. The Master gave her the kind of perspective that relieved some of the pressure under which she habitually worked.

'Abdu'l-Bahá also seemed pleased with Edna's involvement in rehabilitating the French villages and implied that she was doing Bahá'í work by serving others, especially those in distress.

At one time He engaged Corinne and Edna in a discussion concerning the aftermath of the war. He praised America's President, Woodrow Wilson, as a man of vision, someone 'who was ahead of his day'. But He predicted that the League of Nations, which the President helped to create, would collapse as a peace-keeping agency. There were two reasons, he added: not all of the world's nations belonged to the league, and it lacked the ability to enforce its decisions.[10]

On the last day of their pilgrimage, as they were on the point of leaving, with Corinne already in the carriage, Shoghi Effendi came hastening across the road to tell Edna that the Master wanted to see her. In a few minutes she was in His reception room where He was seated in a chair. He motioned to Edna to sit next to Him, on the divan, and Shoghi Effendi sat down on her other side. 'Abdu'l-Bahá looked into her eyes; she began to sob uncontrollably. Lovingly, He patted her arm and said, 'You are My daughter.' When Edna rejoined her mother, Corinne knew that something profoundly good had happened to her, that she would never be the same again. Corinne knew this because she had had a similar experience twelve years before.

Leaving was difficult for Corinne, because everywhere graced by the Master was a blessed spot. Any anxieties she may have had when she arrived now seemed petty. After the first few days in Haifa her frustrations had disappeared. The tension stemming from trying to help the Faith progress in a society that seemed a spiritual desert had vanished. Whatever negative feelings she had harbored toward certain Bahá'ís were drawn from her. Her spirit was refreshed and gladdened by the spirit surrounding her at the World Center. It was an elixir. How could she not be aware? Part of her wanted to stay there forever.

But as much as she wanted to stay with 'Abdu'l-Bahá, there was something within her pulling her back to Chicago. Unlike 1907 when she was overcome with that same desire, Corinne realized that the pilgrimage was an experience of spiritual regeneration; that to be truly faithful was to work in the world as a Bahá'í. She needed to share that special spirit with the friends in Western Michigan, in Chicago and wherever she might travel in America.

It wasn't easy to say goodbye, with Fujita staying and ecstatic to be so close to the Master, and John Esslemont remaining in Haifa for a while, with much to do on his book, and not feeling well. But when he had approached the Master and asked why he should be sick when he was there to write, 'Abdu'l-Bahá had replied: 'I would have you know the perfections of suffering.'[11]

It would be the last time Corinne would see the Master. She and Edna returned home with a message from Him to the American community; but it had nothing to do with the Temple project. It was an appeal to the friends to grow more united and firmer in the Covenant.[12]

13

The First Mashriqu'l-Adhkár in America

When Corinne returned home, she had to find time to share her latest experience with the Master with the friends who could never hear enough about someone's pilgrimage. In some respects that was a strain, because she needed time to take care of the Bahai Temple Unity work she had neglected while away. But nothing gave her more pleasure than sharing her pilgrimage experiences with the believers. It not only inspired them, but it reinforced those wonderful feelings of freedom she experienced while in the Holy Land. And because of that she was better able to keep in focus the new perspective she had gained by being with 'Abdu'l-Bahá.

The atmosphere in the Chicago community was far from perfect. The effects of the Reading Room ordeal were still evident. It was much like the immediate aftermath of a tornado strike. Rebuilding was needed – the rebuilding of community unity.

Interestingly, there was a Tablet from 'Abdu'l-Bahá waiting for her when she arrived at 5338 Kenmore Avenue. It had probably been *en route* while she was on her way to the Holy Land. Corinne had always looked forward eagerly to receiving new messages from the Master. Even though she had just returned from a visit with Him, she approached the Tablet as if it were the first one she had received. This time the emphasis was not on the Temple project or teaching. It dealt with firmness in the Covenant and the means for thwarting attempts to disrupt Bahá'í community unity.

Our hope is that no trace of opposition may remain; but some of the friends in America are restless in their fresh ambitions and strive and seek under the ground and in the air to discover anything that breedeth dissension.

Praise be to God, all such doors are closed in the Cause of Bahá'u'lláh for a special authoritative Centre hath been appointed – a Centre that solveth all difficulties and wardeth off all differences. The Universal House of Justice, likewise, wardeth off all differences and whatever it prescribeth must be accepted and he who transgresseth is rejected. But this Universal House of Justice which is the Legislature hath not yet been instituted.[1]

Progress on the Temple's development was made at the 1920 Bahá'í Temple Unity convention. The delegates finally decided on the design of the House of Worship. A number of eminent architects, Bahá'í and non-Bahá'í, had submitted models. Charles Mason Remey had submitted three and, though none of his was chosen, he approved the Convention's selection of the plan of Louis Bourgeois, a French Canadian believer.[2] It would cost $1,500,000 to build his design.

Mr Bourgeois was sent to Haifa to share his blueprints with the Master. In a letter to the Executive Board, 'Abdu'l-Bahá approved of the basic concept, but recommended that the Temple plan be scaled down, and that no more than $1,000,000 be spent to build it.

With an approved design and, available in the bank, the $200,000 needed for the foundation, building could commence. That delighted Corinne; perhaps the rest of the construction would move ahead swiftly, since in almost every other building effort that's usually the case. That thought was probably prompted by her wish to complete the Temple in 'Abdu'l-Bahá's lifetime.

Since 1903 Corinne had spearheaded the creation of the Mashriqu'l-Adhkár, with continual guidance and encouragement from the Center of the Covenant. To her it was more than another Bahá'í responsibility. It was a divine

THE FIRST MASHRIQU'L-ADHKÁR IN AMERICA   149

mission; for seventeen years she had thought about and worried over the Temple's development, as a mother would over her child.

But about eight months after the 1920 Convention, Corinne received a Tablet from 'Abdu'l-Bahá, in response to her question about the Temple, which was a sign that the Master's consolidation of the North American community was taking effect. America was, indeed, making progress. To Corinne, however, the Tablet was a surprise:

> ... In every respect all the affairs relative to the Mashreq'ul-Azkar are to be referred to the annual Convention. Whatever the Convention, with a majority of opinions, decides, must be accepted and executed.[3]

For so long Corinne had been the link between the Master and the American community in most Temple matters. The friends, even those who resented her seemingly special relationship with 'Abdu'l-Bahá, had grown accustomed to the process. In essence, what the Master had now stated was that the American community was mature enough to administer even its most complicated affairs.

But the new arrangement wasn't easy for Corinne to grasp. When a number of new Temple problems arose, she wrote again to 'Abdu'l-Bahá for advice. He responded by sending a cablegram addressed 'BAGDADI MRS. TRUE KENMORE CHICAGO' and stating: 'ALL AFFAIRS CONCERNING UNIVERSAL TEMPLE REFERRED GENERAL CONVENTION. I CANNOT INTERFERE. SUBMIT EVERYTHING CONVENTION.'[4]

Corinne accepted the message as a command. Difficult as it was, she and the rest of the American community grappled with the remaining problems that the Temple project presented, and managed to solve them. The Master, like a wise father, knew when the child was ready to live on his own.

Personally, the change, at least for a short while, was painful for Corinne. She had grown accustomed to going to 'Abdu'l-Bahá for advice. But it was more than that she received. It was His encouragement, His understanding of aspects of her personality that she wasn't in tune with that helped her to grow. Of course, she was free to write Him about matters other than the Temple, but she knew how busy He was and she didn't want to burden Him with personal concerns. She never received another Tablet. But although the cablegram of February 1921 was her last message from the Master, He had sent in her care just two months earlier a Tablet so significant in its promise as to rejoice and inspire her for the rest of her days:

> . . . Although in the future thousands of Mashriqu'l-Adhkárs will be erected, this Mashriqu'l-Adhkár, because it is the first to be built in America, is very important, and its impact and effect shall be boundless.[5]

14

'In the Center Stands This Youth'

About nine months after 'Abdu'l-Bahá's cablegram to Corinne, word reached America of the Master's passing. It was shocking news, for many believers never dared to think of such an eventuality. To them, He was the Faith. What would happen now? Some wondered and discussed it openly. After all, the Universal House of Justice had not been established.

Corinne, like others, felt the pain of the Master's absence from this earthly plane. But she wasn't crushed. Nearly nineteen years before He had foreseen it, advising her to 'Fear not if this Branch be severed from this material world . . .'[1] Her many Tablets and messages from Him were a continual source of inspiration and, in turn, she became a means of comfort to others. This was certainly evident during that tragic time.

Bahá'ís streamed to her home as the sad news spread throughout the Chicago area. They were drawn there because many sensed a strength in Corinne that they needed to tap; others came to 5338 Kenmore Avenue because the Master had stayed there during His Chicago visit; and there was also the hope that a member of the Bahai Temple Unity's Executive Board might have some idea of what form the world Bahá'í leadership would take.

Though she had no idea at the time, she was certain that the Master had not overlooked that crucial matter. In time, she told the friends, the leadership question would be resolved.

For more than twenty-four hours Bahá'ís packed

Corinne's home, praying continuously. Dr Zia Bagdadi needed special attention, for he was close to collapsing.

When a cablegram from the Greatest Holy Leaf informed the American friends of the Master's appointment of Shoghi Effendi as Guardian of the Cause and Head of the House of Justice, the announcement came as a surprise which affected them in various ways. For most, their sorrow was relieved by the assurance that the future of the Cause was provided for. In the words of 'two pillars of the Faith in America': '. . . how our hearts sang with joy at the news that the Master had not left us comfortless but had made you . . . the centre of the unity of His Cause.' And another expressed the feelings of the great majority: 'Whatever the Guardian of the Cause wishes or advises these servants to do, that is likewise our desire and intention.'[2] But there were others whose doubts were fueled by the youthfulness of the Master's grandson. At 24, he lacked the experience, they felt, to assume the responsibilities 'Abdu'l-Bahá had shouldered, or make the important decisions that might affect the Bahá'í world community for generations. No doubt the Covenant-breaking in Chicago and other centers, which had caused the Master so much anxiety in His later years, was poisoning the minds of some. There was even a story being circulated that 'Abdu'l-Bahá's Will and Testament was a forgery. Ruth White, who had met the Master several times, was among the most vociferous expounders of this outrageous claim.

Though the majority of Bahá'ís remained firm, some left the Faith. All of this was so unnecessary, Corinne felt. Had they been in Haifa and met Shoghi Effendi, and watched him in action, she believed, they would gladly have sacrificed their lives for him. Corinne worked hard at helping the friends cut through rumor and misinformation, anxiety and ignorance, to gain an accurate insight of the Guardianship. She saved many Bahá'ís in Chicago and elsewhere from the clutches of the deluded promulgators of the forgery allegation. The whole matter angered Corinne, but what helped her maintain her emotional equilibrium and clear perspective was her understanding of the Covenant, something the Master had nurtured in her and reinforced in His Tablets. For example, in one of His last messages to her He wrote:

> . . . the ocean of the Covenant is tumultuous and wide. It casteth ashore the foam of violation and thus rest ye assured.[3]

Corinne, trained in the Covenant by the Master Himself, accepted the Guardianship and Shoghi Effendi as Guardian, not because of who he was, but because 'Abdu'l-Bahá had designated him in His Will and Testament. She was certain that His instructions were right for the Faith. To her, the wailing over His passing and the wondering and questioning about His successor wasted precious time and energy that could be used to heed what He wanted the believers to do personally and for the community at large.

Transition is a difficult time for individuals and institutions alike, mainly because of most people's natural reluctance to change. There had been unrest after the Báb's martyrdom. Even after Bahá'u'lláh's passing serious Covenant-breaking occurred. But in time, whatever signs of schism emerged were overcome. The same thing was happening shortly after the Master's death. What was important was that the Guardian had been appointed and was working as the Master did. Corinne was sure that the unrest would pass, as it had after the passing of the Báb and Bahá'u'lláh. But that didn't mean she would stand idly by, while someone in her midst was attacking the Cause. For example, when she heard that an enemy of the Faith was scheduled to address the Woman's Club of Wilmette she attended the meeting. At one point she rose from her seat and in a calm manner defended the Faith. Quickly, two women approached and escorted her from the hall.

Shoghi Effendi's first letter to the Bahá'ís of America was a beacon of hope. In some ways it reflected the sweetness and deep empathy of the Master. Even more, it assured the friends that the Master had been prepared for His passing.

'How well I remember', he wrote, 'when, more than two years ago, the beloved Master turning to a distinguished visitor of His, who was seated by Him in His garden, suddenly broke the silence and said: "My work is now done upon this plane; it is time for me to pass on to the other world."'

A sentence later the young Guardian restored the reader's faith, as well as his confidence in the future, by quoting 'Abdu'l-Bahá again:

> Were ye to know what will come to pass after me, surely would ye pray that my end be hastened.

Those with open minds and pure hearts recognized in Shoghi Effendi's letter a strength they could draw upon. It had the ring of the Master. So to them, his call for unity had positive impact:

> . . . Unity amongst the friends, selflessness in our labors in His Path, detachment from all worldly things, the greatest prudence and caution in every step we take, earnest endeavor to carry out only what is His Holy Will and Pleasure, the constant awareness of His Presence and of the example of His Life, the absolute shunning of whomsoever we feel to be an enemy of the Cause . . . these, and foremost among them is the need for unity, appear to me as our most vital duties, should we dedicate our lives for His service.[4]

Despite his youth and complete unawareness of what he would actually be doing after his Grandfather's passing, Shoghi Effendi undertook his new responsibilities as if he had been trained all his life to be the Guardian. At least this was the impression of the American Bahá'ís he had summoned to Haifa shortly after assuming his new

'IN THE CENTER STANDS THIS YOUTH' 155

position in the Faith. They were Roy Wilhelm, Mountfort Mills and Mason Remey, with Corinne arriving somewhat later. All were members of the Bahai Temple Unity's Executive Board. They weren't the only pilgrims in these early days of the Guardianship. Bahá'ís from Persia, India, Italy, Burma, Egypt, England, France and Germany came also, and several from America, including Corinne's daughter, Katherine.[5]

Any hidden reservations they may have had regarding Shoghi Effendi's ability to lead the Faith quickly vanished upon meeting him. The last time Corinne had seen him, he was preparing to leave for Oxford University, which he had approached with mixed feelings; he didn't want to leave the Master. Her impression of him as the Guardian was comparable to that of Mountfort Mills, which he shared at the Fourteenth Annual American Bahá'í Convention:

> . . . We met Shoghi Effendi, dressed entirely in black, a touching figure. Think of what he stands for today! All the complex problems of the great statesmen of the world are as child's play in comparison with the great problems of this youth, before whom are the problems of the entire world . . .
>
> We received his joyous, hearty hand grasp and our meeting was short. A bouquet was sent to our room in the form of a young tree filled with nectarines or tangerines. It was brought by Mr. Fugeta. We awoke without any sense of sadness. That feeling was entirely gone. The Master is not gone. His Spirit is present with greater intensity and power, freed from bodily limitations. We can take it into our own hearts and reflect it in greater degrees. In the center of this radiation stands this youth, Shoghi Effendi. The Spirit streams forth from this young man. He is indeed young in face, form and manner, yet his heart is the center of the world today . . .[6]

Through this first visit with the Guardian, those summoned to Haifa gained an accurate understanding of his mission.

> The great principles laid down by Baha'Ullah and Abdul-Baha now have their foundation in the external world of God's Kingdom on earth. This foundation is being laid, sure and certain, by Shoghi Effendi in Haifa today.[7]

For Corinne, her meeting with the Guardian was actually a confirmation of her feelings about him before leaving for Haifa. What had impressed her, however, was the atmosphere at the World Center.[8] She knew there would be Covenant-breaking in Akka and Haifa, more than during her previous pilgrimages, because of the transition in the Faith's leadership. But as in 1919 and 1907, there was no apparent negative impact on the way the Faith was being administered from the Holy Land. It was as if Shoghi Effendi was protected from his enemies, known and unknown, by an impregnable, invisible shelter. Not that he was oblivious of the trouble makers. But he wouldn't allow them to impede, in any way, the progress of his work. And part of his work was to sift out whatever poison the Covenant-breakers had spread throughout the body of believers. There was no doubt of who was in charge. Yet his authority wasn't flaunted. When he spoke, people around him listened, not only because of his station as Guardian, but because he made so much sense. And he was a tender teacher, enlightening old and young, from the East and West, anyone who was willing to be taught. Corinne was 60 and he was 24. And she understood, to a degree, Shoghi Effendi's power. In terms of faith, the young Guardian was her father.

She learned from members of the Holy Family how he had cast himself into the position 'Abdu'l-Bahá had created for him. So much depended on him. No wonder the light in his room often burned until 3 a.m. and that after three hours' sleep he was back at work.[9] And it wasn't only writing letters, translating Bahá'u'lláh's

Tablets and receiving the pilgrims. Over the years of his ministry, he had to stimulate and guide the worldwide expansion of the Faith, establish the Administrative Order and, when enough spiritual assemblies were functioning, launch plans in fulfillment of 'Abdu'l-Bahá's Divine Plan Tablets. It was his responsibility, too, to develop the Bahá'í world center into a place worthy of a world religion. The beautification of the Shrines and gardens in Akka and Haifa as the spiritual center of the Cause, and the development of the arc with its Archives Building as the beginning of that great administrative center envisioned by Bahá'u'lláh in the Tablet of Carmel – these too were major tasks he would fulfill in future years.

While Corinne was in Palestine, there was political unrest in that land. Arabs resented the British policy of allowing Jewish immigration in Palestine and clashes between the two religious camps had begun. There was fear among some of the visiting Bahá'ís that the Arab–Jewish feuding could spill over, endangering the local Bahá'ís, even the Guardian.

Shoghi Effendi didn't isolate himself. In fact, almost everything he did in public was a contribution to overcoming religious prejudice and hostility. His peacemaking efforts were manifested in the way he treated people and arranged for them to meet. For example, while Mountfort Mills was in Haifa he attended a tea in honor of the British Governor of Palestine. Among the guests were Muslims, Jews and Christians, some of them religious leaders. In the Guardian's presence, everyone seemed comfortable.[10] Another pilgrim, a few years later, described how Shoghi Effendi had sent aid to both Jews and Arabs in a time of difficulty. His contributions for charitable and educational purposes in the Holy Land were many and much appreciated throughout his ministry.[11]

It was apparent to Corinne that Shoghi Effendi wasn't allowing himself a certain period of time to learn the duties of his office. Actually, he couldn't do that even if he wanted to. For there had never been a Guardian before. He had to establish a mode of operations. Certainly there were Bahá'u'lláh and 'Abdu'l-Bahá to draw from in the spiritual world; but there was another source of assistance to call on in the contingent world. Bahíyyih Khánum was always close by, always willing to help. In a way, she was a mysterious link between him and the Master. Corinne sensed that he was much closer to his great-aunt than to any other member of his family. He confided in her and sought her advice. His relationship with her was unique. When he went away for a period of reflection a few months after the Master's Will and Testament was read, he appointed Bahíyyih Khánum as his representative during his absence. As long as he was gone, she was directing, in consultation with an Assembly he had named, all the affairs of the Faith.

Perhaps one of the most moving moments for Corinne during her 1922 pilgrimage was her visit to the Shrine of the Báb, which at that time was a one-story domeless structure, where, only a few months before, the Master's body had been interred. Going inside must have stirred up emotions experienced only when she recalled her relationship with 'Abdu'l-Bahá through correspondence and face-to-face meetings. For more than twenty years He had lovingly, patiently guided her through life's storms, drawing her closer and closer to the Divine threshold. Along the tortuous way He had helped her to find happiness. Inside the Shrine she discovered one of the things that brought Him joy:

> ... to our astonishment we found two large pictures of the American or 'Mother Mashreq'ul Azkar' (as named by Abdul Baha) hanging on the walls of the two rooms used by the pilgrims who visit the shrine. These are the only pictures on those sacred walls and were placed by the Center of the Covenant, himself.
>
> Members of the Master's family repeatedly told us of his love for the model of this Mashreq'ul Azkar and that they

25. The Bahá'í House of Worship, Wilmette, Illinois, 'the noblest structure reared in the first Bahá'í century' (Shoghi Effendi). It was dedicated to public worship on 2 May 1953.

26. The first gathering of Bahá'ís in Foundation Hall of the House of Worship, 9 July 1922, in commemoration of the anniversary of the martyrdom of the Báb, before the Hall was completed. Corinne True is in the first row (far right), next to Dr Zia Bagdadi. Meetings were not regularly held there until the Guardian advised Corinne during her 1927 pilgrimage that this should be done.

27. Saichiro Fujita and Wyatt Cooper in Wilmette, 1971, whose lives from their youth were intertwined with those of the True family

had heard him tell the architect, Mr. Louis Bourgeois, that its design had come to him from Baha'Ullah.

In moments of overwhelming grief that deluged our hearts while visiting the shrines of the Bab and Abdul Baha, – the one to whom we had turned for so many years for guidance in the path of God, – this sign of Abdul Baha's love for the 'Mother Mashreq'ul Azkar' as indicated by the presence of those pictures lifted our spirits and comforted our hearts. We returned to America to work for the completion of this beautiful edifice with an earnestness and self-sacrifice that we had not realized before. We long to build it now because he loved it and commanded it to be built. Its accomplishment will be a living, thrilling expression of the love and fidelity of the people of Baha for the great Center of the Covenant of Baha'Ullah.[12]

15

'Give Them Love'

When the American delegation was in Haifa meeting with the Guardian, he had told them that the first election of their National Spiritual Assembly should be held at the next annual convention. That directive was followed in March 1922 by a message to the American believers, explaining in general terms the need for such a body and how it was to function.

In 1922 the election procedure reflected the way political elections were held in the United States. Electioneering was allowed. Candidates were nominated. Why, even a straw vote was taken to trim the number of eligible candidates. And there were conservative and liberal wings within the body of Convention delegates. Though it was a far cry from how Bahá'í elections are held today, it was understandable why the American believers employed the electoral method they did. 'Abdu'l-Bahá had never stressed administrative procedure, though he had made provisions for it in His Will and Testament. That was to be one of the Guardian's tasks.

Nevertheless, the election was held and Corinne received the highest number of votes – 55. In many ways the elected body functioned as the Bahai Temple Unity's Executive Board had done in the past. That was reflected in the letterhead it used, which read: 'Bahai Temple Unity – National Spiritual Assembly.' And Corinne was to do what she had been doing for the past thirteen years, functioning as financial secretary.

It was a transitional period and Shoghi Effendi was

patient. He never rebuked the friends. He guided them gently. Two more election attempts – in 1923 and 1924 – were made. Though there was some improvement in the way they were conducted, the Guardian didn't recognize them as bona fide National Spiritual Assembly elections. That didn't mean that he wasn't concerned with what was going on at those conventions. Though in his 1923 Convention message he never mentioned election procedures, his appeal dealt with what would make for acceptable elections in the future:

> THAT THIS YEAR'S CONVENTION MAY THROUGH THE OUTPOURINGS OF HIS GRACE WELD ALL HEARTS TOGETHER, INFUSE THE SOULS WITH A FRESH AND DEEPER CONSCIOUSNESS OF THE SPIRIT OF THE CAUSE AND INAUGURATE AN UNEXAMPLED CAMPAIGN OF TEACHING IS INDEED MY ARDENT PRAYER. LET THIS BE RIDUAN'S MESSAGE: UNITE! DEEPEN! ARISE![1]

The Guardian had sent a personal emissary, Jináb-i-Fáḍil-i-Mázindarání, to speak to the friends about love, not election procedures. Evidently, Shoghi Effendi felt that successful Bahá'í elections were dependent on the degree of love the friends had for each other. During the Riḍván Feast Jináb-i-Fáḍil told stories about 'Abdu'l-Bahá. One in particular stood out:

> In Akka there lived a man who so hated 'Abdu'l-Bahá that he would turn his back when he met Him, fearing lest he lose his hatred. One day they met in such a narrow street that the enemy was forced to meet 'Abdu'l-Bahá face to face. 'Abdu'l-Bahá tapped the man upon the shoulder and said, 'Wait a few moments, until I speak. However great may be your hatred for me it can never be as strong as is my love for you.' The man was startled, awakened, and made to feel the unconquerable power of love.[2]

As far as Shoghi Effendi was concerned, the first truly elected National Spiritual Assembly took place in July 1925, and was recognized as such by him.[3] In that election the secret ballot was employed, as well as other Bahá'í elective procedures presently used.

Corinne True wasn't elected to that National Spiritual Assembly or the previous one. Nor would she ever serve on another.

Though 63 at the time – normally a reasonable retirement age – Corinne didn't even entertain the notion of 'slowing down'. She had recently made her fourth pilgrimage in February 1925, and received the Guardian's guidance for the Temple project. In her mind there was no such thing as retirement in the service of the Faith. She kept doing what she had done for the past sixteen years – the work as financial secretary for the Executive Board of Bahai Temple Unity, and teaching. In 1928 the National Spiritual Assembly changed her title to assistant to the Treasurer, since by then the various separate funds of the Cause came under the heading of the National Bahá'í Fund.

As to teaching, of course nothing could keep her from this; it was as important as breathing. She served as member of the Central States Teaching Committee and in 1928 became chairman of the Temple Program Committee and a member of the Plan for Unified Action Committee.[4] As the years passed there would be more Bahá'í projects and experiences, some coming as a great surprise.

Her daughters were distinguishing themselves. Edna was serving as the Business Manager for the *Star of the West* and was about to launch a successful travel agency. Katherine was in medical school at the University of Pittsburg and would later become a surgeon. Eventually she would be one of only two women elected to the prestigious 500-member American College of Surgeons. As for Arna, she was happily married to Leo, a successful real estate developer; their three adopted children were the joy of their lives. Patty, the oldest, was named after one of Corinne's cousins and Davis and Laurence were named after Arna's brothers.

Corinne adored her grandchildren, and they loved her. A visit with Grandma was an adventure. She had special names for the boys. She called Davis 'Dado' and Laurence

'Larry'. They enjoyed being with her, because she didn't treat them like most of the other adults did. To them she was more than their grandmother. Oh, they respected her, and they quickly sensed when they weren't behaving properly. She would become quiet, her lips tightening and her eyes growing rounder.

Corinne had a knack for becoming totally involved with the children. They knew that when they were with her, they had all of her attention and affection. In a way, they viewed her as a playmate. It wasn't uncommon for her to giggle along with them.

Patty loved to stay overnight at Grandma's house. Early in the morning Patty would jump in bed with her and they would have breakfast together. They both enjoyed munching 'toasty-cream' (milk toast). One morning Patty, who was fascinated by the silk patchwork quilt, asked about its origin. Corinne explained that she had put it together, using parts of clothes belonging to all the members of the True family, including some of Moses' ties.

Playing Grandma's player-piano was always a treat for Patty, even when she had to struggle to reach the foot pedals. Though some in the household found the music disturbing at times, it didn't faze Corinne.

Even on vacations Corinne found time to be with her grandchildren. To Patty, Fruitport was a carnival of fun. She would look forward to the afternoon teas with Grandma – always after her nap, of course – in the grape arbor. Corinne would always dress up for the occasion, wearing freshly polished white shoes. They would sit around a round table, drinking cold water or lemonade, and eating cookies or onion sandwiches. They both loved onion sandwiches. Corinne and her granddaughter would chat about the affairs of the day like two old ladies.

Patty heard expressions from her grandmother that no one she knew used. For example, when she saw someone elegantly dressed, she would say 'she's dressed up like the landlord's daughter'. Or if her hair was messy, she would say, 'I look like a scratch cat.' She never said 'good morning'; it was always 'good mornin'', the way every respectable Kentuckian would say it. To Corinne, a frying pan was a 'spider'.

It was during meals that the children experienced the adult side of their grandma. They often heard her say, 'Clean your plate, now.' Corinne was a good example, because she rarely left a crumb.

Whenever the children stayed with Grandma, there was always the bedtime scrubbing, administered by her. She not only washed their faces and hands, but their feet as well. And in the winter she always made sure that their pajamas were adequately warmed before they put them on.

In Fruitport, she would collect rainwater to wash Patty's hair, and she enjoyed curling it. It was as if she were playing beauty-shop operator. When they walked in the woods together, Corinne would point out the different kinds of flowers and trees, and provide helpful survival tips. The children were able to identify the wintergreens and sassafras leaves, which could be eaten if hunger were to seize them in the forest. And they learned what was poisonous.

After picking flowers together, she would, at times, walk to the school playground, place Patty on the teeter-totter and push the child up and down for a long time, experiencing a thrill every time Patty squealed with delight.

Not many people knew the real Corinne True, not even some who had worked with her for a long time. They attended her regular Friday afternoon teas, which were really firesides or Bahá'í study classes. They respected her knowledge of the teachings and her service to the Faith. And they would come back again and again because being with her was a maturing experience; but few recognized Corinne's caring nature.

One did, however – Vivian Wesson, a black Chicago woman. Mrs Wesson had become a Bahá'í shortly before she went to work for Corinne in 1921 as a cook at 5338

Kenmore Avenue. She was in her early twenties. No other mature white person she had encountered treated her as Corinne did. In her presence, Vivian felt wholeheartedly accepted as a human being, as a child of God, with potential talents. And because of that Vivian felt free. She could be herself, and truly share what was in her heart. And there were times when Vivian didn't have to tell Corinne what was bothering her. She already knew. From Corinne, Vivian developed confidence, an ability to express herself in public, but most important – to trust in Bahá'u'lláh.

Vivian recognized that Corinne was an undemonstrative person; but she was able to see her caring nature, not so much by what Corinne said but by what she did. Corinne was never condescending, nor did she consciously or unconsciously act in a superior manner. Her love for Vivian was genuine and Vivian knew it without question. In fact, Vivian's experience with Corinne had an everlasting effect on her. It allowed her to discover her true self, to transcend much of what racism does to people. She knew that Corinne took an interest in her because she loved her. Vivian's husband felt the same way about Corinne's feelings toward him. In fact, he revealed to his wife that he considered Corinne as his mother.

At first, Vivian was amazed that Corinne could be free of racial prejudice, considering her upbringing and some of the people she associated with. After all, racism seemed to permeate every inch of the prevailing society. But Vivian came to realize why Corinne was the way she was. It was because she was a 'real Bahá'í'. Vivian realized that Corinne was the type of person who embraced wholeheartedly whatever she believed in. If Bahá'u'lláh taught that all humans are members of the same family, then she would accept that without reservation. What Corinne had difficulty with, at times, was understanding why others had reservations, especially some Bahá'ís.

Corinne was not a crusader for social justice. But some

of those who knew her may have thought so; because during the two years Vivian lived with Corinne, and afterwards, there were experiences where racial barriers crumbled when the two of them appeared in places where no blacks had ever been before. And that included some elegant clubs. What Corinne did wasn't calculated. To her, bringing a friend along was a perfectly natural thing to do.

No blacks lived in Fruitport, and most of the villagers had never met any. What they knew about them was based on stories created and passed on by prejudiced men and women. One summer day, Vivian took little Patty for a walk to the village center. Along the way they encountered a cluster of children, who were peering at Vivian. One youngster approached and asked, 'Why are you so dirty? You should wash it off!'

It wasn't something that Vivian hadn't experienced before; fortunately it wasn't a hostile outburst – just an innocent expression by a curious child. Vivian was about to respond when Patty – 5 then – stepped forward and said, 'You see, God made people different colors and He made flowers different colors. He does this because He loves beauty.'

Corinne and Vivian stayed close through the years, as did Katherine, Arna and Edna.

In 1954, during the first year of the Ten Year Crusade, Vivian Wesson decided to pioneer to Togo, in Africa. But before she left, she had to see Corinne. In those days, Corinne's health was fragile. She was 93, and wasn't able to meet as many people as she had been accustomed to do. But when she heard that Vivian wanted to see her, she insisted on their meeting. It was like a mother–daughter reunion. Of course, Corinne was thrilled about Vivian's decision to pioneer. The advice she gave, Vivian took to heart: 'Rely on Bahá'u'lláh. Study the teachings hard. Know your subject when you speak. But don't lecture to people and tell them what they should be. Give them love. And be simple.'[5]

16

The View from Home

America was prospering in the late twenties. It had become the world's industrial giant. There seemed to be a carefree spirit in the land. No wonder the era was called 'The Roaring Twenties'. It was a time when people refused to look back at the recent past. The war that was supposed to end all wars was a convulsion that most people didn't want to recall. They wanted to revel in the present peace and prosperity, and the future looked rosy.

But Corinne and other Bahá'ís knew that the near future appeared grim, that what had occurred between 1914 and 1918 on the European and Asian battlefields would pale in comparison to what was in store for the world in a few years. There was no doubt in Corinne's mind that this would happen, because the Guardian had predicted it.[1]

Despite this awareness, Corinne continued to pursue life in her usual optimistic way. Fretting over matters she could not control was a waste of emotional energy and time, precious time. Progress was being made on the Temple. But as far as she was concerned there should have been greater progress. While in Haifa in 1927, she learned from the Guardian that the American Bahá'ís should start holding meetings in the Temple's Foundation Hall.

The Twentieth American Bahá'í Convention in 1928 was held there. It was a memorable occasion, not only because it was the first convention to be held at the Temple, but because believers could see concrete results of its development. The floors had been laid, and bathrooms installed. There was electric lighting. Foundation Hall, where the four days of the Convention's deliberations took place, was decked out with potted palms and other plants, some in flower. On the wall behind the speaker's table were hung three Persian rugs, the largest and most beautiful having been sent for the Temple with returning pilgrims by the Guardian a few months before. It had been 'used by 'Abdu'l-Bahá at prayer time in the Holy Land, and later hung in His Shrine on Mt. Carmel'. On each side of this rug were two smaller ones, also sent by Shoghi Effendi for the Temple. Above the rugs hung the Greatest Name, and on the floor in front of the speakers stood baskets of roses. The well-attended Convention of 'delegates and friends gathered from far and near, almost every section of the country being represented' was 'an epochal event . . . peerless among the many types of assemblages in the world, for the real purpose' was 'the unity of mankind'.[2]

Corinne participated in the opening ceremony. After several Tablets and prayers of Bahá'u'lláh were recited and chanted, she shared with the friends gifts given to her during her last pilgrimage by Bahíyyih Khánum. First she conveyed the Greatest Holy Leaf's love to them; then she personally poured the tea made from one of the gifts sent for everyone. Parvene Bagdadi, the daughter of Dr Zia Bagdadi, anointed each of the delegates with the attar of rose. That evening of 26 April 1928 at Foundation Hall was a flight into the world of the spirit.

It was time for Corinne to move. She had to be closer to the Mashriqu'l-Adhkár, at least in a spot where she would be able to see its dome. She turned to her son-in-law, Leo Perron, who was in real estate, to help her find land and build a house in Wilmette.

Moving from 5338 Kenmore Avenue wasn't easy, though she knew she shouldn't be attached to worldly things. But so many significant things had happened in that house, some personal and some historical. The Master had stayed there for four days. The Bahai Temple Unity had been founded there, on the last day of the 1909 Convention, and for a while had used it as headquarters. It was a place where many men and women, poor and rich, learned and unschooled, black and white, religious and non-believer, heard of Bahá'u'lláh and eventually embraced His Faith.

In early 1930, she, with Edna and Katherine, moved into 418 Forest Avenue, a sturdy stucco house only five blocks from the unfinished Temple. In the years that followed, it must have thrilled and delighted their hearts to see the unique building gradually take shape, until it stood in all its beauty amid the lovely gardens surrounding it.

In preparing to move, Corinne came upon her old sewing machine. When she opened its cabinet drawer, she found scores of receipts that she had made out to an old friend who had worked for her as a seamstress one or two days a week. Checking them carefully, she noted that Nettie Tobin, a poor woman, had given regularly to the Temple Fund, mostly nickels, dimes and quarters.

Corinne loved Nettie. And Nettie knew that Corinne was a true friend, because she accepted her as she was. Their friendship blossomed despite their different upbringing. Nettie, a former Roman Catholic and a widow, supported herself and her children on the money she made as a seamstress. She lived in a flat in one of Chicago's toughest neighborhoods, a place she viewed as a blessed spot, not a slum. Because she had never attended school, her ability to read and write was limited, and she would often misuse words when she spoke. To those who saw her reality – and Corinne was one of the few who did – she was a wise, generous, compassionate servant of God who believed in Bahá'u'lláh with all her heart and soul. Nettie had become a Bahá'í in the True home, most likely in 1903.

One of Nettie's greatest frustrations was her inability to give as much as she wanted to the Temple Fund. The money she earned each day was barely enough to feed her family and pay the rent. She prayed for the opportunity to provide some significant gift to the Temple. The answer to her prayer has often been described, but the story is still inspiring.[3]

One day, or, as some state, in a dream, she heard a voice commanding her to find a stone. It's possible that Nettie's inspiration came from her understanding of the need for a cornerstone at the Temple site, an understanding awakened by her association with Corinne.

Finding the right stone became her personal mission. One of the first places she looked was a construction site not very far from her apartment. There was a pile of stones near one of the walls being built for a new building. She approached the foreman to see if she could check the pile with the idea of taking one of the stones. He said she could have whatever she wanted since the stones were useless to him. She was thrilled, and rushed home to secure the help of Mírzá Mazlúm, an elderly Persian Bahá'í who lived nearby.

Nettie got one of her old baby carriages from her basement and they wheeled it to the pile of stones. When they had picked the one they wanted, they went to the trolley car line. Somehow she was able to persuade the conductor to allow her to lift the carriage aboard the back platform. That had to be repeated two more times, because to get to the end of the line in northern Evanston they had to transfer twice. Nettie wasn't fazed by what the other passengers thought. She was doing what she knew was right.

In Evanston she pushed the carriage toward the 'Chosen Place' for the Temple. She didn't get very far when the carriage caved in. There wasn't that much further to go, and Nettie wasn't quitting. She hailed a boy pulling a wagon. It didn't take her long to persuade the youngster to help. The three trudged on. When they reached the Temple site, they tried to get to its center, but didn't succeed because the wagon hit something, tipped over and dumped the stone onto the ground. The stone remained on the same spot for about two years, until 'Abdu'l-Bahá noticed it during the Temple dedication ceremony. He asked that it be used as the dedication stone and, with the help of some of the friends, personally placed it in the soil. Those who knew of Nettie Tobin's exploit were amazed at the Master's action, since no one had told Him how that stone got to the Temple site. Corinne had praised Nettie's effort even before the Master's visit to America, for she recognized the purity of her friend's motive. To Corinne, the gift of Nettie's stone was a Temple Fund donation that couldn't be surpassed.

17

Two More Pilgrimages

Living in Wilmette had other advantages than being close to the Temple. Arna and her family were living nearby, in a big house in Winnetka. But there was a death in the Perron family, for Leo died a month before Corinne moved into the house he had helped her build. No one really knew what caused his passing. He had always been a healthy, sturdy man, with considerable energy. About two years before Corinne moved to Wilmette, be began complaining about how tired he was. When he grew weaker, he sought medical help; but no one was able to diagnose his ailment. Not even the best specialists, and he had traveled to the best clinics and hospitals in America.

Arna was a widow with three children. Patty was 12, Davis, 7, and Laurence, 5. For Corinne, Leo's passing was a new challenge; she must try to fill the void that a departed father leaves. Her house on Forest Avenue became one of the children's favorite visiting places. In the summer they could swim in Lake Michigan which was only a block away. During the cold weather, they loved to gather around the fireplace and relax after romping in the snow. Princey, a dog that had belonged to Mr Bourgeois, the architect of the Temple, before he died, was now part of the True household and a favorite playmate of Corinne's grandchildren. Sprawled out before the fire, Princey would usually sneak up on Patty and pull gently on one of her golden curls. Scolding the dog was hopeless, because Princey only understood commands in French, which evidently Mr Bourgeois had spoken to his pet.

For Patty, especially, being close to Grandma was important, because she had a special way of overcoming the girl's fears or fits of temper. Whenever the child was agitated, Corinne would draw Patty to her and recite a prayer. At times there was need for a number of prayers. Invariably, the words of Bahá'u'lláh or the Master would calm the youngster. After a while, when troubled, Patty would search for a prayer book and ask her grandma to help her. Whenever possible Corinne tried to impress upon her grandchildren the Bahá'í standards in dealing with life. She probably felt she had to do that since Arna had adopted a rather liberal attitude toward educating the youngsters as Bahá'ís. Arna based her approach on what the Master had told her: never try to force the Faith upon your children. Corinne was aware of this, but she probably interpreted that guidance differently.

Work had begun on the superstructure of the Temple when Corinne went on pilgrimage with Mrs H. A. Harding of Urbana, Illinois, in March 1931.

For Corinne the trip aboard the *Empress of France* was a joy, mainly because she had met a delightful couple who seemed interested in the Faith. Dr and Mrs Lewis Browne were on their way to the Holy Land to tour the Zionist settlements there. He was an ardent Zionist as well as a famous writer in America, possessing a universal outlook. The Faith's teachings intrigued him. Before leaving the ship he and his wife promised to visit Corinne in Haifa. Thrilled, she said she would try to arrange for them to meet the Guardian.

Greeting Corinne and Mrs Harding at the dock were Fujita and Ruhi Afnan, the Guardian's cousin, who helped them through Customs. Outside was a large automobile in which Fujita drove the ladies to the Pilgrim House. Corinne remembered how much Fujita loved cars, especially big ones. He looked fit and happy and perfectly at home. That pleased Corinne. She had brought him a gift of socks and underwear as well as a shirt.¹

Effie Baker, the Australian Bahá'í in charge of the Pilgrim House, was so happy to see Corinne, as they had become close friends during her last pilgrimage. Now she and Mrs Harding each had single rooms facing the sea. From Corinne's window the Mediterranean looked blue and calm under a brilliant sky. So peaceful. Whatever worries she had in Chicago or aboard ship were gone. She felt so free. But in 1868 the Blessed Beauty wasn't as free, for his view was from a barred window of a prison cell in nearby Akka. That image probably passed through Corinne's mind, as it had in the past.

Corinne could never adequately explain to anyone in America how she felt in Haifa or Bahjí. To her it was the center of the spiritual world, a place of refuge where she could discern the important from the nonessential more easily. Yet, though at ease, she didn't want to relax; she wanted to see and do things.

The Guardian was in Bahjí the afternoon they arrived, directing the restoration of Bahá'u'lláh's Mansion. The Canadian artist and Bahá'í pioneer, Marion Jack, was also at Bahjí painting a picture of a special view from the Mansion, perhaps Bahá'u'lláh's favorite view. That canvas would eventually adorn one of the Mansion's walls.

After lunch Corinne and the other pilgrims, all American women, went to 'Abdu'l-Bahá's house. His sister, the Greatest Holy Leaf, was there and, though physically feeble, was as alert as ever. When she saw Corinne, she greeted her warmly and expressed her delight with the red jacket – Arna's gift sent with Corinne.² Being in the presence of Bahíyyih Khánum must have brought back memories, especially of Corinne's first pilgrimage. She had learned much from that meeting, not only from her words to Corinne, but from her bearing, her gentleness, her calm, her inner strength, and above all the unconditional love that flowed from her. Usually, Bahíyyih Khánum had stayed in the background, serving and caring for others, and always available to 'Abdu'l-Bahá and Shoghi Effendi. Certainly the Guardian knew the value of her quiet counsel. It would be the last time Corinne would see her, for she passed away the following year.

Corinne toured the gardens around the Shrine of the Báb. There were more of them – and more beautiful – than in 1927. Flowers of almost every color were in bloom. The hyacinths, especially, drew Corinne's attention. If there was a paradise on earth, it was where she was. Three rooms, she observed, had been added by the Guardian to the Shrine on the side next the mountain. When she emerged from the Shrine and was putting on her shoes, she heard one of the gardeners call her name, and he appeared with Dr and Mrs Browne following behind. What a surprise! For they had agreed to meet Corinne on Wednesday, but had come now because they had to leave Haifa earlier than originally planned. Corinne had hoped they could meet the Guardian, but he was in Bahjí.

Corinne made the best of it. She guided them through the gardens – a treat for the Brownes, for there was nothing comparable in Haifa. Dr Browne was apparently moved by the experience, because he asked to visit the Shrine. Both he and his wife took off their shoes and reverently entered. Corinne could tell that they were touched – he, a leading Zionist who had studied to be a rabbi, demonstrating such heartfelt respect for the Báb and 'Abdu'l-Bahá.

That evening the pilgrims had dinner with the Guardian, an occasion Corinne looked forward to the moment she set foot on Palestinian soil. He looked well, but was extremely busy. Too busy, she felt. But he seemed happy; that's what mattered most. And why shouldn't he be happy? Progress was being made in consolidating the Faith, the Administrative Order was taking root, and the World Center was taking shape. He was also pleased with the advances made in building the Temple; but he expressed deep regret that Mr Bourgeois wasn't alive to witness the development of his design.

Shoghi Effendi shared with his dinner guests the news that he had found in 'Abdu'l-Bahá's safety-lock box the Báb's original Tablets to the Letters of the Living and to Bahá'u'lláh. He was sending them to America to be reproduced (as they were in *The Dawn-Breakers* in 1932). He also asked about the growth of the Cause in America and if the friends were well and united. It was something the Master had always wanted to know.

More news was revealed that night. One of the rooms added to the Shrine was to be used for an international archives, and Effie Baker was to be its custodian. The Guardian joked about how many keys Effie would have to carry since she was also managing the Pilgrim House.[3]

It was apparent to Corinne that Shoghi Effendi was focused on one thing: the preservation and advancement of God's Cause. It was more than a commitment. It was all he lived for. He was like the candle, mentioned by the Master, that 'weeps its life away drop by drop in order to give forth its flame of light'.[4]

Leaving the Bahá'í World Center was always heart-wrenching. But there was work to be done in America, and knowing this made it a little easier for Corinne to go. It didn't take long to be reminded that the world outside that blessed spot in Haifa was in need of spiritual transformation. The day she arrived in Cairo, a newspaper boy sold her a copy of the local English daily paper. When he disappeared she learned that what she had bought was more than a week old.[5] She was disturbed, but had the same thing happened twenty years earlier she might have been furious. Undoubtedly daily study of the Creative Word had moderated some of her natural inclinations. So the older she became, the calmer she grew. While shedding certain personality characteristics, others developed and her already rock-like steadfastness in the Faith was reinforced. The Guardian had recognized her qualities in 1931 and on 'every visit you pay us', he wrote in his own hand soon after her return. 'Your staunch, unswerving faith, your boundless devotion, and assiduous care to preserve the integrity and extend the bounds of the Cause, are among the most richly valued assets that the Faith of Bahá'u'lláh has in that land.'[6]

One of Corinne's first tasks following her pilgrimage was to make available her pilgrim notes which included such important matters as the definition of the nine Holy Days, celebration of the Day of the Covenant on 26 November, commemoration of the Ascension of 'Abdu'l-Bahá, the function of the Geneva International Bureau, spreading the Cause among young people and in colleges and the duty of Bahá'ís in relation to war.[7] She had already sent to the National Spiritual Assembly from Haifa a number of the Guardian's instructions about the Temple.

When Corinne returned to Wilmette, the Temple's superstructure was completed. She could see it from her home. Though close to 70, and no longer involved directly with the Temple project, she continued to promote it in talks to different communities and letters to individuals throughout the country, for the Guardian had asked her to regard this as her 'first and most sacred obligation . . .'[8] She had set in motion the goal of building the Temple and nothing would stop it, not even the constant struggle for funds. There were slow-ups and deadlines had to be extended but friends continued to send their donations despite the depression that practically crippled the American economy. 'Abdu'l-Bahá's pronouncement at the Temple site in 1912 that 'The Temple is already built'[9] must have fueled her faith that it would come into being. She had done what she was supposed to do, and to the best of her ability. Now it was time for others to take over. She had faith in them.

But Corinne was busy in other ways. In 1929 she had undertaken, as chairman of a small committee, the indexing and editing of unpublished Tablets from 'Abdu'l-Bahá held in the National Archives, and this she worked on for at least five years.[10] The Century of Progress Exposition in Chicago in 1933 brought other responsibilities, such as helping to plan the devotional services in the Temple and speaking at the weekly public meetings in Foundation Hall as one of twelve 'qualified teachers'.[11] She served, too, on Wilmette's Local Spiritual Assembly and held regular classes and firesides in her home. She never forgot the Michigan friends. Many of them received letters from her, and visits, especially in the summer. That nurturing process lasted until she was too feeble to go to Fruitport.

In less than four years Corinne would be back in Haifa with daughters Edna and Katherine, arriving for the first time without having to be taken off a steamer and placed in a smaller boat to reach the shore. At last Haifa had become a full-fledged harbor. A battleship was docked there, as well as the *Jerusalem*, a Jewish-owned large steamer. Once again Fujita was there waiting for his American family.

Getting through Customs was a chore for Corinne. She was impatient, a characteristic she seemed to have conquered back home. Edna and Katherine sensed that the pull of the World Center had simply overcome their mother's normally reserved manner. It was frustrating; so close and yet there were, what seemed to her, meaningless hurdles in the path to Mt Carmel.

Corinne entered the Pilgrim House as if she were visiting a close relative. She was in familiar surroundings, having stayed there her last two pilgrimages. As soon as she set foot in the dwelling, she called out: 'Yoo hoo, Effie, I'm here!' and proceeded to search for her friend.

Effie had lovely rooms arranged for Corinne and her daughters. A vase of fresh flowers was on each dresser.

Corinne was perfectly natural at the World Center, even in the presence of Shoghi Effendi. And it had been no different with 'Abdu'l-Bahá. She wasn't a maudlin person, who would show her emotions when visiting a sacred spot. To her the Bahá'í atmosphere was reality, and she felt most comfortable in it.

While reverent, she felt at ease looking into the Guardian's eyes. In fact, she shared openly her feelings and thoughts with him, even about what most people would view as nonessential matters. For example, during their first dinner with the Guardian, she looked at his plate and then said, 'Shoghi Effendi, you are not eating enough.'

'But Mrs True,' he protested, 'that's all I want.'

'You need to eat more, for eating only twice a day isn't enough.'

At first Edna and Katherine were flabbergasted but they soon realized that the Guardian of the Bahá'í Faith was moved by Corinne's motherly concern for him.[12]

It was wonderful being with Shoghi Effendi again, and to see his eyes light up when he would reveal a recent victory for the Faith. He seemed so pleased by the decision of Egypt's highest court that the Faith wasn't connected with Islam, that it was an independent religion. Now, he said, the believers wouldn't be bound by Muslim law. Bad news sobered him, but he didn't keep it from the pilgrims. One example was the Persian government's closing of the highly successful Bahá'í Tarbíyat School in Tehran, because it wouldn't stay open during Bahá'í holy days.[13]

Corinne felt deeply the absence of Bahíyyih Khánum, whose passing on 15 July 1932 had brought deep sorrow to Shoghi Effendi and shocked the Bahá'í world community. In fact, she noted in her diary: 'The home ['Abdu'l-Bahá's residence] seems so lonely without the Greatest Holy Leaf.'[14]

18

Mother True

There was trouble in the family. Larry had contracted pneumonia, and his doctor was concerned about his chances of surviving. Arna needed as much support as possible, for in 1936 penicillin wasn't available and pneumonia was considered a deadly disease. She had some idea what her mother went through when her brothers and sisters fought for their lives. Helping Arna came naturally to Corinne. She prayed fervently for her grandson and stayed close to her daughter.

Larry weathered the illness; but his doctor told his mother that living in the Chicago area was dangerous for him. His lungs had weakened, and the damp cold winters could set off more infections.

Arna and her children moved to Arizona where the air was clean and dry, and the sunshine plentiful. They settled on a ranch in Wilcox, where the boys took correspondence courses like the ranchers' children. Larry thrived. When Grandma came to see Arna and the children, the boys enjoyed showing off their horse-riding skills to her. She would be perched outside the corral fence watching Larry and Davis do their tricks. Patty, meanwhile, was off to college, attending the University of Arizona in Tucson. About two years later the Perron family set their roots permanently in Claremont, California. Like her own mother, Corinne found herself visiting her daughter, who at times was strapped for money. She would come bearing gifts. For a while the Perrons would go east during the summer, spending most of their time with grandmother.

Corinne missed Arna and the grandchildren when living so far away. But they were healthy and that was more important than having all the family close by. Of course she could move to the West Coast. Actually, there were no commitments to stay in Wilmette. But nothing could draw her away permanently. Besides, she had to stay within the shadow of the Temple.

Though at 75 she was considered an elderly person, she had the energy of a much younger woman. Her curiosity was as keen as ever. She looked forward to reading the newspaper every day. Corinne had a strong interest in world affairs. In 1936 much was happening in the world, a lot of it frightening. The Japanese had invaded Manchuria, a mineral-rich section of China; Italy was trying to seize Ethiopia from Emperor Haile Selassie. Hitler had absorbed Austria into the Third Reich and was building the mightiest military force in Europe. Sadly, the League of Nations, which had been created to keep peace in the world, was helpless in trying to stop the fighting. It would soon collapse. Corinne, of course, was aware of 'Abdu'l-Bahá's prediction that this global forum would fail to maintain peace. She was also aware of Shoghi Effendi's prediction of a greater war than World War I breaking out. What she read in the newspaper, she felt, was a clear sign of an impending worldwide clash. Though she deplored war and the suffering and tragedy it generates, she knew also that from the ashes of disaster many survivors would arise, seeking direction from new sources of light.

In 1938 the family was reunited for a holiday in California where Arna was living in Claremont. From La Jolla Edna sent this description of her mother, then in her 76th year: 'These few days alone here with that precious little Mother o'mine have [been] inexpressibly sweet. We have been quite busy socially – too busy to suit my inclinations for I love best of all just browsing around here – reading, studying and especially learning doing things in little talks with Mother . . .'[1]

But a month later, another blow deprived Corinne of her only brother Tom, after a heart attack when he hovered between life and death. 'Mother is on the train, due in the morning and of course, knows nothing about this. It will be a definite blow to her, as she is deeply attached to this brother but as we know, she has "plenty" to meet this with. Bless her heart, she will probably carry us all through the experience which is apparently inevitable for us –'[2] '. . . Poor little Mother took his going much harder even, than we expected – and we discovered that it was greatly because she had not been able to get him interested in the Cause, although he was a wonderful man. But we think that there was at least a rift in the veil, for one time, near the end, he sent for her and although he could talk very little, he said that he just wanted to tell her that "everything was alright".'[3]

A year later, although no longer 'able to keep the open house I have formally [formerly] done', Corinne's interest in the world around her was as keen as ever. 'These are terrific days and hold untold responsibilities for the Bahá'ís – May the Power of Bahá'u'lláh reinforce us – is our prayer.'[4] And anticipating the Annual Convention of 1939 she wrote: 'How you will love seeing the Temple with so much of its outer dress covering its bare concrete nakedness – Looking forward to wonderful times . . .'[5]

As she entered her 80th year, and just after the 1941 Convention, Edna expressed what all must have felt at that time: 'Yes, Mother is especially marvelous right now, as though (as you said) she had received renewed strength and vigor for her continued service – It is *such* an inspiration and stimulation to live with her – a blessing which you may be sure both Katherine and I fully appreciate and thank God for!'[6] And Corinne herself had written on the previous day: 'We have been coming too [to] since the Convention and trying to get back in our settled habits of Bahá'í work. Our new Local Assembly met last evening and appointed the various Committees to carry on the work in this Community . . . Pray for us that Bahá'u'lláh will give us wisdom and strength to spread His Word all up & down this beautiful North Shore . . . We have begun the new letter from the Guardian [*The Promised Day Is Come*]. There were 27 persons present last Thursday evening & we hope the class will be faithful to this Community Study Class . . .'[7]

About a month after Corinne's 80th birthday, the Japanese bombed Pearl Harbor. The United States had been drawn into World War II, but this time American troops would be fighting on three continents, Asia, Africa and Europe; and civilian population centers would become military targets.

The war touched the lives of Corinne and her daughters directly, especially Arna. Incensed by the sneak attack on Pearl Harbor, Davis quit the University of Arizona and enlisted in the Army Air Corps. He wanted, in the worst way, to be a fighter pilot. Nothing his mother would say could dissuade him from attaining what he desired: Davis had always had an adventurous spirit. He was an extrovert, dashing, a leader among his peers; he possessed a flair for the dramatic. In some ways, he was like his namesake, the uncle he had never met and who died of tuberculosis in 1912.

The urgency of teaching in those closing years of the First Seven Year Plan (1937–1944) was never far from Corinne's thoughts. She had recently studied the Guardian's tremendous book, *The Promised Day Is Come*, with its dire description of the state of humanity, coupled with an assurance of its 'gloriously radiant' future. And she had seen his 'plea' to the 1942 Convention for 'closer communion with the Spirit of Bahá'u'lláh, for more passionate resolve' in the 'crucial year ahead [upon which] hinge the fortunes of this historic crusade.'[8] In a letter a few days after that Convention, she wrote: 'This house is a very deserted home after each annual Convention; we must be very grateful to Baha'u'llah that America still is so bountifully bless [blest] that the Bahais can assembly [assemble] and consult openly about the advancement of God's Kingdom on the Western Hemisphere. We are indeed recipients of very great Bounty but also it demands great gratitude expressed in deeds – Teach! Teach! Teach! This is our great work.'9

In the report of the 1943 Annual Convention, in which Corinne had chaired the memorable Riḍván Feast, this tribute was recorded: 'She is one of the very few people, if not the only one, who has attended all of the thirty-five annual Conventions. Although well in the evening of life one seeing her radiance and hearing her eloquent expressions might think her still in the meridian of life.'10

Larry idolized his older brother, Davis, who had enlisted in the Army Air Corps in 1941, and couldn't wait until he was old enough to enlist and become a fighter pilot too. In 1943, he was in flight training school. But because of a surplus of pilots, he was transferred to the electronics section, an action that pleased his mother. Davis, meanwhile, was in Europe in the thick of a war that was unprecedented in its ferocity. And he was married. Prior to going overseas, he and his girlfriend had eloped, having a simple civil ceremony.

Their grandmother kept in touch by letter, and whenever possible in person. When Larry was stationed in Truax Air Force base in Illinois, she would insist that he spend some of his free time with her. She knew he would love a home-cooked meal and be embraced by a home he had such fond memories of. During the Christmas period of 1943, Corinne, Edna and Katherine went to Springfield, Missouri, a town not far from the Air Force base Larry had been transferred to. He had a two-day pass, and his grandmother and aunts spent that time cheering his spirit. That act of thoughtfulness and generosity came at the right time, for Larry had been feeling terribly low. He never forgot those fun-filled two days. Nor would he forget an incident that someone less sensitive and perceptive might forget. To Larry it epitomized his grandmother's charitable spirit.

It happened at dinner one night while he was visiting her. The True family's cook of the time had a drinking problem, and there were times when she had difficulty doing her job. Larry was there when she spilled a bowl of peas. Instead of getting angry or rebuking the woman, Corinne said gently, 'I don't think she's feeling very well.' What impressed Larry is that she meant what she said; she was trying to turn a negative situation into a positive one. He knew his grandmother's views on alcohol. Yet she showed the cook kindness and understanding; and her attitude influenced everyone at the table to display a similar attitude.

Larry loved to tease his grandmother, especially when she grew older. Maybe because she took everything at face value. At times he would take her for a walk along the lake front. They were an odd couple, he about a foot taller and purposely trying to walk like her, taking tiny steps. It took a while for her to notice what he was doing, but when she caught on she would laugh.

What also impressed Larry was that his grandmother became the center of attention wherever she was, in Bahá'í and non-Bahá'í circles. And she was a quiet woman, who wouldn't try to press her point of view. Yet there was something about her that drew people to her, men, women and children. It was something he couldn't explain.

While the war raged on in early 1944, Bahá'ís – worldwide – were excited about a forthcoming event. It had nothing to do with the war. In fact, it had to do with peace – though most outsiders couldn't see the connection. But the Bahá'ís could. To them, the one hundredth year of the birth of their Faith represented progress in building the foundation of world peace, a condition they felt would be realized in the future. And they believed that with all their heart and soul. The spread of devastation in Africa, Asia and Europe was the prelude to the eventual unification of the planet. Not that they were oblivious to the suffering of millions of people nor immune to it. Bahá'ís were being killed in battle, in bombing raids and some in Nazi concentration camps, left to perish there. But the Bahá'ís had a vision of what the world would be like, and they knew what to do to implement it. And in 1944 there was growing evidence of progress in turning that vision into something substantial. In America, for example, the Faith had spread to every state in the United States and every province in Canada. The number of Local Spiritual Assemblies practically doubled in both countries during the Guardian's First Seven Year Plan, which ended in 1944.

The eyes of the Bahá'í world were focused on Wilmette. For an international celebration of the centenary of the founding of their Faith would take place within the Temple, whose exterior had been completed in time for the observance from 19 through 24 May. Despite severe petroleum rationing, a third of all the Bahá'ís in the United States attended the Centenary celebration; and Bahá'ís from twenty-one Latin American and Caribbean countries streamed to Wilmette.

Corinne had been asked to take part in the celebration ceremonies. The secretary of the National Spiritual Assembly, Horace Holley, had asked her to write a history of the development of the Temple from 1903 to 1915 for a special Centenary publication. She was also invited to speak in the program on 'The Universal House of Worship'. Though 83 at the time, she relished the challenge. After all, it was for the Faith. Her attitude always was that if God wills it, she could do what she was supposed to do. Therefore, she would work as hard as she could to fulfill what the National Spiritual Assembly was expecting of her.

Corinne met both assignments. And the friends were enthralled with her talk, not so much by what she said, but how she said it. Standing very erect, and speaking in a strong voice, she seemed personified spirit, according to one observer. And another has recorded these impressions of that unique talk:

> It gave me profound happiness to see Corinne True at the historic centenary of the Bahá'í Faith in 1944 at the beautiful House of Worship in Wilmette . . . The saintly radiance that emanated from Mrs True reflected the special meaning that this sublime occasion had for her because of the completion of the exterior ornamentation of the House of Worship . . . The Guardian called its termination 'an event of unique and transcendental significance' . . . It was obvious that immortal memories flooded the inner being of Corinne True with light and wonderment . . . depicting a glorious panorama of experiences dating back to thirty-seven years before when she went on her first pilgrimage in 1907 carrying with her for 'Abdu'l-Bahá the scroll signed by early believers requesting His permission to undertake the construction of a Temple in North America . . . The two other majestic implemented goals of the First Seven Year Plan . . . that rejoiced her heart were the establishment of at least one [Spiritual Assembly] in every remaining State in the United States and Province of Canada, and in every Republic of Latin America which had not yet enlisted in the Faith.[11]

After all, she had become a legend, known by Bahá'ís across the country as 'the Mother of the Temple'. Indeed, we are told, it was not long after the inception of the project 'before everyone considered her the focal point . . . and she became known lovingly throughout the Bahá'í world as Mother True. 'Abdu'l-Bahá had designated several of the women believers as "mothers" of various communities, but Corinne was the undisputed "mother" of the Temple.'[12]

It had been a great day for the Bahá'ís. Seeing all of them – the largest gathering of Bahá'ís in the West, many from different lands – had excited her. So had the majestic Temple, towering over the lake front, now the pride of the residents of the area.

As to her history of the Temple, almost everyone was impressed with her article. Some of the exceptions were her daughters. It wasn't her writing style that they objected to; she simply had withheld some of the important facts. And it was done on purpose. Edna, Arna and Katherine were upset that Corinne hadn't mentioned her own contributions to the development of the Ma<u>sh</u>riqu'l-A<u>dh</u>kár.

But the ecstasy of late May was dashed in June. The US War Department contacted Davis's wife about her husband's death. He was returning from a mission inside Germany when his plane was shot down over northern France. The US Eighth Air Force would miss him, because he had flown many successful sorties over enemy territory, downing at least five Nazi fighter planes.

It was a sad time for Arna, Patty and Larry. Davis had been such an energetic young man, so full of life. Gone at such a young age. Gone in an instant, and so far from home. It was difficult to believe because the last time the family saw him he was so animated, so full of hope, and so sure that what he was doing as a fighter pilot was absolutely right. It was as if he just disappeared and never died, because death had usually been equated with illness and the dying person in bed.

It grieved them indescribably to lose Davis, but Arna believed deeply in Bahá'u'lláh; and His teachings on life after death were comforting. So was having her mother to lean on – a pillar of remarkable strength, even in her mid-80s. But what must have hurt most was the fact that Davis had had an opportunity to avoid combat. It had happened while training for overseas duty in Nevada. He was injured in a plane crash. The compound fracture of his arm was so bad that stainless steel screws had to be used to put the arm together. Much of the strength in the arm was gone, and he was removed from the pilots' roster. But Davis was able to persuade his commander to allow him to fly again, even in a war zone.

Because some of the delegates from Latin America had

been unable to attend the Centenary Convention due to transportation difficulties, and the Guardian had stressed that the 'participation of Latin American believers . . . is vital to the future development of the Faith in the Americas',[13] the National Spiritual Assembly arranged a special Centenary session in July 1944. Corinne was invited to address one of the sessions, and we have these notes of her speech from her translator, Gayle Woolson:

> She gave an impressive speech. Just her presence in itself was impressive. The sweet gentleness, humility and devotion combined with spiritual power, strength of faith, and iron firmness were elevating and fortifying . . . Waves of the Holy Spirit seemed to stream forth over the audience as she spoke. The love that poured out from her heart made apparent her exhilaration at witnessing the unity of the Americas . . . Among her words were: 'What deep gratitude we must have in our hearts – both the Bahá'ís of North America and those of Latin America – for the gift of God to humanity which is the Institution of the Guardianship. The love of the chosen branch, Shoghi Effendi, appointed by 'Abdu'l-Bahá, nourishes us and his wisdom leads us to spiritual growth. Upon the foundation of this spiritual development, material progress will also be gained.
>
> 'The Mashriqu'l-Adhkár [The Dawning-Place of the Mention of God] of each Prophet has been the center to unite the children of God. 'Abdu'l-Bahá said to the Bahá'ís that now the Day had come when God's Holy Edifice would be raised in America, and that it is a symbol of the great collective center that is to gather together all humanity, the law of God which brings harmony and union to the hearts. The Center of the Covenant laid its cornerstone and named the Temple the "Mother Temple of the West", and He wrote a Tablet in which He said that from this Temple thousands of Temples would be born.'[14]

In September 1945, on the eve of her return to the pioneer field in Latin America, Mrs Woolson, together with Mrs Dorothy Baker, was a guest in the True home.

'Especially memorable,' she writes, 'were the moments when we were all together at their beautiful, bountiful table. Corinne True related that this was the table at which 'Abdu'l-Bahá sat in 1912 when He was a guest at their home in Chicago at 5338 Kenmore Avenue. While she spoke of Him with such profound devotion, His Spirit seemed to surround her and she brought His holy, sanctified presence close to our hearts.' She also 'seemed electrified by Shoghi Effendi's most recent communications that referred to the new, second Bahá'í century that had commenced just the year before. His words opened up vast new perspectives to our vision. Mrs True's attitude reflected her gratitude that she was living also in this second Bahá'í century as she had in the first and that she was a part of a community upon whom 'Abdu'l-Bahá, in His Divine Plan, had bestowed such an exalted world mission.'[15]

Only a few months later, Corinne had occasion to reaffirm – as indeed her very presence did at all times for those who were privileged to meet her – the deep devotion she felt for the Center of the Covenant, 'Abdu'l-Bahá. On 29 November 1945, she wrote:

> We have just commemorated the Appointment of the Covenant at a Feast meeting in the Temple – the Words of God surely are all powerful, and as they were read by different Bahais from the platform, one could almost see and feel the Holy Presence of Abdul Baha . . . One of the beautiful names given the Revelation of Baha'u'llah is 'The heaven of heavens'. Jesus' Revelation is called the Fourth Heaven but Baha'u'llah's is 'The Heaven of Heavens' – We now know that going to Heaven means turning to the Revelation of Baha'u'llah – and not through the process of physical death – How lovely to turn to God in prayer and know that His Holy Word transforms our hearts and lives – . . . the old Order is crumbling before the Divine Atomic Bomb . . . Please pray for us & we will surely remember you.[16]

28. 418 Forest Avenue, Wilmette, the home of Corinne True and her daughters Edna and Katherine, from 1930. In 1987 it is still Edna's home.

29. Leo Perron, who was married to Arna True in 1912, and inexplicably died in 1929. They had adopted a daughter and two sons, whose ages at his death were from 5 to 12.

30. Davis Perron enlisted in the U.S. Army Air Corps after the attack on Pearl Harbor in December 1941. Newly married, and a daring fighter pilot, he died when his plane was shot down after a mission inside Germany in June 1944.

In the summer of 1947 it was announced that Edna, Chairman of the European Teaching Committee, would 'make a trip to Europe at this time. She will visit each of the European pioneer posts . . . [and] will be accompanied by her mother and Dr Katherine True. Mrs True and Katherine will visit Holland, Belgium, Luxembourg and Switzerland . . . The Trues sail on 23 July on the SS "Noordam".'[17] After their visit to Luxembourg, Corinne and Katherine, accompanied by Virginia Orbison (the 'mother of Spain'), went on to Interlaken, so intimately associated with the Guardian, and at the end of August traveled to Geneva via Montreux, where the Bahá'í International Bureau was established and where, a year later, the first Bahá'í European Conference would be held. Writing from Interlaken, Edna commented: 'This trip has certainly been a "work-out" but *infinitely* worthwhile!'[18] At the end of September, from 'halfway across the ocean' on the SS *America*, Katherine wrote: 'Mother certainly seems none the worse *physically* for her travels this summer, and I can tell you that her *spirits* are greatly uplifted . . . Yesterday we ran into a real storm and last night we practically stood on our heads . . . But we have all come through unscathed . . . and Mother really enjoyed it. What a trooper that gal is —'[19]

In 1950, Corinne had been asked to speak at the Unity Banquet of the European Teaching Conference in Copenhagen, as one of the 'rare few older Bahá'ís attending the Conference who personally knew and met the beloved Master . . .'[20] All the pioneers in Europe were there, together with at least one member of the communities where they were pioneering. Its organizers, who had worked hard to set it up, were anxious about carrying out every detail of their plan. It was one of the biggest teaching conferences ever held in Europe, with nearly 200 in attendance.

On the evening of the festive Banquet, aglow with the

warmth of Bahá'í fellowship, there was one detail that hadn't been dealt with; and it wasn't for lack of trying. It involved Corinne True. No one knew what she was going to talk on. Not even her three daughters who were in Copenhagen. In fact, Edna was Chairman of the European Teaching Committee and she was unable to prise from her mother the nature of her talk. Every time she or her sisters approached their mother on the matter, Corinne would respond calmly: 'I don't know, quite,' or 'It's all taken care of.'

Arna, Edna and Katherine had hoped their mother had prepared a speech, because she was, after all, 88. There was always the chance she could draw a blank, and that could be embarrassing to her and the Conference committee. She had given no indication that she had prepared a thing. Evidently the daughters weren't aware of what the Master had told her about speaking in public. She had never forgotten His instructions.

Presented as a distinguished 'pioneer' who had 'served the Faith since the turn of the century', Corinne arose to speak, empty-handed, her 'gentle presence' conveying to all that 'nobility' to which the Master had referred: 'It is possible so to adjust oneself to the practice of nobility that its atmosphere surrounds and colors every act.'[21] At that point her daughters – all in the audience – knew there was nothing they could do. It was simply in God's hands. Nevertheless, they were anxious.

Corinne smiled at the eager audience and began to speak, calmly, ever so calmly. What flowed from her lips drew her listeners toward her. They literally moved to the edge of their seats.

Sitting next to Edna was David Hofman. He was so stirred that he reached for Edna's hand and, as Corinne spoke on, his grip grew tighter and tighter. One witness said, 'Words fell from her lips like jewels.'[22]

Afterwards people inquired where she gained such wisdom.

'It was 'Abdu'l-Bahá,' she said. 'He told me when I said I could not speak, "Get yourself out of the way and I will come through," so I did just that.'[23]

On her return to Forest Avenue Corinne wrote of this trip with her daughters: 'The Guardian . . . loved my taking my whole family with me, wrote me it was a great example to the younger generation to see & associate with old confirmed Bahais . . . I got as much from participating as any of the younger Pioneers —'[24]

Back home she remained busy. The NSA had appointed her to a special national committee to revise *The Promulgation of Universal Peace*, a book of the Master's talks in North America.

19

A Tower of Strength

The last half of Corinne's Bahá'í life was especially enriched through her contact with the Guardian, Shoghi Effendi. There were the pilgrimages that produced the unforgettable face-to-face meetings with him; there was also the correspondence that spanned more than thirty years. Like her correspondence with the Master, Shoghi Effendi's letters helped to expand her already deep understanding of the Faith, and strengthen her grasp of the Covenant. And there were his writings which she studied in great detail. She never stopped inquiring, learning and growing.

Corinne received more than seventy letters from Shoghi Effendi. For the most part, they were responses to questions about the condition of the Faith in America and the critical issues facing it. While the letters were written by one of his secretaries, Shoghi Effendi rarely missed the opportunity to add a personal note at the end, usually reflecting the major theme of the letter.

Shoghi Effendi encouraged Corinne to write to him. For example, in an early letter he noted:

> . . . I value greatly your views and feelings as they proceed from a heart that is wholly consecrated to His love and a mind that thinks of naught but service to His Cause . . .[1]

Now in her later years Corinne was no longer coordinating the National Fund activities, but she remained keenly interested in how the American treasurer's office was working – and the percentage of giving on the part of the friends. She viewed the latter as a barometer of the American community's spiritual health.

When misundersanding would arise among the believers regarding giving to the Fund, she would often seek clarification from the Guardian. In one instance, he wrote:

> ... With regard to the National Fund, it must not be felt that the believers are *required* to send *unlabelled* contributions to the Fund but that it is only extremely desirable to do so. Individuals are free to specify the purpose of their donations . . .[2]

Clarification on other matters was sought, matters often concerning the application by the Guardian of the administrative principles of the Faith. At times those principles clashed with some of the unofficial practices of many of the communities. One issue was especially testing: could a Bahá'í choose whatever community he wished to be a part of? Previously, as Christians, the friends had had the freedom to select whatever church they wished to worship in, no matter where it was located.

Corinne asked Shoghi Effendi if she and her family could be affiliated with the Chicago community even though they were living outside the boundary of the city. His response, via his secretary, was that they should work to establish a Spiritual Assembly in the town where they were presently living. And then the Guardian added, in his own hand, a note on the importance of taking such matters to the administrative institutions of the Faith:

> I strongly feel that this matter is within the province of the National Assembly. I have laid down the principle in a general way; it is for the local assemblies in collaboration with their national Representatives to apply the principles to the difficult and complex circumstances and situation in their own sphere of activity . . .[3]

That wasn't the last time the Guardian emphasized in his notes to Corinne the importance of taking issues and problems to the administrative institutions. The reminders increased her appreciation of the Faith's Administrative Order and deepened her understanding of how it functioned. Whenever she had the opportunity, she would pass on the Guardian's feelings about the importance of not only respecting the Faith's institutions, but using them to settle disputes, solve problems and organize community events.

Teaching and proclaiming the Faith were also topics Corinne addressed to the Guardian. From his letters she gained insight on how to present the Cause. In one letter written on his behalf, he suggested that holding meetings in the Foundation Hall of the Temple (which he had just recommended to the National Spiritual Assembly through Corinne during her 1927 pilgrimage),

> so parallel in some ways to the gatherings of the early Christians in their catacombs, will keep up enthusiasm and will help to strengthen faith in the onward progress of the Cause.[4]

Corinne's home was a kind of twentieth-century catacomb. While those who attended her firesides in her later years didn't sit on rocks in a cave lit only by candlelight, the Message of Bahá'u'lláh was shared with the same love and reverence as the early followers of Jesus had shared His Message.

In presenting the Faith in public she used as a guide an excerpt from a note from Shoghi Effendi in reference to the kind of talks that should be given at the House of Worship's Foundation Hall:

> The teachings must be referred to, quoted, explained and amplified, and if non-Bahá'í subjects are referred to, they should be considered in the light, and in confirmation, of Bahá'í principles and teachings. We must preserve the identity and purity of the Faith, without restricting it to a rigid and exclusive dogma.[5]

Corinne was always a stickler for using direct quotations from the Central Figures of the Faith in explaining its various aspects, both in public and among Bahá'ís. Her statements were usually sprinkled with terms like, 'Bahá'u'lláh wrote', 'The Master stated', or 'according to the Guardian'. She rarely strayed from the Teachings in her talks and one-on-one explanations. What often disturbed her was for someone to make a statement about the Faith or some subject related to it without proper documentation. That concern was reinforced by guidance from Haifa, as in this case through a letter written on behalf of the Guardian:

> Concerning what Mr. Remey and other believers, whether Americans or otherwise, have told the friends about Melchizedek, and as to their references in regard to the leading religions of the world, and to the symbolism involved in the numerical number of the Temple doors, the Guardian wishes to restate and to reemphasize the general principle that in all such matters of a specific character the friends should be careful not to accept anything as valid and authentic unless it is based on, and corroborated by, a Tablet bearing the signature of the Master. Oral reports and statements cannot be relied upon, since they lead to the same confusions and difficulties into which the followers of former Dispensations have been and are still entangled. It is now, when the Faith is still in its infancy, that extreme caution should be exercised in the apparently unimportant matters. Otherwise, the purity of the Teachings will be beclouded, and the unity of the Cause greatly jeopardized. To protect the Faith from these forms of traditionalism is the duty of the responsible administrators of the Cause, and nothing short of their wisdom, caution and tact in their handling of such delicate matters, can insure the purity and the effectiveness of the Teachings.[6]

News of the Greatest Holy Leaf's passing – 15 July 1932 – stunned Corinne. Her immediate response was to want to reach out to Shoghi Effendi, for she knew how close he was to Bahíyyih Khánum. No one in the world was so close. For almost eleven years she had been for the young Guardian a 'living symbol' and a 'continual reminder' of the departed Master, as well as an affectionate comforter and wise counselor.[7] In a sense, he was now alone, and Corinne felt for him.

Of course, the passing of the Greatest Holy Leaf was a personal loss to Corinne too, for they had forged a close friendship lasting a quarter of a century. But it was to Shoghi Effendi that her heart was drawn. His cabled message deeply moved Corinne:

> 'I FOR MY PART BEWAIL SUDDEN REMOVAL OF MY SOLE EARTHLY SUSTAINER, THE JOY AND SOLACE OF MY LIFE.'[8]

Corinne wrote to the Guardian a few days after hearing the news. She would always cherish his response:

> Dear and precious sister[,]
> I greatly value your words of sympathy as I am fully aware of the Greatest Holy Leaf's attachment to you and of her keen and abiding appreciation of all that you have done for the Cause of her Father. May He enable you to mirror forth the sublimity of her life, and to hand on to future generations her noble heritage.[9]

Corinne was heart-broken that she couldn't attend a special memorial service for the Greatest Holy Leaf, held in the Temple's auditorium. An illness had kept her housebound for weeks.

Perhaps, she thought, a cruise in the Mediterranean would help her to regain her strength. Of course, Haifa – a place she longed to be – bordered on the Mediterranean.

She wrote to the Guardian, asking if she could come to the World Center as soon as possible. Going on pilgrimage would mean foregoing her participation in the presentation of the Faith during the Century of Progress Exposition being held in Chicago.

Shoghi Effendi's response put everything in perspective:

> Dear and valued co-worker:
> Your absence from Chicago, during the Exposition would, I feel certain, leave a gap that few could fill. Your

experience, your exemplary devotion to whatever affects the interests of our beloved Faith, your high purpose and tenacity of faith eminently qualify you to introduce the Cause, explain its aim, reveal its spirit, and demonstrate the significance of its institutions, to the countless visitors who will throng that city this summer. Personally I would prefer to have you and your dear daughter entertained by me and the Master's family in Haifa, but for the sake of the Cause, I feel the urge to address you this request. Your services are engraved upon my heart. I can never forget them or overestimate their value.[10]

While Corinne heeded the Guardian's request, she still longed to see him. Maybe, she thought, he could come to America. His presence, she felt, would generate greater activity among the friends, just as the Master's mission to America had done.

She wrote to Shoghi Effendi, asking him to consider coming to North America.

He responded in his own hand:

Dear and precious co-worker:
I deeply appreciate the sentiments expressed in your letter and am deeply grateful for the services you are rendering and the spirit which animates you in your work. I must feel the urge to undertake the journey to which you refer, otherwise any service I can render will fail to achieve its purpose. The friends in America should concentrate on their task, their glorious and divinely-appointed task, and never allow considerations of my presence or absence to deflect them from their high purpose.[11]

As always, Corinne took the Guardian's response to heart, and continued to the limit of her strength her administrative and teaching work. The fact that Corinne in her old age was active in the Faith didn't surprise the Guardian. He was acquainted with her spirit, the kind of spirit that apostles manifest. What she did for the Faith brought him joy, and he openly shared his thankfulness with her:

> Dear and prized co-worker:
> My heart is filled with gratitude for the fresh evidences of untiring activity, of exemplary loyalty, of steadfastness and devotion that you have so powerfully manifested in recent months. You are truly a tower of strength in these days of stress and trial, worthy of the unquestioning confidence reposed in you by 'Abdu'l-Bahá. Persevere in your meritorious work, and rest assured that my prayers will continue to be offered for you and for your dear daughters.[12]

Corinne's devotion to the Faith was an example to many men and women who knew her or heard about her. She gained their respect through what she did for the Cause she loved with every fiber of her being. There was nothing, absolutely nothing, that meant more to her. Her daughters knew that, and were impressed with their mother's faith, so impressed that they eventually grew to be like her – rock-solid firm in the Covenant, powerful defenders of the Faith, and tireless workers in furthering the interests of the Cause. Arna portrayed her in a letter to Edna, some time after her mother's death: 'I think of certain outstanding qualities that never wavered, like obedience, justice, studying always the Writings themselves, and her unfailing joy in service.'[13] Certainly the Guardian was aware of Corinne's influence on her children. When she was 88 years old, he wrote:

> Dear and valued co-worker:
> I wish to add a few words in person and express to you my abiding and affectionate appreciation of your past and splendid achievements in the service of the Faith, as well as of the services now rendered by your dear and devoted daughters . . .[14]

And eight months later came these words:

> . . . I rejoice that your dear daughters are following in your footsteps, and I will supplicate the Beloved to bless this family that has rendered and is still rendering such

distinguished services to the Cause of Bahá'u'lláh.
Your true and grateful brother,
Shoghi[15]

There were five more letters to Corinne from the Guardian, between 1950 and 1955, chiefly concerning the services of her daughters. But the summit of all the messages Corinne received from him must surely have been his cablegram of 28 February 1952, appointing her a Hand of the Cause of God.[16]

20

The Most Venerable Pioneer

There weren't many American Bahá'ís who had been on pilgrimage as often as Corinne True. She had been to the Holy Land seven times. But at 91 she felt she must go again; and undoubtedly for the last time. It was a need that sprang from a desire to return home. To her, Haifa was her real home. For it had been the source of inspiration for fifty-three years, and her source of life. Deep down she knew that without the steady, loving, patient guidance from 'Abdu'l-Bahá and Shoghi Effendi her life would have taken a different turn than it did.

Edna conveyed her mother's desire to the Guardian and on 4 February he replied: MOTHER WELCOME VISIT SHRINES. Corinne was elated – 'deeply appreciative and grateful', as Edna cabled in her reply, suggesting that she and Katherine also come, and in October, to which the Guardian immediately agreed. The fact that she was in her 90s didn't faze Corinne. She knew she was going to reach Haifa. But, obviously, her daughters were concerned about the 6,000-mile journey; she couldn't go alone.

About three weeks after the second cablegram from the Guardian, another one arrived from him:

> MOVED CONVEY GLAD TIDINGS YOUR ELEVATION RANK HAND CAUSE STOP APPOINTMENT OFFICIALLY ANNOUNCED PUBLIC MESSAGE ADDRESSED ALL NATIONAL ASSEMBLIES STOP MAY SACRED FUNCTION ENABLE YOU ENRICH RECORD SERVICES ALREADY RENDERED FAITH BAHA'U'LLAH[1]

She accepted the appointment without analyzing why

she had been chosen; it wasn't her nature to be analytical. She was certain that the Guardian had his reasons for his decision. Her concern was how she could serve effectively in her new role. For she knew there were no figurehead positions in the Faith. Whatever anyone did for the Cause required work, often hard work.

As a Hand of the Cause, Corinne didn't do anything differently than she had been doing. The Bahá'ís in the Chicago area and elsewhere weren't surprised by her appointment. Many of them were already treating her as someone special, something she probably wasn't aware of.

What excited her most was the prospect of meeting the Guardian again, and returning to the place where her real roots were.

The Trues took their time reaching Haifa. Paris was their first stop, where Corinne relished using the few French phrases she knew, invariably incorrectly, and often amusing her daughters who knew the language. But the startled reaction from the waiters and salesladies didn't faze Corinne.

From France they went to Switzerland for a few days, where the Guardian had spent most of the summer that year working on the Ten Year Crusade plans.

Corinne and her daughters arrived in Haifa a day after Shoghi Effendi. Greeting them at the dock was their old friend Fujita, sporting a wispy beard and a broad smile. To him the Trues were family.

Haifa was a city in a nation that hadn't existed the last time she was on pilgrimage. The sleepy little town on the coast had grown into the country's leading port. And halfway up Mt Carmel was the Shrine of the Báb, taller than before and robed in white. Above – a blue sky was spread as far as the eye could see, and the air was clean. The gardens around the Shrine were in bloom. Paradise. That's what it was – paradise. And she knew it.

Corinne had lived a long life, and had been many places. But there was one place she would never tire of. And she knew that Shoghi Effendi knew how she felt. So she wasn't surprised when he greeted her by saying, 'You've come back to your real home.'²

The highlight of the pilgrimage took place one night at dinner. It may have been one of the most memorable occasions in Corinne's life.

What happened earlier that day had set the tone for what occurred in the evening. Shoghi Effendi had been involved in an event which he considered a great victory for the Faith. Ever since he had been named the Guardian, he had struggled to have the Holy Land's authorities recognize the Bahá'í Faith as a genuine world religion. For thirty years enemies had tried to discredit the Bahá'ís, the Grand Mufti of Jerusalem among them; and Covenant-breakers kept sniping away.

That day the Israeli government reserved a seat of honor for the Guardian at the funeral of Chaim Weizmann, first President of Israel. Throughout the late afternoon and evening the national radio network announced in Arabic and Hebrew that His Eminence Shoghi Effendi Rabbani, the world head of the Bahá'í Faith, was among the dignitaries attending the President's funeral. This recognition of the Faith thrilled the Guardian, for finally it had been legitimized in the eyes of the public.

He came to dinner that night earlier than usual. The Trues were still dressing when Shoghi Effendi arrived in the dining-room. He was smiling, buoyant, eager to be with the believers. After all, the triumph he had experienced a few hours earlier was theirs as well.

When Corinne entered, he greeted her warmly and placed her in the seat of honor, and he sat at her right. There was a twinkle in his eyes when he said to her, 'I understand, Mrs True, you had something to do with the Temple in the United States.'

'Yes, Shoghi Effendi,' she said, rather puzzled.

'Didn't you have something to do with the money?'

'Yes, I received the money and was the financial

secretary.'

At that point he reached into his pocket and pulled out a billfold and said, 'This was the purse carried by 'Abdu'l-Bahá when He visited America.' He placed it in her hands, and told her that he wanted her to keep it. She had been given another link with the Master. There couldn't have been a better gift. Certainly the Guardian knew what could touch her soul. Tears filled her eyes. With love, deep love, she placed the worn leather to her forehead. There was silence for a moment or two; all eyes – some filled with tears – were fixed on the small, elderly lady who had known who her Lord was and had willingly become His captive, serving Him wholeheartedly.

Finally, Shoghi Effendi, obviously moved, urged her to open the billfold. Inside was a gold five-dollar piece with the date 1907 inscribed on it, the year of her first pilgrimage. It's believed that the coin was one of the ten brought to the Master as a gift from the Women's Assembly of Teaching.

That same evening the Guardian talked about the plans of his Ten Year Crusade. He was enthusiastic, full of hope that this expansion campaign would help the Cause spread to places where Bahá'ís had never resided. While talking about the world-wide goals, he suddenly turned to Corinne and asked, 'Mrs True, do you think I am too ambitious?'

Corinne replied: 'No, Shoghi Effendi. But I think we should hurry home and get to work; there is so much work to be done.'

He smiled and that twinkle returned in his eyes. 'Go ahead,' he said, 'and work with your daughters – in Europe, Africa, Asia, and the islands, and even Tibet, you can be a pioneer to any one of those places.'

At first she was speechless. Then a smile crossed her face; she finally realized that he was joking. But he wasn't joking when he suggested that she direct her efforts to helping Bahá'ís become teachers.[3]

Then he described Corinne as a 'spiritual politician', a term none of the Bahá'ís at the table had ever heard before. Rúḥiyyih <u>Kh</u>ánum was there, as well as Leroy Ioas and his wife, and Mason Remey.

Shoghi Effendi looked at Corinne and explained what he meant. 'You have learned to be spiritual and at the same time get things done.'[4] And then he addressed everyone at the table: 'It should be stated that Mrs True is to be regarded as the most venerable figure among the pioneers of the Faith of Bahá'u'lláh in the West.'[5]

That was a strange pronouncement since Corinne True had never lived in a foreign land as a Bahá'í. But she was a pioneer in a different sense. Through her efforts the American community had grown wiser and in numbers. There were those who had disagreed with her, at times vehemently. Nevertheless, she had persevered. Whatever she was asked to do, and whatever she initiated, had been done with determination to succeed, not for personal glory or self-gratification. She had put the Faith first in her life, because she truly understood what it meant to the world. To her, putting anything ahead of the Faith was inconceivable. She had given much to the Cause, much more than most friends and fellow Bahá'ís were aware of. Certainly Bahá'u'lláh and 'Abdu'l-Bahá were aware, and Shoghi Effendi knew. That's all that mattered. There was no need to defend her actions. She tried as hard as she could to please her Lord, at times doing the wrong thing and alienating some people, but never meaning to.

'Abdu'l-Bahá chose her to do what he felt others more experienced in the ways of the world weren't capable of doing. He chose a woman to spearhead the development of the most important single project in the first fifty years of the Faith in America. But there were other things that she was destined to do for the Master; and she probably did them unaware at the time of what her exploits would eventually lead to. Through her efforts the Administrative Order, on a national scale, was started and developed.

31. Corinne True, aged 88, at the European Teaching Conference in Copenhagen, 1950, with a number of distinguished Bahá'í pioneers and European believers. She stands in the first row (3rd from the right) between Arna (on her left) and Marion Little.

32. Corinne's eighth and last pilgrimage, November 1952. She is seated in front of Sylvia Ioas, with Edna on her right and Katherine on her left. Dr Luṭfu'lláh Ḥakím and Mrs Sabet are also with her. The previous February she had been appointed by the Guardian a Hand of the Cause of God.

33. Corinne True attending the public dedication of the Ma<u>sh</u>riqu'l-A<u>dh</u>kár, Wilmette, 2 May 1953, accompanied by (left to right) Katherine, Arna and Edna

34. Corinne with Paul Haney, on the platform of the 1956 Bahá'í National Convention. Horace Holley is seen at the extreme right. All were Hands of the Cause of God.

35. *Corinne with Edna, in front of the National Ḥaẓíratu'l-Quds on Sheridan Avenue, Wilmette, across from the House of Worship*

And 'Abdu'l-Bahá used her to break down the psychological barriers against women in the American Bahá'í community. That was a long and painful experience. Above all she stood firm in the Faith, regardless of the severity of the tests within the Bahá'í community. Nothing could unhinge her attachment to the Cause. It was that, more than anything else, that endeared her to the Master and the Guardian. For it is upon that kind of rock that true Faiths are built.

21

The Hand of the Cause

To a 91-year old, six months isn't a long time. In November of 1952 Corinne had been on pilgrimage. And on 2 May 1953 she was being escorted by her daughters to the Temple – at last completed!

Hailed by the press as an architectural wonder, the Temple drew to itself hundreds of people, black and white, orientals and occidentals, young and old, poor and rich, not only from North America but from other parts of the world. Some of them knew Corinne; others had heard about her involvement with the Temple. Many passed her by unaware of who she was. It was an emotional occasion. For so many had waited so long for the Temple to open its doors. There were so many people there that three special services had to be held. Some wept as they raised their heads toward the dome.

Corinne walked slowly, her head bowed, oblivious of the commotion around her. In fact, she never uttered a word, outside or inside the Temple. There were those who tried to speak to her, but she didn't respond. She wasn't being rude, because she wasn't that way.

As she sat beneath the magnificent dome, and the choir rang out the praises of the Lord, no one knew what dominated her thoughts. A recollection of the fifty-year struggle to build the Temple? At an earlier age, perhaps, but not in 1953. Corinne's consciousness would most likely have been trained on a loftier plane. 'It is done, dear Master,' she might have whispered, 'as you said it would be.'

What else was there to do? Corinne was beyond the twilight of her life. But she was a Hand of the Cause; and the Ten Year Crusade had been launched. So she concentrated on teaching those Bahá'ís who wanted to teach. Young and old called on her, including prospective pioneers. Though at first there were no Auxiliary Board members to guide, she had a part to play, direction coming to the Hands from the Guardian. Despite her inability to attend most of the meetings of the Hands, she kept closely in touch with their actions through the thoughtful visits of her fellow Hand, Horace Holley.

When, in 1954, Auxiliary Board members were appointed to assist the Hands of the Cause, one of those who served in that capacity in Latin America recalls that Corinne True signed every message sent by the American Hands of the Cause, from their cablegram announcing the names of the first nine members for the Americas until her passing in 1961. 'The characteristic steadfastness and perseverance reflected during the early years when Corinne True was involved with the enterprise of the House of Worship in Wilmette was again demonstrated throughout her nine years of service as a Hand of the Cause of God.'[1]

Traveling was becoming more and more difficult. Not that she missed going on long journeys. Corinne never conquered her dislike of travel, but visiting the Temple, which was close by, was a joy. For the National Convention delegates and guests, it was a bounty to have her in their midst. And more than that, for it was a spiritual excursion into the past, an inspirational moment they might never experience again. Some in the audience were aware of her contributions to the Cause. A few understood her value to the Faith. And all were caught up by the rare spirit that could only be generated by someone who had faithfully served the Master and the Guardian, and embraced the Covenant with such unquestionable devotion. In many ways she symbolized the development of the Faith in North America. She was part of the root-system of the Cause in the Western Hemisphere. In 1955 she addressed the Convention. When called on to speak, everyone in Foundation Hall stood up. Frail, and taking short, measured steps, the 94-year old Hand of the Cause was guided onto the platform by daughters Edna and Katherine. She wore a black hat and a royal-blue print dress. A young Bahá'í who was present at that Convention can't recall what she said, for it was so long ago. What he remembered, however, was her expression of faith, her humility, her inner peace. About thirty years later, whenever he thinks of Corinne True, a passage from 'Abdu'l-Bahá's utterances comes to mind: 'The humbler man is in the path of God the more exalted is he; . . . the more he is surrounded with tests and trials the vaster the tranquillity and composure of his spirit.'[2]

During the Riḍván period of 1957, the Hand of the Cause Corinne True had a mission to carry out for the Guardian. She was 95 at the time. It meant long-distance traveling again. This time to the Caribbean, to represent the Guardian in the formation of the National Spiritual Assembly of the Greater Antilles. Katherine and Arna would accompany her.

When their plane landed in Port-au-Prince, Haiti, the site of the Convention, they were greeted by a delegation of Bahá'ís. It was the first time a Hand of the Cause had set foot on that nation's soil. She greeted the friends but could stay only a few hours; for political unrest in Haiti had forced a change in the Convention site. They had to go on to Kingston, Jamaica.

Those friends who attended the Convention were thrilled to have Corinne True with them. To come, many of the Bahá'ís had to overcome great difficulties. Katherine, representing the United States National Spiritual Assembly, opened the Convention, serving as chairman until a permanent one was elected. She introduced her mother, who, after a few words of greeting asked that Arna read the Guardian's message to the Convention.

36. The Hand of the Cause, Corinne True, representing the Guardian of the Faith at the formation of the first National Spiritual Assembly of the Bahá'ís of the Greater Antilles, 22–24 April 1957. Planned for Port-au-Prince, Haiti, it became necessary to hold the Convention in Kingston, Jamaica. Arna and Katherine, the latter representing the National Spiritual Assembly of the United States, attended her.

37. Dr Katherine Knight True (1893–1963)

38. *Arna Corinne True Perron (1890–1975)*

39. Edna Miriam True, who served as a member of the Continental Board of Counsellors for North America and the Trustee of the Continental Fund from 1968 until 1980. Without her generosity and patience in sharing her recollections this book could not have been written.

The next day the election of the National Spiritual Assembly was held. During the ballot counting, the Hand of the Cause Corinne True anointed the friends with attar of rose sent by Shoghi Effendi. Afterwards she spoke briefly, stating that what was taking place that day was a miracle.³ Corinne had lived to see the Faith spread far and wide. Though she knew it would spread even further, she was still thrilled to see natives of tiny islands who had embraced Bahá'u'lláh. Shoghi Effendi was truly the master-builder of the World Order of Bahá'u'lláh! She marveled at his generalship.

About six months later, four days after Corinne's 96th birthday, Rúḥíyyih Khánum called the True home around 2:30 a.m., rousing Edna and Katherine. She shared with Edna the news of Shoghi Effendi's passing.

Dazed, Edna revealed to her sister what she had learned. Katherine, who was Corinne's physician, advised against waking their mother to tell her what had happened in London. The shock, she feared, could kill Corinne, whose health was extremely fragile.

After breakfast, they felt, would be the time to break the news. Even then, they worried about how she would react. She was so close to Shoghi Effendi, closer in some ways than she had been with 'Abdu'l-Bahá. She had known him as a child, watched him mature and cherished him the way a mother would a favorite son. He had strengthened the Faith's unity, successfully led the attack against its enemies, directed its expansion, infused confidence in the believers; taught them, loved them and comforted them in time of crisis. 'With the loss of Shoghi Effendi, what would happen to the Faith – and to them?' Edna and Katherine wondered. Their lives revolved around the Faith. They couldn't sleep that night.

Edna and Katherine took their mother's breakfast to her. She was sitting up; some of her Bahá'í books were on the blanket next to her. Her daughters sat on each side of the bed.

After finishing her breakfast, Corinne was asked by Edna if she had heard the phone ring in the middle of the night.

When Corinne said she hadn't, Edna shared the contents of the call with her.

Corinne lowered her head. There was silence for a moment, maybe longer. Suddenly, she looked up, her face pale, but her eyes ablaze with an assurance her daughters had never seen before. 'You must know that this is the will of God,' she declared.[4]

There was no need for questions. Whatever fear possessed Edna and Katherine vanished. Their mother was a bastion of firmness; and those who visited her felt it.

Her age was finally slowing her down physically. How she wanted to be with her fellow Hands of the Cause of God in Haifa, or traveling about, nurturing the believers around the world. So many of them were troubled. Though confined to her house most of the time, those who called on her were reminded about the importance of winning the goals of the Ten Year Crusade.

Her colleagues knew she was with them in spirit. As Chief Stewards of the Faith, the twenty-seven Hands of the Cause of God had the weighty responsibility of filling, in some measure, the leadership-void created by Shoghi Effendi's passing. Their historic document, 'Proclamation by the Hands of the Cause to the Bahá'ís of East and West,' would provide direction to the friends until the election of the Universal House of Justice. Corinne True was unable to attend that first Conclave of the Hands in Haifa, 'owing to her advanced age of ninety-six and the physical infirmities consequent thereto . . .'[5] But during the 1958 Convention in the United States just a few months later, it was reported, 'Our own dear Hand of the Cause Corinne True shared the rostrum for a brief period.'[6]

The Hands of the Cause kept in contact with her. She received regular reports from Haifa. From time to time they wrote personal letters, like this one from the Hand of the Cause William Sears:

> Dearest Mrs. True:
>   This is a letter of love, to send to you the deepest, heartfelt appreciation for all your great services to our precious Faith. Your devotion and sacrifice in helping to raise up that most Holy House of Worship in Wilmette, is an immortal achievement. The beloved Master said that when the Temple was completed, from that point of light, the Faith of Bahá'u'lláh would be carried to all parts of the world. This prophecy came true in 1953, with the launching of the great World Crusade, and all the victories I have seen and thrilled to can be directly traced back to the building and raising up of that great edifice, with whose name, your own name, will be forever linked.
>   With warmest and deepest personal love,
>   Bill Sears[7]

Two weeks before she passed away, Corinne startled her nurse. While lying in bed she would recite, in a strong voice, memorized passages from Bahá'u'lláh's and 'Abdu'l-Bahá's Writings. At times her recitation would turn into a chant. She would stop for a few minutes, then continue reciting or chanting other passages. The nurse, who had worked for other dying patients, had never experienced such a thing. She didn't know what to make of it.

All three daughters, Edna, Arna and Katherine were present when their mother passed away peacefully on 3 April 1961, seven months short of her hundredth birthday.

Corinne Knight True wasn't a genius endowed with brilliant talents. Nor was she a scholar in a worldly sense, and she had no profession. Neither was she a great beauty. Outwardly she might have seemed a rather ordinary person, reserved by nature, though with an air of quiet dignity, sweet confidence, and friendliness. But her spirit was extraordinary, a spirit tested and strengthened by tragedy, a spirit that searched passionately to express itself through a Divine source. Once found, her spirit surrendered itself to that Divine Will. Perhaps that was her greatest achievement, although not noticeable to most of her contemporaries. But the Master was always aware of it. He knew her as no one else did. That was made evident during the summer of 1909 in Haifa when He asked the pilgrim, Juliet Thompson, about Mrs True.

'I don't know Mrs True,' she replied, 'except through letters.'

'I love Mrs True very much,' said 'Abdu'l-Bahá.[8]

Published Sources

'ABDU'L-BAHÁ. *Selections from the Writings of 'Abdu'l-Bahá.* Compiled by the Research Department of the Universal House of Justice. Translated by a Committee at the Bahá'í World Centre and by Marzieh Gail. Haifa: Bahá'í World Centre, 1978.
—— *Tablets of Abdul-Baha Abbas.* Vol. 1. New York: Baha'i Publishing Committee, 1930.
Bahá'í News. A monthly publication of the National Spiritual Assembly of the Bahá'ís of the United States (until 1948, of the United States and Canada). From the first issue in 1924 until 1930 it was titled *Bahai News Letter.*
Bahá'í World, The. Vol. 2, 1926–1928. New York: Baha'i Publishing Committee, 1928. Vol. 13, 1954–1963, and Vol. 14, 1963–1968. Haifa, Israel: The Universal House of Justice, 1970 and 1974.
Bahíyyih Khánum, The Greatest Holy Leaf. A compilation from Bahá'í sacred texts and writings of the Guardian of the Faith and Bahíyyih Khánum's own letters made by the Research Department at the Bahá'í World Centre. Haifa: Bahá'í World Centre, 1982.
BALYUZI, H. M. *'Abdu'l-Bahá, The Centre of the Covenant of Bahá'u'lláh.* Oxford: George Ronald, 1971.
RABBANI, RÚHÍYYIH. *The Priceless Pearl.* London: Bahá'í Publishing Trust, 1969.
SHOGHI EFFENDI. *Bahá'í Administration.* Selected Messages, 1922–1932. Wilmette, Illinois: Bahá'í Publishing Trust, 1974 edn, 1980 repr.
—— *God Passes By.* Wilmette, Illinois: Bahá'í Publishing Trust, 7th ptg. 1974.
—— *Messages to America, 1932–1946.* Wilmette, Illinois: Bahá'í Publishing Committee, 1947.
—— *The Promised Day Is Come.* Wilmette, Illinois: Bahá'í Publishing Trust, rev. edn 1961.

—— *The World Order of Bahá'u'lláh*. Wilmette, Illinois: Bahá'í Publishing Trust, rev. edn 1955.
SMITH, PETER. 'The American Bahá'í Community, 1894–1917: A Preliminary Survey.' *Studies in Bábí and Bahá'í History*. Vol. 1, ed. M. Momen. Los Angeles: Kalimát Press, 1982.
Star of the West. The Bahá'í Magazine. Published from 1910 to 1933 from Chicago and Washington, DC, by official Bahá'í agencies. First volume entitled *Bahai News*. (Volumes 1 to 14 reprinted in 8 volumes by George Ronald, Oxford.)
STOCKMAN, ROBERT H. *The Bahá'í Faith in America. Origins, 1892–1900*. Vol. 1. Wilmette, Illinois: Bahá'í Publishing Trust, 1985.
THOMPSON, JULIET. *'Abdu'l-Bahá, The Center of the Covenant*. Wilmette, Illinois: Bahá'í Publishing Committee, 1948.
—— *The Diary of Juliet Thompson*. Los Angeles: Kalimát Press, 1983.
TRUE, CORINNE. *Notes Taken at Acca*. Chicago: Bahai Publishing Society, 1907.
WHITE, ROGER. *The Shell and the Pearl*. An Account of the Martyrdom of 'Alí-Aṣghar of Yazd. Oxford: George Ronald, 1984.
WHITMORE, BRUCE W. *The Dawning Place*. The Building of a Temple, the Forging of the North American Bahá'í Community. Wilmette, Illinois: Bahá'í Publishing Trust, 1984.
—— 'Mother of the Temple. The story of Hand of the Cause of God Corinne Knight True.' *Bahá'í News*, No. 538, January 1976, and Part II, No. 539, February 1976. Wilmette, Illinois: National Spiritual Assembly of the Bahá'ís of the United States.

Notes and References

CORINNE KNIGHT'S SOUTHERN HERITAGE

[1] The Constitution of the United States, Article 1, section 2, (3). This clause was set aside by Amendment 13 which abolished slavery in 1865.
[2] Personal journal of Thomas Knight, completed 15 April 1935, p. 13.
[3] Quoted by Honor Kempton, *The Bahá'í World*, vol. 13, p. 846. This memorial article for Mrs True was attributed to Charlotte Linfoot in error, on first publication.

TRAGEDY AND FAITH

[1] See Stockman, *The Bahá'í Faith in America*, vol. 1, chaps. 11 and 12.
[2] *Tablets of Abdul-Baha Abbas*, vol. 1, pp. 85–6. Original translation, Acca; sent to Mrs True, 12 October 1900. Personal papers of Edna M. True.
[3] ibid. p. 86. Original translation dated May 1901 by Mrs True. Personal papers of Edna M. True.

'FOUND YE SPIRITUAL ASSEMBLIES'

[1] See Stockman, *The Bahá'í Faith in America*, vol. 1, p. 160.
[2] *Selections from the Writings of 'Abdu'l-Bahá*, sect. 38, pp. 79–80. Original translation unidentified as to place and undated, but copied by Mrs True in her notebook between her Tablets translated 21 June 1902 and September 1902. Personal papers of Edna M. True.
[3] Tablet of 'Abdu'l-Bahá: 'To the President of the Assembly of Teaching of the Maid Servants of the Merciful Corinne True Chicago.' Original translation, Chicago, September 1902. Personal papers of Edna M. True.
[4] *Selections from the Writings of 'Abdu'l-Bahá*, sect. 122, p. 142. Original translation, Washington, DC, 16 April 1902. Personal papers of Edna M. True.

⁵Edna True, in conversation with Marion Hofman, Zurich, 20 June 1986.

'ABDU'L-BAHÁ'S CALL FOR THE TEMPLE

¹*Selections from the Writings of 'Abdu'l-Bahá*, sect. 141, pp. 162–4. Original translation, Chicago, 21 June 1902. Personal papers of Edna M. True.
²ibid. sect. 91, p. 122. Original translation, Washington, DC, 16 April 1902. Personal papers of Edna M. True.
³ibid. sect. 90, p. 121. Original translation, Chicago, 7 April 1903. Personal papers of Edna M. True.
⁴*Tablets of Abdul-Baha Abbas*, vol. 1, pp. 96–7. Original translation dated 'Acca June 7th 1903'. Personal papers of Edna M. True.
⁵Mrs Charles Lincoln Papers, National Bahá'í Archives, Wilmette, Illinois. Quoted by Whitmore, 'Mother of the Temple', *Bahá'í News*, no. 538, January 1976, pp. 4–5.
⁶*Selections from the Writings of 'Abdu'l-Bahá*, sect. 10, pp. 26–7. Original Tablet 'Revealed in the Holy City Acca. July 4th 1903'. Original translation, Chicago, 29 September [1903]. Personal papers of Edna M. True.
⁷Tablet of 'Abdu'l-Bahá. 'Revealed at Acca Oct. 6th 1904.' Original translation, Chicago, 14 November 1904. Personal papers of Edna M. True. The lines quoted are an approved translation from the Bahá'í World Centre.
⁸Copies of the letters of Edna and Katherine to 'Abdu'l-Bahá are from the personal papers of Edna M. True.
⁹*Tablets of Abdul-Baha Abbas*, vol. 1, pp. 84–5. Original translation, Acca, 9 June 1903. Personal papers of Edna M. True.
¹⁰*The Bahá'í World*, vol. 14, p. 383, and *Tablets of Abdul-Baha Abbas*, vol. 1, p. 85. Original translation, Acca, 9 June 1903. Personal papers of Edna M. True.

SIX DAYS IN AKKA

¹*Tablets of Abdul-Baha Abbas*, vol. 1, p. 99. Original translation, Washington, DC, 4 December 1906. Personal papers of Edna M. True.
²From Curtis Kelsey's interview with Corinne True, Wilmette, undated.
³See Balyuzi, *'Abdu'l-Bahá*, p. 117, also Shoghi Effendi, *God Passes By*, pp. 263, 264, 266.
⁴Corinne True, *Notes Taken at Acca*, p. 17.

NOTES AND REFERENCES TO PAGES 57–83 219

⁵*Selections from the Writings of 'Abdu'l-Bahá*, sect. 234, p. 316. Original translation, Chicago, 7 April 1903. Personal papers of Edna M. True.
⁶Mrs Helen S. Goodall Papers, National Bahá'í Archives, Wilmette, Illinois. Quoted by Whitmore, *The Dawning Place*, p. 29.
⁷See White, *The Shell and the Pearl*, for a detailed description of this event, from which some of these details have come.
⁸Mrs Helen S. Goodall Papers, National Bahá'í Archives, Wilmette, Illinois. Quoted by Whitmore, 'Mother of the Temple', *Bahá'í News*, no. 538, January 1976, p. 7.
⁹ibid. p. 9.
¹⁰See Shoghi Effendi, *God Passes By*, p. 263, and Balyuzi, *'Abdu'l-Bahá*, p. 94.
¹¹Mrs Charles Lincoln Papers, National Bahá'í Archives, Wilmette, Illinois. Quoted by Whitmore, 'Mother of the Temple', *Bahá'í News*, no. 538, January 1976, p. 8.

THE STRUGGLE FOR UNITY

¹Quoted by Whitmore, *The Dawning Place*, p. 36.
²Mrs Helen S. Goodall Papers, National Bahá'í Archives, Wilmette, Illinois. Quoted by Whitmore, 'Mother of the Temple', *Bahá'í News*, no. 538, January 1976, p. 6.
³See Peter Smith, 'The American Bahá'í Community', 1894–1917: A Preliminary Survey', *Studies in Bábí and Bahá'í History*, vol. 1, p. 139.
⁴*Tablets of Abdul-Baha Abbas*, vol. 1, p. 100. Original translation, Acca, 19 June 1908. Personal papers of Edna M. True.
⁵Whitmore, *The Dawning Place*, p. 37.

A WONDERFUL COINCIDENCE

¹Thornton Chase to Hooper Harris, 27 November 1908. Thornton Chase Papers, National Bahá'í Archives, Wilmette, Illinois.
²See *Tablets of Abdul-Baha Abbas*, vol. 1, p. 100, to Corinne True. Original translation, Acca, 19 June 1908. Personal papers of Edna M. True.
³ibid., p. 102, to Corinne True. Original translation, Haifa, 15 September 1908. Personal papers of Edna M. True.
⁴ibid.
⁵Quoted by Whitmore, *The Dawning Place*, p. 50. The author is grateful to Mr Whitmore's valuable book for many of the details concerning this historic Convention.

[6] Shoghi Effendi, *God Passes By*, p. 276.
[7] Original translation, Haifa, 29 July 1909. Personal papers of Edna M. True. The lines quoted are an approved translation from the Bahá'í World Centre.
[8] Mrs Helen S. Goodall Papers, National Bahá'í Archives, Wilmette, Illinois. Quoted by Whitmore, 'Mother of the Temple', *Bahá'í News*, no. 539, February 1976, p. 15.
[9] Horace Holley Papers, National Bahá'í Archives, Wilmette, Illinois. ibid. pp. 15–16.
[10] Original translation, Washington, DC, 4 March 1910. Personal papers of Edna M. True. The lines quoted are an approved translation from the Bahá'í World Centre.
[11] The first volume of *Star of the West* was titled *Bahai News*; it consisted of nineteen issues, from 21 March 1910 to 2 March 1911.
[12] *Star of the West (Bahai News)*, vol. 1, no. 14, 23 November 1910, p. 7. (Reprinted by George Ronald, vol. 1.)

THE MASTER'S PROTECTION AND GUIDANCE

[1] *Star of the West (Bahai News)*, vol. 1, no. 18, 7 February 1911, p. 7. Original translation, Washington, DC, 11 January 1911. Personal papers of Edna M. True. (Reprinted by George Ronald, vol. 1.)
[2] Mrs Helen S. Goodall Papers, National Bahá'í Archives, Wilmette, Illinois. Quoted by Whitmore, 'Mother of the Temple', *Bahá'í News*, no. 539, February 1976, p. 17.
[3] Tablet from 'Abdu'l-Bahá to 'all friends of Abha in America', undated. *Star of the West*, vol. 2, no. 13, 4 November 1911, p. 3. (Reprinted by George Ronald, vol. 2.)
[4] Tablet to the American Friends from 'Abdu'l-Bahá, translated 28 April 1911. *Star of the West*, vol. 2, no. 4, 17 May 1911, p. 7. (Reprinted by George Ronald, vol. 1.)
[5] *Star of the West*, vol. 2, no. 5, 5 June 1911, p. 13. (Reprinted by George Ronald, vol. 1.) Original translation, Chicago, 1 June 1911. Personal papers of Edna M. True.
[6] Wendell Phillips Dodge, ''Abdu'l-Bahá's Arrival in America', *Star of the West*, vol. 3, no. 3, 28 April 1912, p. 4. (Reprinted by George Ronald, vol. 2.)
[7] The author is indebted to Whitmore, *The Dawning Place*, pp. 61–5, for many of the details in this description of the dedication ceremony, including these words of 'Abdu'l-Bahá.
[8] Albert Windust Papers, National Bahá'í Archives, Wilmette,

Illinois. Quoted by Whitmore, 'Mother of the Temple', *Bahá'í News*, no. 539, February 1976, p. 19.
[9]From letter of Corinne True to Marion and David Hofman, 29 November 1945. See also *Star of the West*, vol. 3, no. 12, 16 October 1912, pp. 14–15. (Reprinted by George Ronald, vol. 2.)
[10]See *Star of the West*, vol. 3, no. 9, 20 August 1912, p. 16. (Reprinted by George Ronald, vol. 2.)
[11]ibid., vol. 3, no. 10, 8 September 1912, p. 4.
[12]Personal papers of Albert Windust, prepared by his daughter Isabelle, pp. 15–16, and sent to Edna M. True.
[13]From Maḥmúd's Diary, p. 371, as quoted by Whitmore, 'Mother of the Temple', idem, p. 19.
[14]Personal papers of Albert Windust, idem, p. 17; sent to Edna M. True.
[15]Author's interview with Edna M. True, recorded on tape.

'THE MONEY CAME . . . ROLLING IN'

[1]Letter from Corinne True to Helen Goodall, 5 February 1914. Mrs Helen S. Goodall Papers, National Bahá'í Archives, Wilmette, Illinois.
[2]ibid.
[3]ibid., 28 May 1914.
[4]Tablet of 'Abdu'l-Bahá to Corinne True. Original translation, Washington, DC, 18 November 1909. Personal papers of Edna M. True.
[5]*Star of the West*, vol. 6, no. 7, 13 July 1915, p. 57, from 'Brief History of the Mashrak-el-Azkar in America' by Corinne True. (Reprinted by George Ronald, vol. 4.) See also Whitmore, *The Dawning Place*, p. 69.
[6]Adapted from a taped interview with Wyatt Cooper by Mrs Beth McKenty Smith.
[7]The account of Wyatt Cooper is based on the recollections of Edna M. True and Lawrence Cooper, his son, as well as on the taped interview by Mrs Smith.

TWO KINDS OF WAR

[1]*Star of the West*, vol. 5, no. 4, 17 May 1914, p. 56. (Reprinted by George Ronald, vol. 3.)
[2]See Whitmore, *The Dawning Place*, p. 71.
[3]Tablet of 'Abdu'l-Bahá addressed to Mrs Arna True Perron. Original translation, Tiberias, Syria, 1 June 1914. Personal papers of Edna M. True. The lines quoted are an approved translation from the Bahá'í World Centre.

[4] *Star of the West*, vol. 5, no. 7, 13 July 1914, p. 104, revealed 2 April 1914. The translation used in this chapter is that of the Guardian in *The Passing of 'Abdu'l-Bahá*, Stuttgart, January 1922, pp. 30–31, as published in Balyuzi, *'Abdu'l-Bahá*, pp. 405–6. (*Star of the West* reprinted by George Ronald, vol. 3.)

[5] Mrs Helen S. Goodall Papers, National Bahá'í Archives, Wilmette, Illinois. Letter of Corinne True to Helen Goodall, 28 March 1915.

[6] From two Tablets of 'Abdu'l-Bahá, 21 and 14 April 1914, quoted in *Star of the West*, vol. 5, no. 17, 19 January 1915, pp. 264–5. (Reprinted by George Ronald, vol. 4.)

[7] Mrs Helen S. Goodall Papers, National Bahá'í Archives, Wilmette, Illinois. Letter of Corinne True to Helen Goodall, 20 January 1915.

[8] *Star of the West*, vol. 6, no. 4, 17 May 1915, pp. 26, 28, which include a photograph of the medallion. (Reprinted by George Ronald, vol. 4.)

[9] ibid., vol. 6, no. 7, 13 July 1915, pp. 51, 57.

[10] ibid., vol. 6, no. 5, 5 June 1915, p. 36.

[11] Quoted in Whitmore, *The Dawning Place*, p. 75.

[12] Report of the 1916 Convention, *Star of the West*, vol. 7, no. 7, 13 July 1916, p. 60. (Reprinted by George Ronald, vol. 4.)

[13] *Star of the West*, vol. 6, no. 10, 8 September 1915, p. 74. (Reprinted by George Ronald, vol. 4.)

[14] ibid., vol. 7, no. 10, 8 September 1916, p. 93. (Reprinted by George Ronald, vol. 4.) Original translation, Haifa, 10 July 1916. Personal papers of Edna M. True.

[15] Mrs Helen S. Goodall Papers, National Bahá'í Archives, Wilmette, Illinois. Quoted by Whitmore, 'Mother of the Temple', *Bahá'í News*, no. 539, February 1976, p. 20.

[16] *Star of the West*, vol. 7, no. 16, 31 December 1916, p. 157. (Reprinted by George Ronald, vol. 4.) Words of 'Abdu'l-Bahá as reported in a letter from His secretary.

[17] Report of the Bahá'í Committee of Investigation, presented to the 1918 Annual Bahá'í Convention, Chicago, pp. 4, 10–12.

[18] Smith, 'The American Bahá'í Community, 1894–1917: A Preliminary Survey', *Studies in Bábí and Bahá'í History*, vol. 1, pp. 189–90.

[19] *Star of the West*, vol. 9, no. 5, 5 June 1918, pp. 63–4. (Reprinted by George Ronald, vol. 5.)

[20] Statement of Corinne True, 17 November 1917, to the Committee of Investigation, reporting words of 'Abdu'l-Bahá to her as He was leaving for Cincinnati, 4 November 1912.

21 *Star of the West*, vol. 8, no. 14, 23 November 1917, pp. 202–3. (Reprinted by George Ronald, vol. 5.)
22 Letter from Corinne True to Madie — of Atlanta, Ga., Chicago, 18 December 1918. Author's personal papers.

FAREWELL TO THE MASTER

1 *Star of the West*, vol. 9, no. 19, 2 March 1919, p. 220. (Reprinted by George Ronald, vol. 5.)
2 ibid., vol. 10, no. 1, 21 March 1919, pp. 10–11. (Reprinted by George Ronald, vol. 5.) Original translation, Haifa, 7 February 1919. Personal papers of Edna M. True.
3 ibid., vol. 10, no. 7, 13 July 1919, p. 143. Original translation, Haifa, 30 March 1919. Personal papers of Edna M. True.
4 Cited in letter from Corinne True to Helen S. Goodall, 21 July 1919. Personal papers of the author.
5 *Star of the West*, vol. 10, no. 1, 21 March 1919, pp. 10–11. (Reprinted by George Ronald, vol. 5.) Original translation, Haifa, 7 February 1919. Personal papers of Edna M. True.
6 ibid., vol. 10, no. 7, 13 July 1919, pp. 120–21.
7 See Mrs True's account of their journey and 1919 pilgrimage, *Star of the West*, vol. 10, no. 17, 19 January 1920, pp. 312–13. (Reprinted by George Ronald, vol. 6.)
8 See ibid., vol. 10, no. 3, 28 April 1919, p. 36. (Reprinted by George Ronald, vol. 5.)
9 From Edna True's talk with Marion Hofman, Zurich, 20 June 1986.
10 From taped interview by the author with Edna M. True, reporting 'Abdu'l-Bahá's words during her pilgrimage in 1919.
11 From recollections of Edna M. True, as told to Marion Hofman, Wilmette, March 1987.
12 The message is published in *Star of the West*, vol. 10, no. 17, 19 January 1920, p. 306. (Reprinted by George Ronald, vol. 6.)

THE FIRST MASHRIQU'L-ADHKÁR IN AMERICA

1 *Selections from the Writings of 'Abdu'l-Bahá*, sect. 187, p. 215. Original translation, Acca, 24 July 1919. Personal papers of Edna M. True.
2 In a Tablet to Corinne True, following receipt of her letter reporting the proceedings of the Convention, 'Abdu'l-Bahá praised Mr Remey for this action. Original translation, Haifa, 12 June 1920. Personal papers of Edna M. True.
3 *Star of the West*, vol. 12, no. 1, 21 March 1921, p. 19.

(Reprinted by George Ronald, vol. 7.) Original translation, Mt Carmel, Palestine, 8 December 1920. Personal papers of Edna M. True.

[4] *Star of the West*, ibid., for text of cablegram sent 15 February 1921 from Haifa. Personal papers of Edna M. True for form of address.

[5] Tablet from 'Abdu'l-Bahá: 'Through the revered maidservant of God, Mrs Corinne True, Chicago'; translated Mt Carmel, Palestine, 12 December 1920. *Star of the West*, vol. 12, no. 13, pp. 218–19, the recipient being unnamed. (Reprinted by George Ronald, vol. 7.) The sentence quoted is an approved translation from the Bahá'í World Centre.

'IN THE CENTER STANDS THIS YOUTH'

[1] *Selections from the Writings of 'Abdu'l-Bahá*, sect. 234, p. 316. Original translation, Chicago, 7 April 1903. Personal papers of Edna M. True.

[2] Quoted in Rabbani, *The Priceless Pearl*, pp. 50–51.

[3] *Selections from the Writings of 'Abdu'l-Bahá*, sect. 187, p. 216: Original translation, Bahjeh, Acca, Palestine, 24 July 1919. personal papers of Edna M. True.

[4] *Bahá'í Administration*, pp. 15–16, 21 January 1922, for the three passages quoted.

[5] Rabbani, *The Priceless Pearl*, p. 55.

[6] Quoted by Louis G. Gregory, 'The Bahai Congress for Teaching and the Fourteenth Annual Convention', *Star of the West*, vol. 13, no. 4, 17 May 1922, p. 68. (Reprinted by George Ronald, vol. 7.)

[7] From talk by Mountfort Mills, ibid.

[8] At that time the term 'World Center' was not normally used. Shoghi Effendi described it in 1927 as the 'International Center of the Cause'. See *Baha'i News Letter*, no. 15, June 1927, p. 3.

[9] From talk by Mountfort Mills, idem, p. 69, quoting Rouhi Effendi.

[10] ibid., p. 70.

[11] *Bahá'í News*, no. 52, May 1931, p. 2, and Rabbani, *The Priceless Pearl*, pp. 294–6.

[12] Corinne True, 'Some Striking Connections between The Shrine of the Bab and The Mashreq-ul Azkar of America', *Star of the West*, vol. 13, no. 5, August 1922, pp. 120, 121. (Reprinted by George Ronald, vol. 7.)

'GIVE THEM LOVE'

[1] Cablegram to 'Delegates and Friends at Convention', 21 April 1923, quoted in *Star of the West*, vol. 14, no. 3, June 1923, p. 74. (Reprinted by George Ronald, vol. 8.)
[2] Quoted in Convention report by Louis G. Gregory, *Star of the West*, ibid., p. 69.
[3] For election date of National Spiritual Assembly see *Baha'i News Letter*, no. 6, pp. 2, 5. For year of recognition as the National Spiritual Assembly see Shoghi Effendi, *God Passes By*, p. 333.
[4] *Baha'i News Letter*, no. 27, October 1928, p. 2, and no. 28, November 1928, p. 1.
[5] From author's interview with Vivian Wesson, Palo Alto, California, 19 November 1984.

THE VIEW FROM HOME

[1] Letter from Marion Yazdi to Corinne True, 27 October 1928. Personal papers of Edna M. True, held by the author. See Shoghi Effendi's letter, 28 November 1931, entitled 'The Goal of a New World Order', in *The World Order of Bahá'u'lláh*, p. 46.
[2] See *Star of the West*, vol. 19, no. 3, June 1928, pp. 80–81, for a description of the Convention and illustration of the assembled Bahá'ís in Foundation Hall; also *The Bahá'í World*, vol. 2, p. 180, for illustration.
[3] The following account of Nettie Tobin's gift of a stone is derived by the author from talks with Edna M. True, and from a tape recording of Wyatt Cooper in which he stated that Nettie Tobin told him about the episode. Several versions of the story exist. The Cooper tape is held by the author.

TWO MORE PILGRIMAGES

[1] Letter from Corinne True to her daughters, 14 March 1931.
[2] ibid.
[3] From Corinne True's diary regarding her 1931 and 1935 pilgrimages.
[4] Thompson, *'Abdu'l-Bahá – The Center of the Covenant*, p. 15.
[5] Letter from Corinne True to her daughters, 8 April 1931, from Cairo.
[6] From a letter written by the Guardian to Mrs Corinne True, 29 August 1931. *Bahá'í News*, no. 57, December 1931, p. 4, authenticated at the Bahá'í World Centre.
[7] *Bahá'í News*, ibid.

⁸ibid., no. 61, April 1932, p. 3.
⁹Quoted by Whitmore, *The Dawning Place*, p. 65.
¹⁰*Bahá'í News*, no. 33, July 1929, pp. 4, 5, and no. 79, Supplement, November 1933, p. 1.
¹¹ibid., no. 72, April 1933, p. 6, and no. 74, May 1933, p. 8.
¹²From taped interview by the author with Edna M. True, July 1983.
¹³From Corinne True's diary regarding her 1935 pilgrimage.
¹⁴ibid.

MOTHER TRUE

¹12 March 1938. Personal papers of Marion Holley Hofman.
²Edna M. True, 13 April 1938; ibid.
³April 1938, after Annual Bahá'í Convention; ibid.
⁴Corinne True, 17 April 1939; ibid.
⁵23 April 1939; ibid.
⁶Edna M. True, 8 May 1941; ibid.
⁷Corinne True, 7 May 1941; ibid.
⁸*Messages to America, 1932–1946*, p. 55.
⁹Corinne True, 9 May 1942. Personal papers of Marion Holley Hofman.
¹⁰*Bahá'í News*, no. 164, July 1943, p. 6.
¹¹Gayle Woolson, 'Memories of the Hand of the Cause of God Mrs. Corinne True'; sent to Edna M. True, 27 March 1985, pp. 2–3.
¹²Whitmore, 'Mother of the Temple', *Bahá'í News*, no. 538, January 1976, p. 10.
¹³*Messages to America, 1932–1946*, p. 68.
¹⁴Gayle Woolson, idem, pp. 5–6.
¹⁵Gayle Woolson, 'My contact with Mrs. Corinne True as a Guest in Her Home in Wilmette in 1945'; sent to Edna M. True, 15 July 1985, p. 4.
¹⁶29 November 1945, to Marion and David Hofman. Personal papers of Marion Holley Hofman.
¹⁷*Bahá'í News*, no. 198, August 1947, p. 2.
¹⁸27 August 1947. Personal papers of Marion Holley Hofman.
¹⁹30 September 1947; ibid.
²⁰*Bahá'í News*, no. 234, August 1950, p. 8.
²¹ibid., no. 236, October 1950, p. 11.
²²*The Bahá'í World*, vol. 13, p. 848. Memorial article by Honor Kempton.
²³ibid. Also from author's taped interview with Edna M. True, July 1983.

NOTES AND REFERENCES TO PAGES 193–206

[24] 27 October 1950. Personal papers of Marion Holley Hofman.

A TOWER OF STRENGTH

[1] From a letter written by the Guardian to Corinne True, 16 February 1924. The extracts from the Guardian's letters to Mrs True, quoted in this chapter, are from the personal papers of Edna M. True, authenticated at the Bahá'í World Centre.
[2] ibid., 19 February 1926.
[3] ibid., 2 February 1927.
[4] From a letter written on behalf of the Guardian, 20 March 1928.
[5] From a letter written by the Guardian, 1 May 1929.
[6] From a letter written on behalf of the Guardian, 10 November 1933.
[7] From the Guardian's letter addressed to 'Brethren and fellow-mourners in the Faith of Bahá'u'lláh!' *Bahíyyih Khánum, The Greatest Holy Leaf,* p. 31.
[8] Shoghi Effendi, *Messages to America, 1932–1946,* p. 1.
[9] From a letter written by the Guardian to Corinne True, 23 August 1932.
[10] ibid., 11 January 1933.
[11] ibid., 15 April 1933.
[12] ibid., 26 April 1936.
[13] Letter of Arna True Perron. Personal papers of Edna M. True.
[14] From a letter written by the Guardian to Corinne True, 24 February 1947.
[15] ibid., 19 October 1947.
[16] From records held at the Bahá'í World Centre. For text of cable see p. 202.

THE MOST VENERABLE PIONEER

[1] Cablegram, 28 February 1952. Personal papers of Edna M. True, and authenticated at the Bahá'í World Centre.
[2] From author's taped interview with Edna M. True, July 1984.
[3] Recorded by Edna M. True, November 1952.
[4] Notes taken by Katherine True at the dinner table, November 1952. Personal papers of Edna M. True.
[5] ibid. See also *The Bahá'í World,* vol. 13, p. 848, col. 1.

THE HAND OF THE CAUSE

[1] Gayle Woolson, 'My Contact with Hand of the Cause of God Mrs. Corinne True, While I Was an Auxiliary Board Member Serving in Latin America'; sent to Edna M. True, 17 June 1985, p. 5.

[2] *Star of the West*, vol. 13, no. 5, August 1922, p. 104. (Reprinted by George Ronald, vol. 7.) From a talk by 'Abdu'l-Bahá on Mt Carmel to a group of college students, undated.

[3] *Bahá'í News*, no. 317, July 1957, pp. 13–14.

[4] From address by the Hand of the Cause Paul Haney at the memorial service for Mrs True in the Ma<u>sh</u>riqu'l-A<u>dh</u>kár, 28 April 1961. *Bahá'í News*, no. 363, June 1961, p. 13. Also, from the recollections of Edna M. True as told to the author.

[5] From an article by the Hand of the Cause Paul Haney, *The Bahá'í World*, vol. 13, p. 345, col. 1.

[6] *Bahá'í News*, no. 328, June 1958, p. 14.

[7] From the personal papers of Edna M. True.

[8] *The Diary of Juliet Thompson*, p. 57.